Rick

SNAPSHOT

Copenhagen & the Best of Denmark

CONTENTS

INTRODUCTION

This Snapshot guide, excerpted from my guidebook *Rick Steves' Scandinavia*, introduces you to one of the most technologically advanced, yet traditional and welcoming nations in Europe—Denmark. There's a lot more here than just Hans Christian Andersen stories, sweet breakfast pastries, and rolling farmlands. Start with the livable Danish capital, Copenhagen, where you can experience the classic Tivoli Gardens amusement park, Europe's first pedestrian shopping mall, a warrior-king's Renaissance castle, and a free-spirited squatters' colony. You can side-trip to nearby Roskilde to see millennium-old Viking ships, or head to Frederiksborg Castle to tour Denmark's Versailles.

Beyond the capital, make time for the rest of Denmark—rugged islands, salty harbors, and windswept sandy coasts. The isle of Ærø is your time-warp experience back into a cozy 18th-century town and a chance to unwind in an utterly authentic Danish environment. To complete your visit, check out Hans Christian Andersen's house in Odense and stop in Denmark's "second city"—Aarhus—with its open-air folk museum and wildly contemporary art museum.

To help you have the best trip possible, I've included the following topics in this book:

• **Planning Your Time,** with advice on how to make the most of your limited time

• **Orientation,** including tourist information (abbreviated as TI), tips on public transportation, local tour options, and helpful hints

• **Sights** with ratings:

▲▲▲—Don't miss

▲▲—Try hard to see

▲—Worthwhile if you can make it

No rating—Worth knowing about

• **Sleeping** and **Eating,** with good-value recommendations in every price range

• **Connections,** with tips on trains, buses, and driving

Practicalities, near the end of this book, has information on money, phoning, hotel reservations, transportation, and more, plus Danish survival phrases.

To travel smartly, read this little book in its entirety before you go. It's my hope that this guide will make your trip more meaningful and rewarding. Traveling like a temporary local, you'll get the absolute most out of every mile, minute, and dollar.

God rejse! Happy travels!
Rick Steves

DENMARK

DENMARK

Danmark

 Denmark is by far the smallest of the Scandi-
navian countries, but in the 16th century, it
was the largest—at one time, Denmark ruled
all of Norway and the three southern provinces of Sweden. Danes are proud of their
mighty history and are the first to remind you
that they were a lot bigger and a lot stronger
in the good old days. And yet, they're a remarkably mellow, well-
adjusted lot—organized without being uptight, and easygoing
with a delightfully wry sense of humor.

In the 10th century, before its heyday as a Scan-superpower,
Denmark was, like Norway and Sweden, home to the Vikings.
More than anything else, these fierce warriors were known
for their great shipbuilding, which enabled them to travel far.
Denmark's Vikings journeyed west to Great Britain and Ireland
(where they founded Dublin) and brought back various influences,
including Christianity.

Denmark is composed of many islands, a peninsula (Jutland)
that juts up from northern Germany, Greenland, and the Faroe
Islands. The two main islands
are Zealand (Sjælland in Danish), where Copenhagen is
located, and Funen (Fyn in
Danish), where Hans Christian
Andersen (or, as Danes call him,
simply "H. C.") was born. Out of
the hundreds of smaller islands,
ship-in-bottle-cute Ærø is my

favorite. The Danish landscape is gentle compared to the dramatic
fjords, mountains, and vast lakes of other Scandinavian nations.
Danes (not to mention Swedes and Norwegians) like to joke about
the flat Danish landscape, saying that you can stand on a case of
beer and see from one end of the country to the other. Denmark's
highest point in Jutland is only 560 feet above sea level, and no
part of the country is more than 30 miles from the ocean.

In contrast to the rest of Scandinavia, much of Denmark is
arable. The landscape consists of rolling hills, small thatched-roof

farmhouses, beech forests, and whitewashed churches with characteristic stairstep gables. Red brick, which was a favorite material of the nation-building King Christian IV, is everywhere—especially in major civic buildings such as city halls and train stations.

Like the other Scandinavian countries, Denmark is predominantly Lutheran, but only a small minority attend church regularly. The majority are ethnic Danes, and many (but certainly not all) of them have the stereotypical blond hair and blue eyes. Two out of three Danes have last names ending in "-sen." The assimilation of ethnic groups into this homogeneous society, which began in earnest in the 1980s, is a source of some controversy. But in general, most Danes have a live-and-let-live attitude and enjoy one of the highest standards of living in the world. Taxes are high in this welfare state, but education is free and medical care highly subsidized. Generous paternity leave extends to both men and women.

DENMARK

Denmark Almanac

Official Name: Kongeriget Danmark—the Kingdom of Denmark—or simply Denmark.

Population: Denmark's 5.5 million people are mainly of Scandinavian descent, with immigrants—mostly German, Turkish, Iranian, and Somali—making up 10 percent of the population. Greenland is home to the indigenous Inuit, and the Faroe Islands to people of Nordic heritage. Most Danes speak both Danish and English, with a small minority speaking German, Inuit, or Faroese. The population is 90 percent Protestant—mostly Evangelical Lutheran—and 10 percent "other."

Latitude and Longitude: 56°N and 10°E, similar latitude to northern Alberta, Canada.

Area: 16,600 square miles, roughly twice the size of Massachusetts.

Geography: Denmark includes the Jutland peninsula in northern Europe. Situated between the North Sea and the Baltic Sea, it shares a 42-mile border with Germany. In addition to Greenland and the Faroe Islands, Denmark also encompasses 400 islands (78 of which are inhabited). Altogether Denmark has 4,544 miles of coastline. The mainland is mostly flat, and nearly two-thirds of the land is cultivated.

Biggest Cities: Denmark's capital city, Copenhagen (pop. 1 million), is located on the island of Zealand (Sjælland). Aarhus (on the mainland) has 243,000 and Odense (on Funen/Fyn) has 168,000.

Denmark, one of the most environmentally conscious European countries, is a front-runner in renewable energy, recycling, and organic farming. You'll see lots of modern windmills dotting the countryside. Since the country lacks other sources of power, wind power accounts for 20 percent of Denmark's energy today, with a goal of 50 percent by 2030. Half of all waste is recycled. In grocery stores, organic products are shelved right alongside non-organic ones—for the same price.

Denmark's Queen Margrethe II is a very popular and talented woman who, along with her royal duties, has designed coins, stamps, and book illustrations. Danes gather around the TV on New Year's Eve to hear her annual speech to the nation and flock to the Royal Palace in Copenhagen on April 16 to sing her "Happy Birthday." Her son, Crown Prince Frederik, married Australian Mary Donaldson in 2004. Their

Economy: Denmark's modern economy is holding its own, with a Gross Domestic Product of just under $210 billion. Denmark's top exports include pharmaceuticals, oil, machinery, and food products. It is also one of the world's leaders in exports of wind turbine technology. The GDP per capita is about $37,600.

Currency: 6 Danish kroner (kr, officially DKK) = about $1.

Government: Denmark is a constitutional monarchy. Queen Margrethe II is the head of state, but the head of government is the prime minister, a post held since October 2011 by Helle Thorning-Schmidt. The 179-member parliament (Folketinget) is elected every four years.

Flag: The Danish flag is red with a white cross.

The Average Dane: He or she is 41 years old, has 1.74 children, and will live to be 78. About 74 percent of Danish women are employed outside the home. About 53 percent of Danes own a home or apartment, 83 percent own a mobile phone, and 90 percent have Internet access.

son Christian's birth in 2005 was cause for a national celebration.

The Danes are proud of their royal family and of the flag, a white cross on a red background. Legend says it fell from the sky during a 13th-century battle in Estonia, making it Europe's oldest continuously used flag. You'll see it everywhere—decorating cakes, on clothing, or fluttering in the breeze atop government buildings. It's as much a decorative symbol as a patriotic one.

You'll also notice that the Danes have an odd fixation on two animals: elephants and polar bears, both of which are symbols of national (especially royal) pride. The Order of the Elephant is the highest honor that the Danish monarch can bestow on someone; if you see an emblematic elephant, you know somebody very important is involved. And the polar bear represents the Danish protectorate of Greenland—a welcome reminder to Danes that their nation is more than just

DENMARK

Jutland and a bunch of flat little islands.

From an early age, Danes develop a passion for soccer. You may see red-and-white-clad fans singing on their way to a match. Despite the country's small size, the Danish national team does well in international competition. Other popular sports include sailing, cycling, badminton, and team handball.

The Danish language, with its three extra vowels (Æ, Ø, and Å), is notoriously difficult for foreigners to pronounce. Even seemingly predictable consonants can be tricky. For example, the letter "d" is often dropped, so the word *gade* (street)—which you'll see, hear, and say constantly—is pronounced "gah-eh." Luckily for us, almost everyone also speaks English and is heroically patient with thick-tongued foreigners. Danes have playful fun teasing tourists who make the brave attempt to say Danish words. The hardest phrase, *rød grød med fløde* (a delightful red fruit porridge topped with cream), is nearly impossible for a non-Dane to pronounce. Ask a local to help you.

Sample Denmark's sweet treats at one of the many bakeries you'll see. The pastries that we call "Danish" in the US are called *wienerbrød* in Denmark. Bakeries line their display cases with several varieties of *wienerbrød* and other delectable sweets. Try *kringle, snegle,* or *Napoleonshatte,* or find your own favorite. (Chances are it will be easier to enjoy than to pronounce.)

Two important words to know are *skål* ("cheers," a ritual always done with serious eye contact) and *hyggelig* (pronounced HEW-glee), meaning warm and cozy. Danes treat their home like a sanctuary and spend a great deal of time improving their gardens and houses—inside and out. Cozying up one's personal space (a national obsession) is something the Danes do best. If you have the opportunity, have some Danes adopt you while you are in Denmark so you can enjoy their warm hospitality.

Heaven to a Dane is returning home after a walk in a beloved beech forest to enjoy open-faced sandwiches washed down with beer among good friends. Around the *hyggelig* candlelit table, there will be a spirited discussion of the issues of the day, plenty of laughter, and probably a few good-natured jokes about the Swedes or Norwegians. *Skål!*

COPENHAGEN

København

Copenhagen, Denmark's capital, is the gateway to Scandinavia. It's an improbable combination of corny Danish clichés, well-dressed executives having a business lunch amid cutting-edge contemporary architecture, and some of the funkiest counterculture in Europe. And yet, it all just works so tidily together. With the Øresund Bridge connecting Sweden and Denmark (creating the region's largest metropolitan area), Copenhagen is energized and ready to dethrone Stockholm as Scandinavia's powerhouse city.

A busy day cruising the canals, wandering through the palace, and taking an old-town walk will give you your historical bearings. Then, after another day strolling the Strøget (STROY-et, Europe's first and greatest pedestrian shopping mall), biking the canals, and sampling the Danish good life (including sampling a gooey Danish), you'll feel

right at home. Live it up in Scandinavia's cheapest and most fun-loving capital.

Planning Your Time

A first visit deserves a minimum of two days. Note that many sights are closed on Monday year-round or in the off-season.

Day 1: Catch a 10:30 city walking tour with Richard Karpen (Mon-Sat mid-May-mid-Sept; described later under "Tours in

COPENHAGEN

The Story of Copenhagen

If you study your map carefully, you can read the history of Copenhagen in today's street plan. København (literally, "Merchants' Harbor") was born on the little island of Slotsholmen—today home of Christiansborg Palace—in 1167. What was Copenhagen's medieval moat is now a string of pleasant lakes and parks, including Tivoli Gardens. You can still make out some of the zigzag pattern of the moats and ramparts in the city's greenbelt.

Many of these fortifications—and several other landmarks—were built by Denmark's most memorable king. You need to remember only one character in Copenhagen's history: Christian IV. Ruling from 1588 to 1648, he was Denmark's Renaissance king and a royal party animal (see the "King Christian IV" sidebar, later). The personal energy of this "Builder King" sparked a Golden Age when Copenhagen prospered and many of the city's grandest buildings were erected. In the 17th century, Christian IV extended the city fortifications to the north, doubling the size of the city, while adding a grid plan of streets and his Rosenborg Castle. This old "new town" has the Amalienborg Palace and *The Little Mermaid* site.

In 1850, Copenhagen's 140,000 residents all lived within this defensive system. Building in the no-man's-land outside the walls was only allowed with the understanding that in the event of an attack, you'd burn your dwellings to clear the way for a good defense.

Most of the city's historic buildings still in existence were built within the medieval walls, but conditions became too crowded, and outbreaks of disease forced Copenhagen to spread outside the walls. Ultimately those walls were torn down and replaced with "rampart streets" that define today's city center: Vestervoldgade (literally, "West Rampart Street"), Nørrevoldgade ("North"), and Østervoldgade ("East"). The fourth side is the harbor and the island of Slotsholmen, where København was born.

Copenhagen"). After lunch at Riz-Raz, catch the relaxing canal-boat tour out to *The Little Mermaid* site and back. Enjoy the rest of the afternoon tracing Denmark's cultural roots in the National Museum and visiting the Ny Carlsberg Glyptotek art gallery (Impressionists and Danish artists). Spend the evening strolling the Strøget (follow my self-guided walk).

Day 2: At 10:00, go Neoclassical at Thorvaldsen's Museum (closed Mon), and tour the royal reception rooms at the adjacent Christiansborg Palace. After a *smørrebrød* lunch, spend the afternoon seeing the Rosenborg Castle/crown jewels. Spend the evening at Tivoli Gardens.

Christiania—the hippie squatters' community—is not for everyone. But it's worth considering if you're intrigued by alternative lifestyles, or simply want a break from the museums. During a busy trip, Christiania fits best in the evening.

Budget Itinerary Tip: Remember the efficiency and cost-effectiveness of sleeping while traveling in and out of town (saving time and hotel costs). Consider taking an overnight train to Stockholm or Oslo, or cruise up to Oslo on a night boat. Kamikaze sightseers on tight budgets see Copenhagen as a useful Scandinavian bottleneck. They sleep heading into town on a train, tour the city during the day, and sleep heading north into Scandinavia on a boat or train to their next destination. At the end of their Scandinavian travels, they do the same thing in reverse. The result is two days and no nights in Copenhagen (you can check your bag and take a shower at the train station). Considering the joy of Oslo and Stockholm, this isn't all that crazy if you have limited time and can sleep on a moving train or boat.

Orientation to Copenhagen

Copenhagen is huge (with a million people), but for most visitors, the walkable core is the diagonal axis formed by the train station, Tivoli Gardens, Rådhuspladsen (City Hall Square), and the Strøget pedestrian street, ending at the colorful old Nyhavn sailors' harbor. Bubbling with street life, colorful pedestrian zones, and most of the city's sightseeing, the Strøget is fun (and most of it is covered by my self-guided walk in this chapter). But also be sure to get off the main drag and explore. By doing things by bike or on foot, you'll stumble onto some charming bits of Copenhagen that many travelers miss.

Outside of the old city center are three areas of interest to tourists:

1. To the north are Rosenborg Castle and *The Little Mermaid* area (Amalienborg Palace and Museum of Danish Resistance).

COPENHAGEN

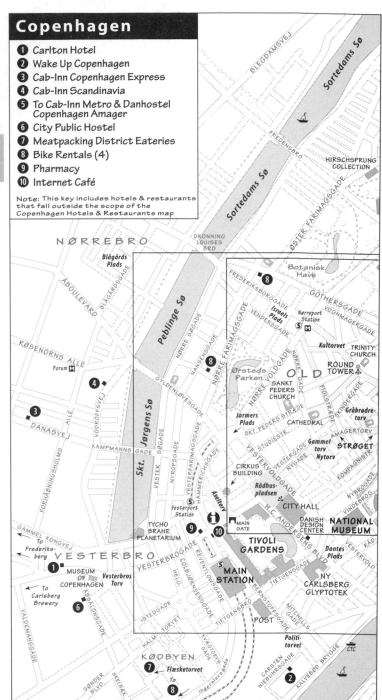

Copenhagen

1 Carlton Hotel
2 Wake Up Copenhagen
3 Cab-Inn Copenhagen Express
4 Cab-Inn Scandinavia
5 To Cab-Inn Metro & Danhostel Copenhagen Amager
6 City Public Hostel
7 Meatpacking District Eateries
8 Bike Rentals (4)
9 Pharmacy
10 Internet Café

Note: This key includes hotels & restaurants that fall outside the scope of the Copenhagen Hotels & Restaurants map

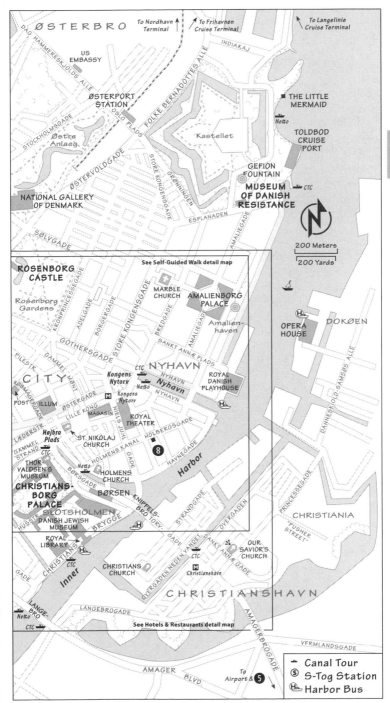

COPENHAGEN

2. To the east, across the harbor, are Christianshavn (Copenhagen's "Little Amsterdam" district) and the alternative enclave of Christiania.

3. To the west (behind the train station) is Vesterbro, a young and trendy part of town with lots of cafés, bars, and boutiques (including the hip Meatpacking District, called Kødbyen); the picnic-friendly Frederiksberg park; and the Carlsberg Brewery.

All of these sights are walkable from the Strøget, but taking a bike, bus, or taxi is more efficient. I rent a bike for my entire visit (for about the cost of a single cab ride per day) and park it safely in my hotel courtyard. I get anywhere in the town center literally faster than by taxi (nearly anything is within a 10-minute pedal). In good weather, the city is an absolute delight by bike (for more on biking in Copenhagen, see "Getting Around Copenhagen: By Bike," later).

Tourist Information

Copenhagen's questionable excuse for a TI, which bills itself as "Wonderful Copenhagen," is actually a blatantly for-profit company. As in a (sadly) increasing number of big European cities, it provides information only about businesses that pay a hefty display fee of thousands of dollars each year. This colors the advice and information the office provides. While they can answer basic questions and have a room-booking service (for a 100-kr fee), the office is worthwhile mostly as a big rack of advertising brochures—you can pick up the free map at many hotels and other places in town (May-June Mon-Sat 9:00-18:00, closed Sun; July-Aug Mon-Sat 9:00-20:00, Sun 10:00-18:00; Sept-April Mon-Fri 9:00-16:00, Sat 9:00-14:00, closed Sun; just up the street from train station—to the left as you exit the station—at Vesterbrogade 4A, good Lagkagehuset bakery in building, tel. 70 22 24 42, www.visit copenhagen.com).

The **Copenhagen Card,** which includes free entry to many of the city's sights (including expensive ones, like Tivoli and Rosenborg Castle) and all local transportation throughout the greater Copenhagen area, can save busy sightseers some money; if you're planning on visiting a lot of attractions with steep entry prices, do the arithmetic to see if buying this pass adds up (249 kr/24 hours, 479 kr/72 hours, 699 kr/120 hours—sold at the TI and some hotels).

Alternative Sources of Tourist Information: As the TI's bottom line competes with its mission to help tourists, you may want to seek out other ways to inform yourself. The local English-language newspaper, *The Copenhagen Post,* has good articles about what's going on in town (comes out each Thursday, often available free at TI or some hotels, or buy it at a newsstand, www.cph

post.dk). The witty alternative website, **www.aok.dk,** has several articles in English (and many more in Danish—readable and very insightful if you translate them in Google Translate).

Arrival in Copenhagen
By Train

The main train station is called Hovedbanegården (HOETH-bahn-gorn; look for *København H* on signs and schedules). It's

a temple of travel and a hive of travel-related activity (and 24-hour thievery). Kiosks and fast-food eateries cluster in the middle of the main arrivals hall. The **ticket office** is on the left (as you face the front of the hall), and a **train information** kiosk is right in the middle of the hall.

Within the station, you'll find **baggage storage** (go down stairs at back of station marked *Bagagebokse;* lockers cost 40-50 kr/day, and the checkroom/*garderobe* costs 45-55 kr/day per bag; both open Mon-Sat 5:30-1:00 in the morning, Sun 6:00-1:00 in the morning); pay **WCs** (right side of station, near ticket offices); a **post office** (back of station, Mon-Fri 8:00-21:00, Sat-Sun 10:00-16:00); a branch of the recommended **Lagkagehuset** bakery; and lots more. At both the front and the back of the station, you'll find **ATMs** and **Forex** exchange desks (the least expensive place in town to change money, daily 8:00-21:00).

The tracks at the back of the station (tracks 9-10 and 11-12) are for the suburban train (S-tog).

Tickets: While you're in the station, you can plan for your departure by reserving your overnight train seat or *couchette* at the *Billetsalg* office (daily 9:30-18:00). Some international rides and high-speed InterCity trains require reservations (usually 25-55 kr), but railpass-holders can ride any Danish train without a reservation. The *Kviksalg* office, with longer hours, sells tickets within Denmark (plus the regional train to Malmö, Sweden). This "quick sale" office will also help you with reservations for international trips if the *Billetsalg* office is closed, or if you're departing by train within one hour or early the next day. If you're heading into Sweden, you can also buy tickets at the *SJ Rejsebutik* (Swedish Railways) office, near the back of the station.

Getting into Town: If you want to get right to sightseeing, you're within easy walking distance of downtown. Just walk out the front door and you'll run into one of the entrances for Tivoli amusement park; if you go around its left side and up a couple of blocks, you'll be at Rådhuspladsen, where my self-guided walk begins.

Hotels are scattered far and wide around town. It's best to get arrival instructions from your hotelier, but if you're on your own, here are some tips:

To reach hotels **behind the station,** slip out the back door—just go down the stairs at the back of the station marked *Reventlowsgade.*

For hotels **near Nørreport** (Ibsens and Jørgensen), ride the S-tog from the station two stops to Nørreport, within about a 10-minute walk of the hotels.

For hotels **near Nyhavn** (71 Nyhavn and Bethel Sømandshjem), you can take the S-tog to Nørreport, then transfer to the Metro one stop to Kongens Nytorv, within a 10-minute walk of Nyhavn. Or you can take bus #11A or #15 (or #26 from around the corner) to Kongens Nytorv, next to Nyhavn.

Note: If you're staying near Nørreport (or near Nyhavn, an easy Metro connection from Nørreport), check your train schedule carefully; many local trains (such as some from Roskilde) continue through the main train station to the Nørreport station, saving you an extra step.

By Plane

Kastrup, Copenhagen's international airport, is a traveler's dream, with a TI, baggage check, bank, ATMs, post office, shopping mall, grocery store, bakery, and more. There are three check-in terminals, within walking distance of each other (departures screens tell you which terminal to go to). But on arrival, all flights feed into one big arrivals lobby in Terminal 3. When you pop out here, there's a TI kiosk on your left, taxis out the door on your right, trains straight ahead, and shops and eateries filling the atrium above you. You can use dollars or euros at the airport, but you'll get change back in kroner (airport code: CPH, airport info tel. 32 31 32 31, www.cph.dk).

To get from the airport to downtown, your options include the Metro, trains, and taxis. There are also buses into town, but the train/Metro is generally better.

The **Metro** runs directly from the airport to Christianshavn, Kongens Nytorv (near Nyhavn), and Nørreport, making it the best choice for getting into town if you're staying in any of these areas (36-kr three-zone ticket, yellow M2 line, direction: Vanløse, 4-10/hour, 11 minutes to Christianshavn). The Metro station is located at the end of Terminal 3 and is covered by the roof of the terminal.

Convenient **trains** also connect the airport with downtown (36-kr three-zone ticket, covered by railpass, 4/hour, 12 minutes). Buy your ticket from the ground-level ticket booth (look for *DSB:*

Tickets for Train, Metro & Bus signs) before riding the escalator down to the tracks. Track 2 has trains going into the city (track 1 is for trains going east, to Sweden). Trains into town stop at the main train station (signed *København H;* handy if you're sleeping at my recommended hotels behind the train station), as well as the Nørreport and Østerport stations. At Nørreport, you can connect to the Metro for Kongens Nytorv (near Nyhavn) and Christianshavn.

With the train/Metro trip being so quick, frequent, and cheap, I see no reason to take a taxi here. But if you do, **taxis** are fast, civil, accept credit cards, and charge about 250 kr for a ride to the town center.

By Boat
For information on Copenhagen's cruise terminals, see the end of this chapter.

Helpful Hints
Emergencies: Dial 112 and specify fire, police, or ambulance. Emergency calls from public phones are free.

Pharmacy: Steno Apotek is across from the train station (open 24 hours, Vesterbrogade 6C, tel. 33 14 82 66).

Blue Monday: As you plan, remember that most sights close on Monday, but these attractions remain open: Amalienborg Palace Museum (closed Mon Nov-April), Christiansborg Palace (closed Mon Oct-April), City Hall, Danish Design Center, Museum of Copenhagen, Rosenborg Castle (closed Mon Nov-April), Round Tower, Royal Library, Our Savior's Church, Tivoli Gardens (generally closed late Sept-mid-April), canal tours, and walking or bike tours. You can explore Christiania, but Monday is its rest day ("resting" from what, I'm not sure), so it's unusually quiet and some restaurants are closed.

Telephones: Use the telephone liberally—everyone speaks English. Calls anywhere in Denmark are cheap; calls to Norway and Sweden cost 6 kr per minute from a booth (half that from a private home). Get a phone card (sold at newsstands, starting at 30 kr). To make inexpensive international calls, buy an international phone card. There are a variety to choose from, varying in price. (7-Eleven stores give you a voucher that acts as the calling card, with instructions and your PIN code.)

Internet Access: Wi-Fi is easy to find in Copenhagen (available free at virtually all hotels and many cafés). **Telestation,** tucked behind the train station kitty-corner from the TI, is a call shop with several Internet terminals (10 kr/15 minutes,

15 kr/30 minutes, 25 kr/1 hour; Mon-Sat 10:00-21:00—until 19:00 in winter, Sun 11:00-20:00—until 18:00 in winter, Banegårdspladsen 1, tel. 33 93 00 02). Additionally, several places offer free Internet access (designed for quick info and email checks): **Copenhagen Central Library** (most terminals, least wait, midway between Nørreport and the Strøget at Krystalgade 15, Mon-Fri 10:00-19:00, Sat 10:00-14:00, closed Sun); **"Black Diamond" library** (2 stand-up terminals on the skyway over the street nearest the harbor); and the main **university building** (corner of Nørregade and Sankt Peders Stræde, 2 terminals just inside the door).

Laundry: Pams Møntvask is a good coin-op laundry near Nørreport (31 kr/load wash, 6 kr for soap, 2 kr/minute to dry, daily 6:00-21:00, 50 yards from Ibsens Hotel at 86 Nansensgade). **Tre Stjernet Møntvask** ("Three Star Laundry") is a few blocks behind the train station at Istedgade 45, near the Meatpacking District (wash-27 kr/load, soap-5 kr, dry-1 kr/1.5 minutes, daily 6:00-21:00). *Vaskel* is wash, *torring* is dry, and *sæbe* is soap.

Ferries: Book any ferries now that you plan to take later in Scandinavia. Visit a travel agent or call direct. For the Copenhagen-Oslo overnight ferry, call **DFDS** (Mon-Fri 9:30-17:00, tel. 33 42 30 00, www.dfdsseaways .com) or visit the **DSB Resjebureau** at the main train station. For the boat from Stockholm to Helsinki, contact **Viking Line** (08/452-4000, www.vikingline.fi) or **Tallink Silja** (tel. 08 22 21 40, www.tallinksilja.com). For the boat to St. Petersburg, contact **St. Peter Line** (www.stpeterline.com).

Jazz Festival: The Copenhagen Jazz Festival—10 days in early July—puts the town in a rollicking slide-trombone mood. The Danes are Europe's jazz enthusiasts, and this music festival fills the town with happiness. The TI prints up an extensive listing of each year's festival events, or get the latest at www .jazz.dk. There's also a winter jazz festival in February.

Updates to This Book: For news about changes to this book's coverage since it was published, see www.ricksteves.com/update.

Getting Around Copenhagen

By Public Transit: It's easy to navigate Copenhagen, with its fine buses, Metro, and S-tog (a suburban train system with stops in the city; Eurail valid on S-tog). For a helpful website that covers public-transport options (nationwide) in English, consult www .rejseplanen.dk.

The same **tickets** are used throughout the system. A 24-kr, two-zone ticket gets you an hour's travel within the center—pay as you board buses, or buy from station ticket offices or vending machines for the Metro. (Automated ticket machines may not accept American credit cards, but I was able to use an American debit card with a PIN, and most machines also take Danish cash; if you want to use your credit card and the machine won't take it, find a cashier.) Assume you'll be within the middle two zones unless traveling to or from the airport, which requires a three-zone ticket (36 kr).

One handy option is the blue, two-zone *klippekort,* which can be shared—for example, two people can take five rides each (145 kr for 10 rides, insert it in the validation box each time you board a train and it'll snip off one of your rides).

If you're traveling exclusively in central Copenhagen, the **City Pass** is a good value (75 kr/24 hours, 190 kr/72 hours, covers travel within zones 1-4, including the airport). To travel throughout the greater Copenhagen region—including side-trips such as Roskilde, Frederiksborg Castle, Louisiana, and Kronborg Castle—you'll need to pay more for a **"24-hour ticket"** (130 kr) or a **"7-day flexicard"** (225 kr—can be a good value even for less than a week). All passes are sold at stations, the TI, 7-Elevens, and other kiosks. Validate any all-day or multi-day ticket by stamping it in the yellow machine on the bus or at the station.

While the train system is slick (Metro and S-tog, described later), its usefulness is limited for the typical tourist—but **buses**

serve all of the major sights in town every five to eight minutes during daytime hours. If you're not riding a bike everywhere, get comfortable with the buses. Bus drivers are patient, have change, and speak English. City maps list bus routes. Locals are usually friendly and helpful. There's also a floating "Harbor Bus."

Bus lines that end with "A" (such as #1A) use quiet, eco-friendly, electric buses that are smaller than normal buses, allowing access into the narrower streets of the old town. Designed for tourists, these provide an easy overview to the city center. Among these, the following are particularly useful:

Bus **#1A** loops from the train station up to Kongens Nytorv (near Nyhavn) and then farther north, to Østerport.

Bus **#2A** goes from Christianshavn to the city center, then onward to points west.

Bus **#5A** connects the station more or less directly to Nørreport.

Bus **#6A** also connects the station to Nørreport, but on a much more roundabout route that twists through the central core (with several sightseeing-handy stops).

Bus **#11A** does a big loop from the train station through the core of town up to Nørreport, then down to Nyhavn before retracing its steps back via Nørreport to the train station.

Other, non-"A" buses, which are bigger and tend to be more direct, can be faster for some trips:

Bus **#14** runs from Nørreport (and near my recommended hotels) down to the city center, stopping near the Strøget and Slotsholmen Island, and eventually going near the main train station.

Buses **#15** and **#26** run a handy route right through the main tourist zone: train station/Tivoli to Slotsholmen Island to Kongens Nytorv (near Nyhavn) to the Amalienborg Palace/*Little Mermaid* area. Bus #26 continues even farther northward to the city's cruise ports, but the line splits, so pay attention to which bus you're on: Those marked *Langelinie* go to the Langelinie Pier, while *Færgehavn Nord* heads for Frihavnen. Note that bus #26 does not run on weekends.

Bus **#29** goes from Nyhavn to Slotsholmen Island to Tivoli.

Copenhagen's **Metro** line, while simple, is super-futuristic and growing. For most tourists' purposes, only the airport and three consecutive stops within the city matter: Nørreport (connected every few minutes by the S-tog to the main train station), Kongens Nytorv (near Nyhavn and the Strøget's north end), and Christianshavn. Nearly all recommended hotels are within walking distance of the main train station or these three stops.

The city is busy at work on the new Cityringen (City Circle) Metro line. When it opens in 2018, the Metro will instantly become far handier for tourists—linking the train station, Rådhuspladsen, Gammel Strand (near Slotsholmen Island), and Kongens Nytorv (near Nyhavn). In the meantime, you can expect to see massive construction zones at each of those locations. Eventually the Metro will also extend to Ørestad, the industrial and business center created after the Øresund Bridge was built between Denmark and Sweden (for the latest on the Metro, see www.m.dk).

The **S-tog** is basically a commuter line that links stations on the main train line through Copenhagen; for those visiting the city, the most important stops are the main train station and Nørreport (where it ties into the Metro system). However, the S-tog is very handy for reaching many of the outlying sights.

By Boat: The hop-on, hop-off "Harbor Bus" (Havnebus) boat stops at the "Black Diamond" library, Christianshavn (near Knippels Bridge), Nyhavn, the Opera House, and Nordre Tolbod, which is a short walk from *The Little Mermaid* site. The boat is actually part of the city bus system (lines #901 and #902) and covered by the tickets described earlier. Taking a long ride on this boat—from the library to the end of the line—is the "poor man's cruise," without commentary, of course (runs 6:00-19:00). Or, for a true sightseeing trip, consider a guided harbor cruise (described later under "Tours in Copenhagen").

By Taxi: Taxis are plentiful, easy to call or flag down, and pricey (26-kr pickup charge and then 13 kr/kilometer). For a short ride, four people spend about the same by taxi as by bus. Calling 35 35 35 35 will get you a taxi within minutes...with the meter already well on its way.

By Bike: Cyclists see more, save time and money, and really feel like locals. With a bike, you have Copenhagen at your command. I'd rather have a bike than a car and driver at my disposal. Virtually every street has a dedicated bike lane (complete with bike signal lights). Police issue 500-kr tickets to anyone riding on sidewalks or through pedestrian zones. Note also that bikes can't be parked just anywhere. Observe others and park your bike among other bikes. The simple built-in lock that binds the back tire is adequate.

Your best bet for renting a bike is to ask your hotelier first. Many rent decent bikes at reasonable rates to their guests, saving you a trip to a bike-rental outlet and letting you hit the road the moment you arrive.

For an (often) better-quality bike and advice from someone with more cycle expertise, consider one of these rental outfits in or near the city center:

• **Baisikeli Bike Rental,** behind Ørsteds Park just south of Nørreport (budget bike: 50 kr/6 hours, 80 kr/24 hours, 35 kr/extra day; better "standard" bike: 80 kr/6 hours, 110 kr/24 hours, 50 kr/extra day; daily 10:00-18:00; Turesensgade 10—tel. 53 71 02 29, this location closed in winter; second location tucked behind the Kødbyen district and train station at Ingerslevsgade 80; www.cph-bike-rental.dk). *Baisikeli* means "bike" in Swahili, and this company donates their refurbished used bikes to Africa.

• **Københavens Cyklebørs,** also near Nørreport (75 kr/1 day, 140 kr/2 days, 200 kr/3 days, 350 kr/week, Mon-Fri 9:00-17:30, Sat 10:00-13:30-but you can return bike until 21:00, closed Sun, Gothersgade 157—tel. 33 14 07 17, www.cykelborsen.dk).

• **Gammel Holm Cykler,** near Nyhavn (Holbergsgade 12—tel. 33 33 83 84).

From May through November, 2,400 clunky but practical little **free bikes** are scattered around the old town center (basically

COPENHAGEN

the terrain covered in the Copenhagen map in this chapter). Simply locate one of the hundred-some racks, unlock a bike by popping a 20-kr coin into the handlebar, and pedal away. When you're done, plug your bike back into any other rack, and your deposit coin will pop back out; if you can't find a rack, just abandon your bike and someone will take it back and pocket your coin. These simple bikes come with theft-proof parts (unusable on regular bikes) and—they claim—embedded computer chips so that bike patrols can trace and retrieve strays. The bikes are funded by advertisements painted on the wheels and by a progressive electorate. Copenhagen's radical city-bike program is a clever idea, but in practice, it doesn't work great for sightseers. It's hard to find bikes in working order, and when you get to the sight and park your bike, it'll be gone by the time you're ready to pedal on. (The 20-kr deposit coin acts as an incentive for any kid or homeless person to pick up city bikes not plugged back into their special racks.) Use the free bikes for a one-way pedal here and there. For efficiency, pay to rent one.

Tours in Copenhagen

On Foot

Copenhagen is an ideal city to get to know by foot. You have two good options:

▲▲**Hans Christian Andersen Tours by Richard Karpen**— Once upon a time, American Richard Karpen visited Copenhagen and fell in love with the city. Now, dressed as Hans Christian Andersen in a 19th-century top hat and long coat, he leads one-hour tours that wander in and out of buildings, courtyards, back streets, and unusual parts of the old town. Along the way, he gives insightful and humorous background on the history, culture, and contemporary life of Denmark, Copenhagen, and the Danes.

Richard offers three entertaining and informative walks: "Castles and Kings," "Royal Copenhagen," and "Romantic Copenhagen." Each walk includes a stroll of a little more than a mile (with breaks) and covers different parts of the historic center (100 kr apiece, kids under 12 free; departs from the TI, up the street from the main train station at Vesterbrogade 4A—at the corner with Bernstorffsgade and directly across from Hard Rock Café; mid-May-mid-Sept Mon-Sat at 10:30, none on Sun; departs promptly—if you miss him try to catch up with the tour at the next stop on Rådhuspladsen). Richard's tours, while all different, complement each other and are of equal introductory value. Go whichever day is convenient for you. The earlier you take this tour, the earlier you'll have a good historical orientation.

Richard also does excellent tours of Rosenborg Castle (80 kr, doesn't include castle entry, mid-May-mid-Sept Mon and Thu at 13:30, one hour, led by dapper Renaissance "Sir Richard," meet outside castle ticket office). You can also hire him for a private tour of the city or of Rosenborg Castle (1,000 kr, or save a bit by paying $165 in US dollars, May-Sept, advance notice required, mobile 60 43 48 26, copenhagenwalks@yahoo.com).

For details, see www.copenhagenwalks.com. No reservations are needed for Richard's scheduled tours—just show up.

▲▲**Copenhagen History Tours**—Christian Donatzky, a charming young Dane with a master's degree in history, runs a walking tour on Saturday mornings. Themes vary by month: In April and May, Christian offers "Reformed Copenhagen" (covering the period from 1400-1600); in June and July, he runs the "King's Copenhagen" (1600-1800); and in August and September, he leads special themed tours—in 2013, he will focus on Danish philosopher Søren Kierkegaard (in honor of the thinker's 200th birthday), while in 2014 and beyond, the tour will feature "Hans Christian Andersen's Copenhagen" (1800-present). The tours are thoughtfully designed, and those with a serious interest in Danish history find them time well spent. Strolling with Christian is like walking with your own private Danish encyclopedia (80 kr, Sat at 10:00, approximately 1.5 hours, small groups of 5-15 people, tours depart from statue of Bishop Absalon on Højbro Plads between the Strøget and Christiansborg Palace, English only, no reservations necessary—just show up, tel. 28 49 44 35, www.history tours.dk, info@historytours.dk).

By Boat

For many, the best way to experience the city's canals and harbor is by canal boat. Two companies offer essentially the same live, three-language, one-hour cruises. Both

Hans Christian Andersen
(1805-1875)

The author of such classic fairy tales as *The Ugly Duckling* was an ugly duckling himself—a misfit who blossomed. Hans Christian

Andersen (called H. C., pronounced "hoe see" by the Danes) was born to a poor shoemaker in Odense. As a child he was gangly, high-strung, and effeminate. He avoided school because the kids laughed at him, so he spent his time in a fantasy world of books and plays. When his father died, the 11-year-old was on his own, forced into manual labor. He loved playing with a marionette theater that his father had made for him, sparking a lifelong love affair with the theater. In 1819, at the age of 14, he moved to Copenhagen to pursue an acting career and worked as a boy soprano for the Royal Theater. When his voice changed, the director encouraged him to return to school. He dutifully attended—a teenager among boys—and eventually went on to the university. As rejections piled up for his acting aspirations, Andersen began to shift his theatrical ambitions to playwriting.

After graduation, Andersen won a two-year scholarship to travel around Europe, the first of many trips he'd make and write about. His experiences abroad were highly formative, providing inspiration for many of his tales. Still in his 20s, he published an (obviously autobiographical) novel, *The Improvisatore*, about a poor young man who comes into his own while traveling in Italy. The novel launched his writing career, and soon he was hobnobbing with the international crowd—Charles Dickens, Victor Hugo, Franz Liszt, Richard Wagner, Henrik Ibsen, and Edvard Grieg.

Despite his many famous friends, Andersen remained a

boats leave at least twice an hour from Nyhavn and Christiansborg Palace, cruise around the palace and Christianshavn area, and then proceed into the wide-open harbor. Best on a sunny day, it's a relaxing way to see *The Little Mermaid* and munch on a lazy picnic during the slow-moving narration.

▲Netto-Bådene—These inexpensive cruises cost about half the price of their rival, Canal Tours Copenhagen. Go with Netto; there's no reason to pay double (45 kr, mid-March–mid-Oct daily 10:00-17:00, runs later in summer, sign at dock shows next departure, generally every 20 minutes, dress warmly—boats lonely soul who never married. Of uncertain sexuality, he had very close male friendships and journaled about unrequited love affairs with several women, including the famous opera star of the day, Jenny Lind, the "Swedish Nightingale." (For more on this aspect of his life, see the sidebar on page 37.) Without a family of his own, he became very close with the children of his friends—and, through his fairy tales, with a vast extended family of kids around the world.

Though he wrote novels, plays, and travel literature, it was his fairy tales, including *The Ugly Duckling*, *The Emperor's New Clothes*, *The Princess and the Pea*, *The Little Mermaid*, and *The Red Shoes*, that made him famous in Denmark and abroad. They made him Denmark's best-known author, the "Danish Charles Dickens." Some stories are based on earlier folk tales, and others came straight from his inventive mind, all written in an informal, conversational style that was considered unusual and even surprising at the time.

Andersen's compelling tales appeal to children and adults alike. They're full of magic and touch on strong, universal emotions—the pain of being different, the joy of self-discovery, and the struggle to fit in. The ugly duckling, for example, is teased by his fellow ducks before he finally discovers his true identity as a beautiful swan. In *The Emperor's New Clothes*, a boy is derided by everyone for speaking the simple, self-evident truth that the emperor is fooling himself. Harry Potter author J. K. Rowling recently said, "The indelible characters he created are so deeply implanted in our subconscious that we sometimes forget that we were not born with the stories." (For more on Andersen's famous story *The Little Mermaid*—and what it might tell us about his life—see page 37.)

By the time of his death, the poor shoemaker's son was wealthy, cultured, and had been knighted. His rise through traditional class barriers mirrors the social progress of the 19th century.

are open-top until Sept, tel. 32 54 41 02, www.havnerundfart .dk). Netto boats often make two stops where passengers can get off, then hop back on a later boat—at the bridge near *The Little Mermaid*, and at the Langebro bridge near Danhostel. Not every boat makes these stops; check the clock on the bridges for the next departure time.

Don't confuse the cheaper Netto and pricier Canal Tours Copenhagen boats: At Nyhavn, the Netto dock is midway down the canal (on the city side), while the Canal Tours Copenhagen dock is at the head of the canal. Near Christiansborg Palace, the

Netto boats leave from Holmen's Bridge in front of the palace, while Canal Tours Copenhagen boats depart from Gammel Strand, 200 yards away. Boats leaving from Christiansborg are generally less crowded than those leaving from Nyhavn.

Canal Tours Copenhagen—This more expensive option does the same cruise as Netto for 70 kr (daily March-late Oct 9:30-17:00, until 20:00 late June-late Aug; late-Oct-Dec 10:00-15:00, no tours Jan-Feb, boats are sometimes covered if it's raining, tel. 32 96 30 00, www.stromma.dk).

In summer, Canal Tours Copenhagen also runs unguided hop-on, hop-off **"water bus"** tours (40 kr/single trip, 70 kr/24 hours, daily late May-early Sept 10:15-18:45) and 1.5-hour evening **jazz cruises** (see "Nightlife in Copenhagen").

By Bus

Hop-on, Hop-off Bus Tours—These offer a basic 1.25- to 1.5-hour circle of the city sights, allowing you to get on and off as you like: Tivoli Gardens, Gammel Strand near Christiansborg Palace, *The Little Mermaid* site, Rosenborg Castle, Nyhavn sailors' quarter, and more, with recorded narration. The options include **City Sightseeing** (red buses, 155 kr, 185 kr includes Carlsberg and Christiania routes, ticket good for 24 hours, 2/hour, May-Aug daily 10:00-16:30, shorter hours off-season, bus departs City Hall below the *Lur Blowers* statue—to the left of City Hall—or at many other stops throughout city, pay driver, tel. 25 55 66 88, www.city-sightseeing.dk) and **Open Top Tours** (green buses, 175 kr, 35 kr more to add cruise on Canal Tours Copenhagen, ticket good for 24 hours, 2/hour, departures 10:00-16:00, www.stromma.dk/en/opentoptours). Another operation—called **Step On Step Off**—does a similar route with slightly lower frequency (every 45 minutes in summer, hourly in winter; 170 kr/1 day, 200 kr/2 days, www.steponstepoff.dk).

City Sightseeing also runs jaunts into the countryside, with themes such as Vikings, castles, and Hamlet. There are other companies as well; a variety of guided bus tours depart from Rådhuspladsen in front of the Palace Hotel.

By Bike

▲Bike Copenhagen with Mike—Mike Sommerville offers a good three-hour, guided tour of the city daily at 10:30 (with a second departure at 14:30 Tue-Wed, Fri, and Sat in June-Aug, and on Sat in Sept; 290 kr including bike rental, cash only). A Copenhagen native, Mike enjoys showing off his city to visitors by biking at a leisurely pace, "along the high roads, low roads, in-roads, and off-roads of Copenhagen." All tours are in English, and depart from the Bike Copenhagen with Mike tour base at Sankt Peders Straede 47, in the Latin Quarter. Mike also offers a night tour, a countryside tour, and private tours; see the details at www. bikecopenhagenwithmike.dk.

Self-Guided Walk

The Strøget and Copenhagen's Heart and Soul

Start from Rådhuspladsen (City Hall Square), the bustling heart of Copenhagen, dominated by the tower of the City Hall. Today this square always seems to be hosting some lively community event, but it was once Copenhagen's fortified west end. For 700 years, Copenhagen was contained within its city walls. By the mid-1800s, 140,000 people were packed inside. The overcrowding led to hygiene problems. (A cholera outbreak killed 5,000.) It was clear: The walls needed to come down...and they did. Those formidable town walls survive today only in echoes—a circular series of roads and the remnants of moats, now people-friendly city lakes (see "The Story of Copenhagen" sidebar, earlier).

• *Stand 50 yards in front of City Hall and turn clockwise for a...*

Rådhuspladsen Spin-Tour

The **City Hall,** or Rådhus, is worth a visit. Old **Hans Christian Andersen** sits to the right of City Hall, almost begging to be in another photo (as he used to in real life). Climb onto his well-worn knee. (While up there, you might take off your shirt for a racy photo, as many Danes enjoy doing.)

The wooded area behind Andersen is **Tivoli Gardens.** In 1843, magazine publisher Georg Carstensen convinced the king to let him build a pleasure garden outside the walls of crowded Copenhagen. The king quickly agreed, knowing that happy people care less about fighting for democracy. Tivoli became Europe's first great public amusement park. When the train lines came, the station was placed just beyond Tivoli.

The big, broad boulevard is **Vesterbrogade** ("Western Way"), which led to the western gate of the medieval city (behind you, where the pedestrian boulevard begins). Here, in the traffic hub of this huge city, you'll notice...not many cars. Denmark's 180 percent tax on car purchases makes the bus, Metro, or bike a sweeter option.

Down Vesterbrogade towers the **SAS building,** Copenhagen's only skyscraper. Locals say it seems so tall because the clouds hang so low. When it was built in 1960, Copenhageners took one look and decided—that's enough of a skyline.

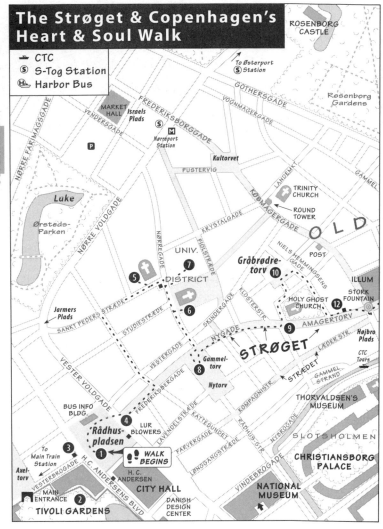

The Strøget & Copenhagen's Heart & Soul Walk

- CTC
- ⑤ S-Tog Station
- Harbor Bus

ROSENBORG CASTLE

To Østerport ⑤ Station

GOTHERSGADE

Rosenborg Gardens

FREDERIKSBORGGADE   VOGNMAGERGADE

MARKET HALL   Israels Plads

VENDERSGADE

Nørreport Station Ⓜ

Kultorvet

PUSTERVIG

LANDEMÆRKET   GAMMEL

TRINITY CHURCH

ROUND TOWER

Luke

Ørsteds-Parken

NØRRE VOLDGADE

KØBMAGERGADE

KRYSTALGADE

OLD

NØRREGADE

FIOLSTRÆDE

NIELS HEMMINGSENS GADE

POST

UNIV.

⑦

Gråbrødre-torv ⑩

⑤

DISTRICT

⑥

HOLY GHOST CHURCH

ILLUM

STORK FOUNTAIN

⑫

Jarmers Plads

SANKT PEDERS STRÆDE   STUDIESTRÆDE

SKINDERGADE   KLOSTERSTR.

AMAGERTORV

⑨

Højbro Plads

NYGADE

STRØGET

LÆDERSTR.

CTC Tours

VESTER VOLDGADE

VESTERGADE

FREDERIKSBERGGADE

Gammel-torv   ⑧

Nytorv

GAMMEL STRAND

KOMPAGNISTR.   STRÆDET

RÅDHUS-STR.

THORVALDSEN'S MUSEUM

SLOTSHOLMEN

BUS INFO BLDG.

LUR BLOWERS

LAVENDELSTRÆDE   KATTESUNDET

FARVERGADE   LØNGANGSTRÆDE

NYBROGADE

CHRISTIANSBORG PALACE

Rådhus-pladsen ①

④

WALK BEGINS

③

To Main Train Station

Axel-torv

VESTERBROGADE   H.C. ANDERSENS GADE

②

H.C. ANDERSEN

CITY HALL

DANISH DESIGN CENTER

TIVOLI GARDENS

MAIN ENTRANCE

H.C. ANDERSENS BLVD

VINDEBROGADE

NATIONAL MUSEUM

COPENHAGEN

The golden **weather girls** (on the corner, high above Vesterbrogade) indicate the weather: on a bike (fair weather) or with an umbrella. These two have been called the only women in Copenhagen you can trust, but for years they've been stuck in almost-sunny mode...with the bike just peeking out. Notice that the red temperature dots max out at 28° Celsius (that's 82° Fahrenheit).

To the right, just down the street, is the Tiger Store (a popular local dime store...everything is priced at 10 or 20 kr). The next street (once the local Fleet Street, with the big newspapers) still

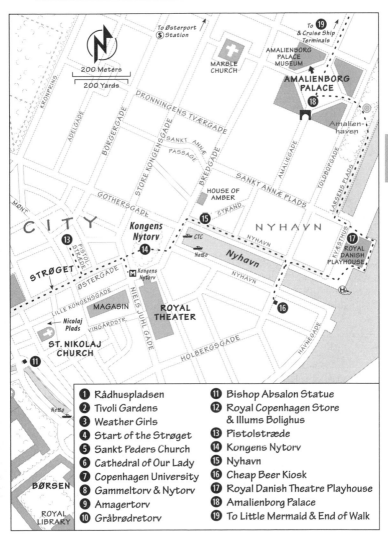

To Østerport Ⓢ Station

To ⑲ & Cruise Ship Terminals

AMALIENBORG PALACE MUSEUM

MARBLE CHURCH

AMALIENBORG PALACE

⑱

Amalienhaven

COPENHAGEN

200 Meters
200 Yards

KRONPRINS

KRONPRINS

ADELGADE

BORGERGADE

DRONNINGENS TVÆRGADE

STORE KONGENSGADE

SANKT ANNÆ PASSAGE

BREDGADE

SANKT ANNÆ PLADS

AMALIEGADE

TOLDBODGADE

Larsens Plads

GOTHERSGADE

MØNT

C I T Y

HOUSE OF AMBER

STRAND

Kongens Nytorv

⑬

PISTOLSTRÆDE

N Y H A V N

⑮

⑰

ROYAL DANISH PLAYHOUSE

KVÆSTHUS

STRØGET

ØSTERGADE

Ⓜ Kongens Nytorv

⑭

CTC

Netto

Nyhavn

NYHAVN

NYHAVN

LILLE KONGENSGADE

NIELS JUHL GADE

VINGÅRDSTR.

MAGASIN

ROYAL THEATER

HAVNEGADE

⑯

Ⓗ

Nicolaj Plads

ST. NIKOLAJ CHURCH

HOLBERGSGADE

⑪

Netto

BØRSEN

ROYAL LIBRARY

❶ Rådhuspladsen	⓫ Bishop Absalon Statue
❷ Tivoli Gardens	⓬ Royal Copenhagen Store & Illums Bolighus
❸ Weather Girls	
❹ Start of the Strøget	⓭ Pistolstræde
❺ Sankt Peders Church	⓮ Kongens Nytorv
❻ Cathedral of Our Lady	⓯ Nyhavn
❼ Copenhagen University	⓰ Cheap Beer Kiosk
❽ Gammeltorv & Nytorv	⓱ Royal Danish Theatre Playhouse
❾ Amagertorv	⓲ Amalienborg Palace
❿ Gråbrødretorv	⓳ To Little Mermaid & End of Walk

has the offices for *Politiken* (the leading Danish newspaper) and the best bookstore in town, Boghallen.

As you spin farther right, three fast-food joints stand at the entry to the Strøget (STROY-et), Copenhagen's grand pedestrian boulevard—where we're heading next. Just beyond that and the Art Deco-style Palace Hotel (with a tower to serve as a sister to the City Hall) is the ***Lur Blowers* sculpture,** which honors the earliest warrior Danes. The *lur* is a curvy, trombone-sounding horn that was used to call soldiers to battle or to accompany pagan religious processions. The earliest bronze *lurs* date as far back as 3,500 years ago. Later, the Vikings used a wood version of the *lur*. The ancient originals, which still play, are displayed in the National Museum. (City tour buses leave from below these Vikings.)

• *Now head down the pedestrian boulevard.*

The Strøget

The American trio of Burger King, 7-Eleven, and KFC marks the start of this otherwise charming pedestrian street. Finished in 1962, Copenhagen's experimental, tremendously successful, and much-copied pedestrian shopping mall is a string of lively (and individually named) streets and lovely squares that bunny-hop through the old town from City Hall to the Nyhavn quarter, a 20-minute stroll away.

As you wander down this street, remember that the commercial focus of a historic street like the Strøget drives up the land value, which generally trashes the charm and tears down the old buildings. Look above the modern window displays and street-level advertising to discover bits of 19th-century character that still survive. Though the Strøget has become hamburgerized, historic bits and attractive pieces of old Copenhagen are just off this commercial cancan.

After one block (at Kattesundet), make a side-trip three blocks left into Copenhagen's colorful **university district.** Formerly the old brothel neighborhood, later the heart of Copenhagen's hippie community in the 1960s, today this "Latin Quarter" is Soho chic. At Sankt Peders Stræde, turn right and walk to the end of the street.

Along the way, look for large mansions that once circled expansive **courtyards.** As the population grew, the city walls constricted Copenhagen's physical size. The courtyards were gradually filled with higgledy-piggledy secondary buildings. Today throughout the old center, you can step off a busy pedestrian mall and back in time into these characteristic half-timbered time warps. Replace the parked car with a tired horse and the bikes with a line of outhouses, and you're in 19th-century Copenhagen. If you see an open courtyard door, you're welcome to discreetly wander in and look around.

You'll also pass funky shops, and the big brick **Sankt Peders Church**—the old German merchant community's church, which still holds services in German. Its crypt (filling a ground-floor building out back due to the boggy nature of the soil) is filled with fancy German tombs (fee to enter).

• *When Sankt Peders Stræde intersects with Nørregade, look right to find the big, Neoclassical...*

Cathedral of Our Lady (Vor Frue Kirche)

The obelisk-like **Reformation Memorial** across the street from the cathedral celebrates Denmark's break from the Roman Catholic Church to become Lutheran in 1536. Walk around and study the reliefs of great Danish reformers protesting from their pulpits. The relief facing the church shows King Christian III presiding over the pivotal town council meeting when they decided to break away from Rome. As a young man, Prince Christian had traveled to Germany, where he was influenced by Martin Luther. He returned to take the Danish throne by force, despite Catholic opposition. Realizing the advantages of being the head of his own state church, Christian confiscated church property and established the state Lutheran Church. King Christian was crowned inside this cathedral. Because of the reforms of 1536, there's no Mary in the Cathedral of Our Lady.

The cathedral's **facade** looks like a Greek temple. (Two blocks to the right, in the distance, notice more Neoclassicism—the law courts.) You can see why Golden Age Copenhagen (early 1800s) fancied itself a Nordic Athens. Old Testament figures (King David and Moses) flank the cathedral's entryway. Above, John the Baptist stands where you'd expect to see Greek gods. He invites you in...to the New Testament.

The **interior** is a world of Neoclassical serenity. Go inside (free, open daily 8:00-17:00). This pagan temple now houses

Christianity. The nave is lined by the 12 apostles, clad in classical robes—masterpieces by the great Danish sculptor Bertel Thorvaldsen. Each strikes a meditative pose, carrying his identifying symbol: Peter with keys, Andrew with the X-shaped cross of his execution, Matthew and John writing their books, and so on. They lead to a statue of the *Risen Christ*, standing where the statue of Zeus would have been: inside a temple-like niche, flanked by columns, and topped with a pediment. Rather than wearing a royal robe, Jesus wears his burial shroud, opens his arms wide, and says, "Come to me." (Mormons will recognize this statue—a

replica stands in the visitors center at Salt Lake City's Temple Square and is often reproduced in church publications.) The marvelous acoustics are demonstrated in free organ concerts Saturdays in July and August at noon. Notice how, in good Protestant style, only the front half of the pews are "reversible," allowing the congregation to flip around and face the pulpit (in the middle of the church) to better hear the sermon.

• *Head back outside. If you face the facade and look to the left (across the square called Frue Plads), you'll see...*

Copenhagen University

Now home to 30,000 students, this university was founded by the king in the 15th century to stop the Danish brain drain to Paris.

Today tuition is free (but room, board, and beer are not). Locals say it's easy to get in, but, given the wonderful lifestyle, very hard to get out.

Step up the middle steps of the university's big building and enter a colorful lobby, starring Athena and Apollo. The frescoes celebrate high thinking, with themes such as the triumph of wisdom over barbarism. Notice how harmoniously the architecture, sculpture, and painting work together. (Just inside the door are two stand-up terminals offering free Internet access.)

Outside, busts honor great minds from the faculty, including (at the end) Niels Bohr, a professor who won the 1922 Nobel Prize for theoretical physics. He evaded the clutches of the Nazi science labs by fleeing to America in 1943, where he helped develop the atomic bomb.

• *Rejoin the Strøget (down where you saw the law courts) at the twin squares called...*

Gammeltorv and Nytorv

This was the old town center. In Gammeltorv ("Old Square"), the Fountain of Charity (Caritas) is named for the figure of Charity on top. It has provided drinking water to locals since the early 1600s. Featuring a pregnant woman squirting water from her breasts next to a boy urinating, this was just too much for people of the Victorian Age. They corked both figures and raised the statue to what they hoped would be out of view. The Asian-looking kiosk was one of the city's first community telephone centers from the days before phones were privately owned. Look at the reliefs ringing its top: an airplane with bird wings (c. 1900) and two women talking on the newfangled phone. (It was thought business would popularize the telephone, but actually it was women.)

While Gammeltorv was a place of happiness and merriment, Nytorv ("New Square") was a place of severity and judgment.

Walk to the small raised area in front of the old ancient-Greek-style former City Hall. Do a 360. The square is Neoclassical (built mostly around 1800). Read the old Danish on the City Hall facade: "With Law Shall Man Build the Land." Look down at the pavement and read the plaque: "Here stood the town's *Kag* (whipping post) until 1780."

• *Now walk down the next stretch of the Strøget to reach...*

Amagertorv

This is prime real estate for talented street entertainers and pickpockets. Walk to the stately brick Holy Ghost church (Helligåndskirken). The fine spire is typical of old Danish churches. Under the stepped gable was a medieval hospital run by monks (one of the oldest buildings in town, dating from the 12th century).

A block behind the church (walk down Valkendorfsgade—the street just before the church—and through a passage under the rust-colored building at #32) is the leafy and caffeine-stained **Gråbrødretorv.** This "Grey Friars' Square," surrounded by fine

old buildings, is a popular place for an outdoor meal or drink in the summer. At the end of the square, the street Niels Hemmingsens Gade returns (past the recommended Copenhagen Jazz House, a good place for live music nightly) to the Strøget.

Once at the Strøget, turn left and continue down Amagertorv, with its fine inlaid Italian granite stonework, to the next square with the "stork" fountain (actually three herons). From the fountain, you can see the imposing Parliament building, Christiansborg Palace (with its "three crowns" spire) and an equestrian statue of Bishop Absalon, the city's founder (canal boat tours depart

Copenhagen at a Glance

▲▲▲**Tivoli Gardens** Copenhagen's classic amusement park, with rides, music, food, and other fun. **Hours:** Mid-April-late Sept daily 11:00-22:00, later Fri-Sat and mid-June-late Aug, also open daily 11:00-22:00 for a week in mid-Oct and mid-Nov-late Dec. See page 38.

▲▲▲**National Museum** History of Danish civilization with tourable 19th-century Victorian Apartment. **Hours:** Museum— Tue-Sun 10:00-17:00, closed Mon; Victorian Apartment—tours June-Sept Sat at 14:00. See page 42.

▲▲▲**Rosenborg Castle and Treasury** Renaissance castle of larger-than-life "warrior king" Christian IV. **Hours:** June-Aug daily 10:00-17:00; May and Sept-Oct daily 10:00-16:00; Nov-Dec Tue-Sun 11:00-14:00 (treasury until 16:00), closed Mon; Jan-April Tue-Sun 11:00-16:00, closed Mon. See page 53.

▲▲▲**Christiania** Colorful counterculture squatters' colony. **Hours:** Always open. See page 62.

▲▲**Christiansborg Palace** Royal reception rooms with dazzling tapestries. **Hours:** Palace—daily 10:00-17:00 except closed Mon Oct-April; stables—daily 13:30-16:00 except closed Mon Oct-April. See page 45.

▲▲**Museum of Danish Resistance** Chronicle of Denmark's struggle against the Nazis. **Hours:** May be closed; if open May-Sept Tue-Sun 10:00-16:00, Oct-April Tue-Sun 10:00-15:00, closed Mon year-round. See page 51.

▲▲**Thorvaldsen's Museum** Works of the Danish Neoclassical sculptor. **Hours:** Tue-Sun 10:00-17:00, closed Mon. See page 47.

▲**City Hall** Copenhagen's landmark, packed with Danish history and symbolism and topped with a tower. **Hours:** Mon-Fri 8:30-

nearby). The Victorian WCs here (steps down from fountain, 2 kr, free urinals) are a delight.

Amagertorv is a highlight for shoppers, with the Royal Copenhagen store—stacked with three floors of porcelain— and Illums Bolighus' three floors of modern Danish design (see "Shopping in Copenhagen," later). A block toward the canal— running parallel to the Strøget—starts Strædet, which is a "second Strøget" featuring cafés, antique shops, and no fast food.

North of Amagertorv, a broad pedestrian mall called **Købmagergade** leads past a fine modern bakery (Illum Bager,

16:30, some Sat 10:00-13:00, closed Sun. See page 40.

▲**Ny Carlsberg Glyptotek** Scandinavia's top art gallery, featuring Egyptians, Greeks, Etruscans, French, and Danes. **Hours:** Tue-Sun 11:00-17:00, closed Mon. See page 41.

▲**Museum of Copenhagen** The story of Copenhagen, displayed in an old house. **Hours:** Daily 10:00-17:00. See page 45.

▲**Danish Jewish Museum** Exhibit tracing the 400-year history of Danish Jews, in a unique building by American architect Daniel Libeskind. **Hours:** June-Aug Tue-Sun 10:00-17:00; Sept-May Tue-Fri 13:00-16:00, Sat-Sun 12:00-17:00; closed Mon year-round. See page 50.

▲**Amalienborg Palace Museum** Quick and intimate look at Denmark's royal family. **Hours:** May-Oct daily 10:00-16:00; Nov-April Tue-Sun 11:00-16:00, closed Mon. See page 51.

▲**Rosenborg Gardens** Park surrounding Rosenborg Castle, filled with statues and statuesque Danes. **Hours:** Always open. See page 59.

▲**National Gallery of Denmark** Good Danish and Modernist collections. **Hours:** Tue-Sun 10:00-17:00, Wed until 20:00, closed Mon. See page 60.

▲**Our Savior's Church** Spiral-spired church with bright Baroque interior. **Hours:** Church—daily 11:00-15:30 but may close for special services; tower—July-mid-Sept Mon-Sat 10:00-19:00, Sun 10:30-19:00; April-June and mid-Sept-Nov daily until 16:00, closed Dec-March and in bad weather. See page 61.

next to McDonald's; salads, sandwiches, and traditional pastries) to Christian IV's Round Tower and the Latin Quarter (university district). The recommended Café Norden overlooks the fountain— a good place for a meal or coffee with a view. The second floor offers the best vantage point.

The final stretch of the Strøget leads to **Pistolstræde** (leading off the Strøget to the left from Østergade at #24, just after crossing the busy street), a cute lane of shops in restored 18th-century buildings. Wander back into the half-timbered section.

• *Continuing along the Strøget, passing major department stores (see "Shopping in Copenhagen," later), you'll come to the biggest square in town...*

Kongens Nytorv

The "King's New Square" is home to the National Theater, French embassy, and venerable Hotel d'Angleterre. In the mid-1600s the city expanded, pushing its wall farther east. The equestrian statue in the middle of the square celebrates Christian V, who made this square the city's geographical and cultural center. In 1676, King Christian rode off to reconquer the southern tip of Sweden and reclaim Denmark's dominance.

He returned empty-handed and broke. Denmark became a second-rate power, but Copenhagen prospered. In the winter this square becomes a popular ice-skating rink.

Before entering the square, walk to the right, toward the small glass pyramids (marking the Metro). Wander into **Hviids Vinstue,** the town's oldest wine cellar (from 1723, before the Metro station, at #19, under the Bali Restaurant) to check out its characteristic interior and fascinating old Copenhagen photos. It's a colorful spot for an open-face sandwich and a beer (three sandwiches and a beer for 65 kr at lunchtime). Their wintertime *gløgg* (hot spiced wine) is legendary. Across the street, towering above the Metro station, is Magasin du Nord, the grandest old department store in town.

The **Metro** that runs underground here features state-of-the-art technology (automated cars, no driver...sit in front to watch the tracks coming at you). As the cars come and go without drivers, compare this system to the public transit in your town.

• *Back up at ground level, walk across the square to the trendy harbor of...*

Nyhavn

Established in the 1670s along with Kongens Nytorv, Nyhavn ("New Harbor") is a recently gentrified sailors' quarter. (Hong Kong is the last of the nasty bars from the rough old days.) With its trendy cafés, jazz clubs, and tattoo shops (pop into Tattoo Ole at #17—fun photos, very traditional), Nyhavn is a wonderful place to hang out. The canal is filled with glamorous old sailboats of all sizes. Historic sloops are welcome to moor here in Copenhagen's ever-changing boat museum. Hans Christian Andersen lived and wrote his first stories here (in the red double-gabled building on the right at #20). A miniscule amber museum is above the House of Amber at the head of the canal.

Wander the quay, enjoying the frat-party parade of tattoos (hotter weather reveals more tattoos). Celtic and Nordic mythological designs are in (as is bodybuilding, by the looks of things). The place thrives—with the cheap-beer drinkers dockside and the richer and older ones looking on from comfier cafés.

A note about all this public beer-drinking: There's no more beer consumption here than in the US; it's just out in public. Many

young Danes can't afford to drink in a bar, so they "picnic drink" their beers in squares and along canals, spending a quarter of the bar price for a bottle from a nearby kiosk. Consider grabbing a cold 10-kr beer yourself and joining the scene (the kiosk is on Holbergsgade, just over the bridge and on the left, open daily until 24:00).

From the end of Nyhavn canal, turn left around the **Royal Danish Theatre's Playhouse.** Continuing north along the har-

bor, you'll stroll a delightful waterfront promenade to the modern fountain of Amaliehaven Park, immediately across the harbor from Copenhagen's slick Opera House. The Opera House is bigger than it looks because much of it is underground. Its striking design is controversial. Completed in 2005 by Henning Larsen, it was a $400 million gift to the nation from an oil-shipping magnate.

• *A block inland (behind the fountain) is the orderly...*

Amalienborg Palace and Square

Queen Margrethe II and her husband live in the mansion to your immediate left as you enter the square from the harborside. (If the flag's flying, she's home.) Her son and heir to the throne, Crown Prince Frederik, recently moved into the mansion across the

street with his wife, Australian businesswoman Mary Donaldson, and their four children.

Though the guards change with royal fanfare at noon only when the queen is in residence, they shower every morning. The royal guard often has a police escort when it marches through town on special occasions—leading locals to joke that theirs is "the only army in the world that needs police protection."

The small **Amalienborg Palace Museum** offers an intimate look at royal living (far side of square).

The equestrian statue of Frederick V is a reminder that this square was the centerpiece of a planned town he envisioned in 1750. It was named for him—Frederikstaden. During the 18th century, Denmark's population grew and the country thrived (as trade flourished and its neutrality kept it out of the costly wars impoverishing much of Europe). Frederikstaden, with its strong Neoclassical harmony, was designed as a luxury neighborhood for the city's business elite. Nobility and other big shots moved in, but the king came here only after his other palace burned down in a 1794 fire.

Just inland, the striking Frederikskirke—better known as the **Marble Church**—was designed to fit this ritzy new quarter. If it's open, step inside to bask in its vast, serene, Pantheon-esque atmosphere (free, Mon-Thu 10:00-17:00, Fri-Sun 12:00-17:00).

• *From the square, Amaliegade leads two blocks north to...*

Kastellet Park

In this park, you'll find some worthwhile sightseeing. Just before the park's entrance, look for Denmark's fascinating (and free) WWII-era **Museum of Danish Resistance**. Beyond that is the

1908 **Gefion Fountain,** which illustrates the myth of the goddess who was given one night to carve a hunk out of Sweden to make into Denmark's main island, Sjælland (or "Zealand" in English), which you're on. Gefion transformed her four sons into oxen to do the job,  and the chunk she removed from Sweden is supposedly Vänern, Sweden's largest lake. If you look at a map showing Sweden and Denmark, the island and the lake are, in fact, roughly the same shape.

Next to the fountain is an Anglican church built of flint. Climb up the stairs by the fountain and continue along the top of the rampart about five minutes to reach the harborfront site

The Little Mermaid and Hans Christian Andersen

"Far out in the ocean, where the water is as blue as a cornflower, as clear as crystal, and very, very deep..." there lived a young mermaid. So begins one of Hans Christian Andersen's (1805-1875) best-known stories. The plot line starts much like the Disney children's movie, but it's spiced with poetic description and philosophical dialogue about the immortal soul.

The mermaid's story goes like this: One day, a young mermaid spies a passing ship and falls in love with a handsome human prince. The ship is wrecked in a storm, and she saves the prince's life. To be with the prince, the mermaid asks a sea witch to give her human legs. In exchange, she agrees to give up her voice and the chance of ever returning to the sea. And, the witch tells her, if the prince doesn't marry her, she will immediately die heartbroken and without an immortal soul. The mermaid agrees, and her fish tail becomes a pair of beautiful but painful legs. She woos the prince—who loves her in return—but he eventually marries another. Heartbroken, the mermaid prepares to die. She's given one last chance to save herself: She must kill the prince on his wedding night. She sneaks into the bedchamber with a knife...but can't bear to kill the man she loves. The mermaid throws herself into the sea to die. Suddenly, she's miraculously carried up by the mermaids of the air, who give her an immortal soul as a reward for her long-suffering love.

The tale of unrequited love mirrors Andersen's own sad love life. He had two major crushes—one of them for the famous opera singer, Jenny Lind—but he was turned down both times, and he never married. Scholars with access to Andersen's diary believe he was bisexual and died a virgin. The great author is said to have feared he'd lose his artistic drive if he ever actually made love to another person. His dearest male friend, Edvard Collin, inherited Andersen's entire estate (which was not unusual in the Romantic 19th century, when men tended to have more emotional and intimate friendships than today).

of the overrated, overfondled, and overphotographed symbol of Copenhagen, ***Den Lille Havfrue—The Little Mermaid***. *The Little Mermaid* statue was a gift to the city of Copenhagen in 1909 from brewing magnate Carl Jacobsen (whose art collection forms the basis of the Ny Carlsberg Glyptotek). Inspired by a ballet performance of Andersen's story, Jacobsen hired the young sculptor Edvard Eriksen to immortalize the mermaid as a statue. Eriksen used his wife Eline as the model.

For the non-Disneyfied *Little Mermaid* story—and insights into Hans Christian Andersen—see the sidebar.

• *Our walking tour is finished. You can get back downtown on foot, by taxi, or on bus #1A or #15 from Store Kongensgade on the other side of Kastellet Park, or bus #26 from farther north, along Folke Bernadottes Allé.*

Sights in Copenhagen

Near the Train Station

Copenhagen's great train station, the Hovedbanegården, is a fascinating mesh of Scandinavian culture and transportation efficiency. From the station, delightful sights fan out into the old city. The following attractions are listed roughly in order from the train station to Slotsholmen Island.

▲▲▲**Tivoli Gardens**—The world's grand old amusement park—since 1843—is 20 acres, 110,000 lanterns, and countless ice cream

cones of fun. You pay one admission price and find yourself lost in a Hans Christian Andersen wonderland of rides, restaurants, games, marching bands, roulette wheels, and funny mirrors. A roller coaster screams through the middle of a tranquil Asian food court, the Small-World-inspired Den Flyvende Kuffert ride floats through Hans Christian Andersen fairy tales, and a fancy pavilion hides one of the most respected restaurants in Copenhagen. It's a children's fantasyland midday, but it becomes more adult-oriented later on. With or without kids, this place is a true magic kingdom. Tivoli doesn't try to be Disney. It's wonderfully and happily Danish. I find it worth the admission just to see Danes—young and old—at play.

Cost: 95 kr, free for kids under 8. To go on rides, you'll buy ride tickets from the automated machines (25 kr, color-coded rides cost 1, 2, or 3 tickets apiece); or you can buy an all-day ride pass for 199 kr. If you'll be using at least eight tickets, buy the ride pass

instead. To leave and come back later, you'll have to buy a 15-kr re-entry ticket before you exit. Tel. 33 15 10 01, www.tivoli.dk.

Hours: Mid-April-late Sept daily 11:00-22:00, later Fri-Sat and mid-June-late Aug. In winter, Tivoli opens daily 11:00-22:00 for a week in mid-October for Halloween, then again from mid-November to New Year's Day for a Christmas market with *gløgg* (hot spiced wine) and ice-skating on Tivoli Lake. Dress warm for chilly evenings any time of year. There are lockers by each entrance.

COPENHAGEN

Getting There: Tivoli is across Bernstoffsgade from the train station. If you're catching an overnight train, this is *the* place to spend your last Copenhagen hours.

Entertainment at Tivoli: Upon arrival (through main entrance, on left in the service center), pick up a map and look for the events schedule. Take a moment to sit down and plan your entertainment for the evening. Events are spread between 15:00 and 23:00; the 19:30 concert in the concert hall can be as little as 50 kr or as much as 1,200 kr, depending on the performer (box office tel. 33 15 10 12). If the Tivoli Symphony is playing, it's worth paying for. The ticket box office is outside, just to the left of the main entrance (daily 10:00-20:00; if you buy a concert ticket you get into Tivoli for free).

Free concerts, pantomime theater, ballet, acrobats, puppets, and other shows pop up all over the park, and a well-organized visitor can enjoy an exciting evening of entertainment without spending a single krone beyond the entry fee. Friday evenings feature a (usually free) rock or pop show at 22:00. People gather around the lake 45 minutes before closing time for the "Tivoli Illuminations" (except on Fri, when there's no show). Fireworks blast a few nights each summer. The park is particularly romantic at dusk, when the lights go on.

Eating at Tivoli: Inside the park, expect to pay amusement-park prices for amusement-park-quality food. Still, a meal here is part of the fun. **Søcafeen** serves only traditional open-face sandwiches in a fun beer garden with lakeside ambience. They allow picnics if you buy a drink (and will rent you plates and silverware for 10 kr per person). The *pølse* (sausage) stands are cheap, and there's a bagel sandwich place in the amusements corner. **Færgekroen** offers a quiet, classy lakeside escape from the amusement-park intensity, with traditional dishes washed down by its own microbrew (190-265-kr hearty pub grub). They host live piano on Thursday, Friday, and Saturday evenings from 20:00, often resulting in an impromptu sing-along with a bunch of very happy Danes. **Wagamama,** a modern pan-Asian slurpathon from the UK, serves healthy noodle dishes (at the far back side of the park, also possible to enter from outside, 100-130-kr meals). **Nimb's Terrasse** has dignified French food in a garden setting (175-225-kr dishes). **Café Georg,** to the left of the concert hall, has tasty 75-kr sandwiches and a lake view (also 100-kr salads and omelets). The kid-pleasing **Piratiriet** lets you dine on a pirate ship (140-170-kr main dishes).

For something more upscale, consider the complex of Nimb restaurants, in the big Taj Mahal-like pavilion near the entrance facing the train station. **Nimb's Louise** is Tivoli's big splurge, with seasonal menus that are well-regarded even by non-parkgoers (lunch: three courses-495 kr; dinner: four courses-750 kr, eight courses-1125 kr). **Nimb's Brasserie,** sharing the same lobby, has more affordable prices (175-235-kr main dishes).

If it's chilly, you'll find plenty of **Mamma Mokka** coffee take-away stands. If you get a drink "to go," you'll pay an extra 5-kr deposit for the cup, which you can recoup by inserting the empty cup into an automated machine (marked on maps).

▲**City Hall (Rådhus)**—This city landmark, between the train station/Tivoli and the Strøget, is free and open to the public; you can wander throughout the building and into the peaceful garden out back. It also offers private tours and trips up its 345-foot-tall tower.

Cost and Hours: Free, Mon-Fri 8:30-16:30; you can usually slip in Sat 10:00-13:00 when weddings are going on, or join the Sat tour; closed Sun. Guided English-language tours-30 kr, 45 minutes, gets you into more private, official rooms; Mon-Fri at 15:00, Sat at 10:00. Tower-20 kr, 300 steps for the best aerial view of Copenhagen, June-Sept Mon-Fri at 11:00 and 14:00, Sat at 12:00, closed Sun and Oct-May. Tel. 33 66 33 66.

Visiting City Hall: It's draped, inside and out, in Danish symbolism. The city's founder, Bishop Absalon, stands over the door. Absalon (c. 1128-1201)—bishop, soldier, and foreign-policy wonk—was King Valdemar I's right-hand man. In Copenhagen, he drove out pirates and built a fort to guard the harbor, turning a miserable fishing village into a humming Baltic seaport. The polar bears climbing on the roof-top symbolize the giant Danish protectorate of Greenland. Six night watchmen flank the city's gold-and-green seal under the Danish flag.

Step inside. The info desk

(on the left as you enter) has racks of tourist information (city maps and other brochures). The building and its huge tower were inspired by the city hall in Siena, Italy (with the necessary bad-weather addition of a glass roof). Enormous functions fill this grand hall (the iron grate in the center of the floor is an elevator for bringing up 1,200 chairs), while the busts of four illustrious local boys—fairy-tale writer Hans Christian Andersen, sculptor Bertel Thorvaldsen, physicist Niels Bohr, and the building's archi-tect, Martin Nyrop—look on. Underneath the floor are national archives dating back to 1275, popular with Danes researching their family roots.

Danish Design Center—This center shows off the best in Danish design as well as top examples from around the world, including architecture, fashion, and graphic arts. A visit to this low-key dis-play for sleek Scandinavian objects offers an interesting glimpse into a culture that takes pride in functionalism and minimalism. The ground and upper floors are filled with changing exhibits; the basement houses the "semipermanent" Denmark by Design exhibit (likely through sometime in 2013), with samples of Danish design from 1950 to 2000. The boutique next to the ticket counter features three themes: travel light (chic travel accessories and gad-gets), modern Danish classics, and books and posters. Sometimes it feels a bit like an Ikea showroom—suggesting the prevalence of Scandinavian design in our everyday lives. But perusing the exhib-its here, you'll come to see design not just as something pleasing to the eye, but as an invaluable tool that can improve lives and solve problems.

Cost and Hours: 55 kr, Mon-Fri 10:00-17:00, Wed until 21:00, Sat-Sun 11:00-16:00—July-Aug until 17:00, across from Tivoli Gardens and down the street from City Hall at H. C. Andersen Boulevard 27, tel. 33 69 33 69, www.ddc.dk.

Eating: The café on the main level, under the atrium, serves light lunches (55-65-kr sandwiches and salads, three *smørrebrød* for 125 kr).

▲Ny Carlsberg Glyptotek—Scandinavia's top art gallery is an impressive example of what beer money can do. Brewer Carl Jacobsen (son of J. C. Jacobsen, who funded the Museum of

National History at Frederiksborg Castle) was an avid collec-tor and patron of the arts. (Carl also donated *The Little Mermaid* statue to the city.) His namesake museum has intoxicating artifacts from the ancient world, along with some fine art from our own times. The next time you sip a

Carlsberg beer, drink a toast to Carl Jacobsen and his marvelous collection. *Skål!*

Cost and Hours: 75 kr, free Sun; open Tue-Sun 11:00-17:00, closed Mon, classy cafeteria under palms, behind Tivoli at Dantes Plads 7, tel. 33 41 81 41, www.glyptoteket.com.

Visiting the Museum: Pick up a floor plan as you enter to help navigate the confusing layout. For a chronological swing, start with Egypt (mummy coffins and sarcophagi, a 5,000-year-old hippo statue), Greece (red-and-black painted vases, statues), the Etruscan world (Greek-looking vases), and Rome (grittily realistic statues and portrait busts). The sober realism of 19th-century Danish Golden Age painting reflects the introspection of a once-powerful nation reduced to second-class status—and ultimately embracing what made them unique. The "French Wing" (just inside the front door) has Rodin statues. A heady, if small, exhibit of 19th-century French paintings (in a modern building within the back

courtyard) shows how Realism morphed into Impressionism and Post-Impressionism, and includes a couple of canvases apiece by Géricault, Delacroix, Monet, Manet, Millet, Courbet, Degas, Pissarro, Cézanne, Van Gogh, Picasso, Renoir, and Toulouse-Lautrec. Look for art by Gauguin—from before Tahiti (when he lived in Copenhagen with his Danish wife and their five children) and after Tahiti. There's also a fine collection of modern (post-Thorvaldsen) Danish sculpture.

Linger with marble gods under the palm leaves and glass dome of the very soothing winter garden. Designers, figuring Danes would be more interested in a lush garden than in classical art, used this wonderful space as leafy bait to cleverly introduce locals to a few Greek and Roman statues. (It works for tourists, too.) One of the original *Thinker* sculptures by Rodin (wondering how to scale the Tivoli fence?) is in the museum's backyard.

▲▲▲National Museum—Focus on this museum's excellent and curiously enjoyable Danish collection, which traces this civilization from its ancient beginnings. Its prehistoric collection is the best of its kind in Scandinavia. Exhibits are laid out chronologically and are eloquently described in English.

Cost and Hours: Free, Tue-Sun 10:00-17:00, closed Mon, mandatory lockers take a 10-kr coin that will be returned, enter at Ny Vestergade 10, tel. 33 13 44 11, www.natmus.dk. The café overlooking the entry hall serves coffee, pastries, and lunch (90-145 kr).

⊙ Self-Guided Tour: Pick up the museum map as you enter, and head for the Danish history exhibit. It fills three floors, from the bottom up: prehistory, the Middle Ages and Renaissance, and modern times (1660-2000).

Start before history did, in the **Danish Prehistory** exhibit (on the right side of the main entrance hall). Recently updated, this collection is slick and extremely well-presented.

In the Stone Age section, you'll see primitive tools and still-clothed skeletons of Scandinavia's reindeer-hunters. The oak coffins were originally covered by burial mounds (called "barrows"). People put valuable items into the coffins with the dead, such as a folding chair (which, back then, was a real status symbol). In the farming section, ogle the ceremonial axes and amber necklaces.

The Bronze Age brought the sword (several are on display).

The "Chariot of the Sun"—a small statue of a horse pulling the sun across the sky—likely had religious significance for early Scandinavians (whose descendants continue to celebrate the solstice with fervor). In the same room are those iconic horned helmets. Contrary to popular belief (and countless tourist shops), these helmets were not worn by the Vikings, but by their predecessors—for ceremonial purposes, centuries earlier. In the next room are huge cases filled with still-playable *lur* horns. Another room shows off a bitchin' collection of well-translated rune stones proclaiming heroic deeds.

This leads to the Iron Age and an object that's neither Iron nor Danish: the 2,000-year-old Gundestrup Cauldron of art-textbook fame. This 20-pound, soup-kitchen-size bowl made of silver was found in a Danish bog, but its symbolism suggests it was originally from Thrace (in northeast Greece) or Celtic Ireland. On the sides, hunters slay bulls, and gods cavort with stags, horses, dogs, and dragons. It's both mysterious and fascinating.

Prehistoric Danes were fascinated by bogs. To make iron, you need ore—and Denmark's many bogs provided that critical material in abundance, leading people to believe that the gods dwelled there. These Danes appeased the gods by sacrificing valuable items (and even people) into bogs. Fortunately for modern archaeologists, bogs happen to be an ideal environment for preserving fragile objects. One bog alone—the Nydam bog—has yielded thousands of items, including three whole ships.

No longer bogged down in prehistory, the people of Scandinavia came into contact with Roman civilization. At about this time, the Viking culture rose; you'll see the remains of an old warship. The Vikings, so feared in most of Europe, are still thought of fondly here in their homeland. You'll notice the descriptions straining to defend them: Sure, they'd pillage, rape, and plunder. But they also founded thriving, wealthy, and cultured trade towns. Love the Vikings or hate them, it's impossible to deny their massive reach—Norse Vikings even carved runes into the walls of the Hagia Sophia church (in today's Istanbul).

Next, go upstairs. You'll enter (awkwardly) right between the **Middle Ages and Renaissance** sections; to go in chronologi-

cal order, go left, cover your eyes, and walk through the exhibits to the start of the Middle Ages and the coming of Christianity. Then retrace your steps through the Middle Ages (eyes open this time). Here you'll find lots of bits and pieces of old churches, such as golden altars and *aquamaniles*, pitchers used for ritual hand-washing. The Dagmar Cross is the prototype for a popular form of crucifix worn by many Danes (Room 102, small glass display case, smallest of the three crosses in this case—with colorful enamel paintings). Another cross in this case (the Roskilde Cross, studded with gemstones) was found inside the wooden head of Christ displayed high on the opposite wall. There are also exhibits on tools and trade, weapons, drinking horns, and fine, wood-carved winged altarpieces. Carry on to find fascinating material on the Reformation, an exhibit on everyday town life in the 16th and 17th centuries, and, in Room 126, a unique "cylinder perspective" of the noble family (from 1656) and two peep shows. (Don't get too excited—they're just church interiors.)

The next floor takes you into **modern times,** with historic toys and a slice-of-Danish-life (1600-2000) gallery where you'll see everything from rifles and old bras to early jukeboxes. You'll learn that the Danish Golden Age (which dominates most art museums in Denmark) captured the everyday pastoral beauty of the countryside, celebrated Denmark's smallness and peace-loving

nature, and mixed in some Nordic mythology. With industrialization came the labor movement and trade unions. After delving into the World Wars, Baby Boomers, creation of the postwar welfare state, and the "Depressed Decade" of the 1980s (when Denmark suffered high unemployment), the collection is capped off by a stall that, until recently, was used for selling marijuana in the squatters' community of Christiania.

The Rest of the Museum: If you're eager for more, there's plenty left to see. The National Museum also has exhibits on the history of this building (the Prince's Palace), a large ethnology collection, antiquities, coins and medallions, temporary exhibits, and a good children's museum. The floor plan will lead you to what you want to see.

▲**National Museum's Victorian Apartment**—The National Museum (listed above) inherited an incredible Victorian apartment just around the corner. The wealthy Christensen family managed to keep its plush living quarters a 19th-century time capsule until the granddaughters passed away in 1963. Since then, it's been part of the National Museum, with all but two of its rooms looking just as they did around 1890.

Cost and Hours: 50 kr, required one-hour tours in English leave from museum reception desk, June-Sept Sat only at 14:00.

▲**Museum of Copenhagen (Københavns Museum)**—This fine old house is filled with an entertaining and creative exhibit telling the story of Copenhagen. The ground floor covers the city's origins, the upper floor is dedicated to the 19th century, and the top floor includes a fun year-by-year walk through Copenhagen's 20th century, with lots of fun insights into contemporary culture.

Cost and Hours: 20 kr, daily 10:00-17:00, behind the train station at Vesterbrogade 59, tel. 33 21 07 72, www.copenhagen.dk.

On Slotsholmen Island

This island, where Copenhagen began in the 12th century, is a short walk from the train station and Tivoli, just across the bridge from the National Museum. It's dominated by Christiansborg Palace and several other royal and governmental buildings.

▲▲**Christiansborg Palace**—A complex of government buildings stands on the ruins of Copenhagen's original 12th-century fortress: the Parliament, Supreme Court, prime minister's office, royal reception rooms, royal library, several museums, and royal stables. Although the current palace dates only from 1928 and the royal family moved out 200 years ago, this building—the sixth to stand here in 800 years—is rich with tradition.

Three palace sights (the reception rooms, old castle ruins, and stables) are open to the public, giving us commoners a glimpse of the royal life.

Cost and Hours: Reception rooms-80 kr, ruins-40 kr, stables-40 kr, combo-ticket for all three-110 kr; reception rooms and ruins open daily 10:00-17:00 except closed Mon Oct-April, reception rooms may close at any time for royal events; stables and carriage museum daily 13:30-16:00 except closed Mon Oct-April; tel. 33 92 64 92, www.christiansborgslot.dk.

Visiting the Palace: From the equestrian statue in front, go through the wooden door; the entrance to the ruins is in the corridor on the right, and the door to the reception rooms is out in the next courtyard, also on the right.

Royal Reception Rooms: While these don't quite rank among Europe's best palace rooms, they're worth a look. This is still the place where Queen Margrethe II impresses visiting dignitaries. The information-packed 50-minute English tours of the rooms are excellent (included in ticket, daily at 15:00). At other times, you'll wander the rooms on your own, reading the sparse English descriptions. As you slip-slide on protect-the-floor slippers through 22 rooms, you'll gain a good feel for Danish history, royalty, and politics. For instance, the family portrait of King Christian IX illustrates why he's called the "father-in-law of Europe"—his children eventually became or married royalty in Denmark, Russia, Greece, Britain, France, Germany, and Norway. You'll see the Throne Room; the balcony where new monarchs are proclaimed (most recently in 1972); the Velvet Room, where royals privately greet VIP guests before big functions; and the grand Main Hall lined with boldly colorful (almost gaudy) tapestries. The palace highlight is this dazzling set of modern tapestries—Danish-designed but Gobelin-made in Paris. This gift, given to the queen on her 60th birthday in 2000, celebrates 1,000 years of Danish history, from the Viking age to our chaotic times...and into the future. Borrow the laminated descriptions for blow-by-blow explanations of the whole epic saga.

Castle Ruins: An exhibit in the scant remains of the first fortress built by Bishop Absalon, the 12th-century founder of Copenhagen, lies under the palace. A long passage connects to another set of ruins, from the 14th-century Copenhagen Castle. There's precious little to see, but it is, um, old and well-described.

A video covers more recent palace history.

Royal Stables and Carriages Museum: This facility is still home to the horses that pull the Queen's carriage on festive days, as well as a collection of historic carriages.

Old Stock Exchange (Børsen)—The eye-catching red-brick stock exchange was inspired by the Dutch Renaissance, like much of 17th-century Copenhagen. Built to promote the mercantile ambitions of Denmark in the 1600s, it was the "World Trade Center" of Scandinavia. The facade reads, "For the profitable use of buyer and seller." The dragon-tail spire with three crowns represents the Danish aspiration to rule a united Scandinavia—or at least be its commercial capital. The Børsen (which is not open to tourists) symbolically connected Christianshavn (the harbor, also inspired by the Dutch) with the rest of the city, in an age when trade was a very big deal.

▲▲**Thorvaldsen's Museum**—This museum, which has some of the best swoon-worthy art you'll see anywhere, tells the story

and shows the monumental work of the great Danish Neoclassical sculptor Bertel Thorvaldsen (see sidebar). Considered Canova's equal among Neoclassical sculptors, Thorvaldsen spent 40 years in Rome. He was lured home to Copenhagen with the promise to showcase his work in a fine museum, which opened in the revolutionary year of 1848 as Denmark's first public art gallery. Of the 500 or so sculptures Thorvaldsen completed in his life—including 90 major statues—this museum has most of them, in one form or another (the plaster model used to make the original, the original marble, or a copy done in marble or bronze).

Cost and Hours: 40 kr, free Wed, includes excellent audio-guide on request, Tue-Sun 10:00-17:00, closed Mon, located in Neoclassical building with colorful walls next to Christiansborg Palace, tel. 33 32 15 32, www.thorvaldsensmuseum.dk.

Visiting the Museum: The ground floor showcases his statues. After buying your ticket, go straight in and ask to borrow a free iPod audioguide at the desk. This provides a wonderful statue-by-statue narration of the museum's key works.

Just past the audioguide desk, turn left into the Great Hall,

COPENHAGEN

Bertel Thorvaldsen
(1770-1844)

Bertel Thorvaldsen was born, raised, educated, and buried in Copenhagen, but his most productive years were spent in Rome. There he soaked up the prevailing style of the time: Neoclassical. He studied ancient Greek and Roman statues, copying their balance, grace, and impassive beauty. The simple-but-noble style suited the patriotism of the era, and Thorvaldsen got rich off it. Public squares throughout Europe are dotted with his works, celebrating local rulers, patriots, and historical figures looking like Greek heroes or Roman conquerors.

In 1819, at the height of his fame and power, Thorvaldsen returned to Copenhagen. He was asked to decorate the most important parts of the recently bombed, newly rebuilt Cathedral of Our Lady: the main altar and nave. His *Risen Christ* on the altar (along with the 12 apostles lining the nave) became his most famous and reproduced work—without even realizing it, most people imagine the caring features of Thorvaldsen's Christ when picturing what Jesus looked like.

The prolific Thorvaldsen depicted a range of subjects. His grand statues of historical figures (Copernicus in Warsaw, Maximilian I in Munich) were intended for public squares. Portrait busts of his contemporaries were usually done in the style of Roman emperors. Thorvaldsen carved the *Lion Monument*, depicting a weeping lion, into a cliff in Luzern, Switzerland. He did religious statues, like the *Risen Christ*. Thorvaldsen's most accessible works are from Greek mythology—*The Three Graces*, naked *Jason with the Golden Fleece*, or Ganymede crouching down to feed the eagle Jupiter.

Though many of his statues are of gleaming white marble, Thorvaldsen was not a chiseler of stone. Like Rodin and Canova, Thorvaldsen left the grunt work to others. He fashioned a life-sized model in plaster, which could then be reproduced in marble or bronze by his assistants. Multiple copies were often made, even in his lifetime.

Thorvaldsen epitomized the Neoclassical style. His statues assume perfectly balanced poses—maybe even a bit stiff, say critics. They don't flail their arms dramatically or emote passionately. As you look into their faces, they seem lost in thought, as though contemplating deep spiritual truths.

In Copenhagen, catch Thorvaldsen's *Risen Christ* at the Cathedral of Our Lady, his portrait bust at City Hall, and the full range of his long career at the Thorvaldsen's Museum.

which was the original entryway of the museum. It's filled with replicas of some of Thorvaldsen's biggest and grandest statues—national heroes who still stand in the prominent squares of their major cities (Munich, Warsaw, the Vatican, and others). Two great equestrian statues stare each other down from across the hall; while they both take the classic, self-assured pose of looking one way while pointing another (think Babe Ruth calling his home run), one of them (Jozef Poniatowski) is modeled after the ancient Roman general Marcus Aurelius, while the other (Bavaria's Maximilian I) wears modern garb.

Then take a spin through the smaller rooms that ring the central courtyard. Each of these is dominated by one big work—mostly

classical subjects drawn from mythology. At the far end of the building stand the plaster models for the iconic *Risen Christ* and the 12 Apostles (the final marble versions stand in the Cathedral of Our Lady). Peek into the central courtyard to see the tomb of Thorvaldsen himself.

Speaking of which, continuing into the next row of rooms, look for Thorvaldsen's (very flattering) self portrait, leaning buffly against a partially finished sculpture.

Upstairs, get into the mind of the artist by perusing his personal possessions and the private collection of paintings from which he drew inspiration.

Royal Library—Copenhagen's "Black Diamond" (Den Sorte Diamant) library is a striking, supermodern building made of shiny black granite, leaning over the harbor at the edge of the palace complex. From the inviting lounge chairs, you can ponder this stretch of harborfront, which serves as a showcase for architects. Inside, wander through the old and new sections, catch the fine view from the "G" level, read a magazine, surf the Internet (free terminals in the skyway lobby over the street nearest the harbor), and enjoy a classy—and pricey—lunch.

Cost and Hours: Free, special exhibitions generally 30 kr; reading room open generally Mon-Fri 9:00-21:00, Sat 10:00-17:00, closed Sun; different parts of the library have varying hours, tel. 33 47 47 47, www.kb.dk.

▲**Danish Jewish Museum (Dansk Jødisk Museum)**—This museum, which opened in 2004 in a striking building by American architect Daniel Libeskind, offers a very small but well-exhibited display of 400 years of the life and impact of Jews in Denmark.

Cost and Hours: 50 kr; June-Aug Tue-Sun 10:00-17:00; Sept-May Tue-Fri 13:00-16:00, Sat-Sun 12:00-17:00; closed Mon year-round; behind the Royal Library's "Black Diamond" branch at Proviantpassagen 6—enter from the courtyard behind the red-brick, ivy-covered building; tel. 33 11 22 18, www.jewmus.dk.

Visiting the Museum: Frankly, the architecture overshadows the humble exhibits. Libeskind—who created the equally conceptual Jewish Museum in Berlin, and whose design is the basis for redeveloping the World Trade Center site in New York City—has literally written Jewish culture into this building. The floor plan, a seemingly random squiggle, is actually in the shape of the Hebrew characters for *Mitzvah*, which loosely translated means "act of kindness."

Be sure to watch the two introductory films about the Jews' migration to Denmark, and about the architect Libeskind (12-minute loop total, English subtitles, plays continuously). As you tour the collection, the uneven floors and asymmetrical walls give you the feeling that what lies around the corner is completely unknown...much like the life and history of Danish Jews. Another interpretation might be that the uneven floors give you the sense of motion, like waves on the sea—a reminder that despite Nazi occupation in 1943, nearly 7,000 Danish Jews were ferried across the waves by fishermen to safety in neutral Sweden.

Near the Strøget

Round Tower—Built in 1642 by Christian IV, the tower con-

nects a church, library, and observatory (the oldest functioning observatory in Europe) with a ramp that spirals up to a fine view of Copenhagen (though the view from atop Our Savior's Church is far better).

Cost and Hours: 25 kr, nothing to see inside but the ramp and the view; tower—daily June-Sept 10:00-20:00, Oct-May 10:00-17:00; observatory—summer Sun 13:00-16:00 and mid-Oct-mid-March Tue-Wed 19:00-22:00; just off the Strøget on Købmagergade.

Amalienborg Palace and Nearby

For more information on this palace and nearby attractions, including the famous *Little Mermaid* statue, see the end of my self-guided walk.

▲**Amalienborg Palace Museum (Amalienborgmuseet)**— While Queen Margrethe II and her husband live quite privately in one of the four mansions that make up the palace complex, another mansion has been open to the public since 1994. It displays the private studies of four kings of the House of Glucksborg, who ruled from 1863-1972 (the immediate predecessors of today's Queen). Your visit is short—six or eight rooms on one floor—but it affords an intimate and unique peek into Denmark's royal family. You'll see the private study of each of the last four kings of Denmark. They feel particularly lived-in—with cluttered pipe collections and bookcases jammed with family pictures—because they were. It's easy to imagine these blue-blooded folks just hanging out here, even today. The earliest study, Frederik VIII's (c. 1869), feels much older and more "royal"—with Renaissance gilded walls, heavy drapes, and a polar bear rug. Temporary exhibits fill the larger halls.

Cost and Hours: 80 kr, or 110-kr combo-ticket with Rosenborg Palace; May-Oct daily 10:00-16:00; Nov-April Tue-Sun 11:00-16:00, closed Mon; with your back to the harbor, the entrance is at the far end of the square on the right; tel. 33 15 32 86, www.dkks.dk.

Amalienborg Palace Changing of the Guard—This noontime event is boring in the summer, when the queen is not in residence—

the guards just change places. (This goes on for quite a long time—no need to rush here at the stroke of noon, or to crowd in during the first few minutes; you'll have plenty of good photo ops.) If the queen's at home (indicated by a flag flying above her home), the changing of the guard is accompanied by a military band.

▲▲**Museum of Danish Resistance (Frihedsmuseet)**—On April 9, 1940, Hitler's Nazis violated a peace treaty and invaded Denmark, overrunning the tiny nation in mere hours. This museum tells what happened next—the compelling story of Denmark's heroic Nazi-resistance struggle (1940-1945). While relatively small, the museum rewards those who take the time to read the English explanations and understand the fascinating artifacts. Video touchscreens let you hear interviews with the participants of history (dubbed into English).

Cost and Hours: Free; due to a fire it may be closed, call or visit website to check status; if open hours may be May-Sept Tue-Sun 10:00-16:00, Oct-April Tue-Sun 10:00-15:00, closed Mon year-round; guided tours June-Aug Tue, Thu, and Sun at 14:00; on Churchillparken between Amalienborg Palace and *The Little Mermaid* site; bus #1A or #15 from downtown/Tivoli/train station stops right in front, a 10-minute walk from Østerport S-tog station, or bus #26 from Langelinie cruise port or downtown; tel. 41 20 62 91, www.frihedsmuseet.dk.

● **Self-Guided Tour:** From the main hall, you'll take a counterclockwise spin through the collection. The first sec-

tion, **Adaptation to Avoid Nazification,** examines the unenviable situation in which the Danes found themselves in in 1940: Cooperate with the Nazis (at least symbolically) to preserve some measure of self-determination, or stand up to them and surely be crushed by their military might. Denmark opted for the first option, but kept a fierce resistance always at a rolling boil. Be sure to carefully examine the odd, sometimes macabre items from this period: A delicate, miniature rose made of chewed bread, given as a gift to an inmate at Ravensbrück Concentration Camp; Himmler's eye patch, worn as a disguise; actual human skin tattooed with the SS symbol, removed from a reformed Nazi after the war (at his own request); the pistol of the Danish Nazi leader, Fritz Clausen; RAF (British Royal Air Force) caps and stars-and-stripes bowties, worn as a symbol of resistance and rebellion by young people in the early days of Nazi occupation; cheaply made aluminum Nazi coins, crudely imprinted with messages of Danish resistance; and an old printing press used to produce anti-Nazi leaflets.

Moving down the hallway, you pass into the next section, **Resistance and Sabotage.** You'll learn how the Danish resistance, supported by the SOE (Special Operations Executive, a British governmental agency tasked with subverting Nazi control), bravely stood up to the Nazis, with occasional supplies airlifted in by the Allies. On display are many items used during the resistance, including slugs and bullet casings from a shootout between the resistance and Nazi-friendly forces, and a clandestine radio and telegraph. You'll also learn about everyday life (shortages and rationings for the Nazi war effort), and see a Nazi plate and cutlery emblazoned with a swastika.

The next section, **German Terror,** explains the Nazis' campaign of extermination against Jewish people, and details the valiant Danish effort to rescue some 7,000 Jews by ferrying them across the sea to neutral Sweden; only 481 were murdered by the Nazis (a tiny fraction of the toll in most countries). You'll see articles of the Jewish faith left behind by a refugee (who didn't want to be discovered with them, putting himself at greater risk), and some identification armbands from a concentration camp. You'll also see exhibits on industrial sabotage, and the growth of the underground army in the waning days of the war.

Finally we end at **The Liberation** (May 5, 1945). A giant stained-glass window in the lobby honors the victims of the Nazis. The moving, handwritten letters in the display cases in front (translated into English) are the final messages of Danes who had been sentenced to death by the Nazis.

Rosenborg Castle and Nearby

▲▲▲**Rosenborg Castle (Rosenborg Slot) and Treasury**— This finely furnished Dutch Renaissance-style castle was built by King Christian IV in the early 1600s as a summer residence. Rosenborg was his favorite residence and where he chose to die. Open to the public since 1838, it houses the Danish crown jewels and 500 years of royal knickknacks. While the old palace interior is a bit dark and not as immediately impressive as many of Europe's later Baroque masterpieces, it has a certain lived-in charm. It oozes the personality of the fascinating Christian IV and has one of  the finest treasury collections in Europe. Notice that this is one of the only major sights in town open on Mondays (in summer only).

Cost and Hours: 80 kr, 110-kr ticket also includes Amalienborg Palace Museum, 20 kr for permission to take photos; June-Aug daily 10:00-17:00; May and Sept-Oct daily 10:00-16:00; Nov-Dec Tue-Sun 11:00-14:00 (treasury until 16:00), closed Mon; Jan-April Tue-Sun 11:00-16:00, closed Mon; mandatory lockers take 20-kr coin, which will be returned; Metro or S-tog: Nørreport, then 5-minute walk on Østervoldgade and through park; tel. 33 15 32 86, www.dkks.dk.

Tours: Richard Karpen leads fascinating one-hour tours in princely garb (mid-May-mid-Sept Mon and Thu at 13:30, 80 kr plus entry fee, see "Tours in Copenhagen," earlier). Or take the following self-guided tour that I've woven together from the

King Christian IV:
A Lover and a Fighter

King Christian IV (1577-1648) inherited Denmark at the peak of its power, lived his life with the exuberance of the age, and went to his grave with the country in decline. His legacy is obvious to every tourist—Rosenborg Castle, Frederiksborg Palace, the Round Tower, Christianshavn, and on and on. Look for his logo adorning many buildings: the letter "C" with a "4" inside it and a crown on top. Thanks to both his place in history and his passionate personality, Danes today regard Christian IV as one of their greatest monarchs.

During his 60-year reign, Christian IV reformed the government, rebuilt the army, established a trading post in India, and tried to expand Denmark's territory. He took Kalmar from Sweden and captured strategic points in northern Germany. The king was a large man who also lived large. A skilled horseman and avid hunter, he could drink his companions under the table. He spoke several languages and gained a reputation as outgoing and humorous. His lavish banquets were legendary, and his romantic affairs were numerous.

But Christian's appetite for war proved destructive. In 1626, Denmark again attacked northern Germany, but was beaten back. In 1643, Sweden launched a sneak attack, and despite Christian's personal bravery (he lost an eye), the war went badly. By the end of his life, Christian was tired and bitter, and Denmark was drained.

The heroics of Christian and his sailors live on in the Danish national anthem, "King Christian Stood by the Lofty Mast."

highlights of Richard's walk. If you have a mobile device, you can take advantage of the palace's free Wi-Fi signal, which is intended to let you follow the "Konge Connect" step-by-step tour through the palace highlights (with text explanations on your phone; for instructions, pick up the brochure at the ticket desk).

○ **Self-Guided Tour:** Buy your ticket, then head back out and look for the *castle* sign. You'll tour the ground floor room by room, then climb to the third floor for the big throne room. After a quick sweep of the middle floor, finish in the basement (enter from outside) for the jewels. Begin the tour on the palace's ground floor (turn right as you enter), in the Winter Room.

Ground Floor: Here in the wood-paneled **Winter Room,**

all eyes were on King Christian IV. Today, your eyes should be on him, too. Take a close look at his bust by the fireplace (if it's not here, look for it out in the corridor by the ticket-taker). Check this guy out—earring and fashionable braid, hard drinker, hard lover, energetic statesman, and warrior king. Christian IV was dynamism in the flesh, wearing a toga: a true Renaissance guy. During his reign, Copenhagen doubled in size. You're surrounded by Dutch paintings (the Dutch had a huge influence on 17th-century Denmark). Note the smaller statue of the 19-year-old king, showing him jousting jauntily on his coronation day. In another case, the golden astronomical clock—with musical works and moving figures—did everything you can imagine. Flanking the fireplace (opposite where you entered), beneath the windows, look for the panels in the tile floor that could be removed to let the music performed by the band in the basement waft in. (Who wants the actual musicians in the dining room?) The audio holes were also used to call servants.

The **study** (or "writing closet," nearest where you entered) was small (and easy to heat). Kings did a lot of corresponding. We know a lot about Christian because 3,000 of his handwritten letters survive. The painting on the right wall shows Christian at age eight. Three years later, his father died, and little Christian technically ascended the throne,

though Denmark was actually ruled by a regency until Christian was 19. A portrait of his mother hangs above the boy, and opposite is a portrait of Christian in his prime—having just conquered Sweden—standing alongside the incredible coronation crown you'll see later.

Going back through the Winter Room, head for the door to Christian's **bedroom.** Before entering, notice the little peephole in the door (used by the king to spy on those in this room—well-

camouflaged by the painting, and more easily seen from the other side), and the big cabinet doors for Christian's clothes and accessories, flanking the bedroom door (notice the hinges and keyholes). Heading into the bedroom, you'll see paintings showing the king as an old man...and as a dead man. (Christian died in this room.) In the case are the clothes he wore at his finest hour. During a naval battle against Sweden (1644), Christian stood directing the action when an explosion ripped across the deck, sending him sprawling and riddling him with shrapnel. Unfazed, the 67-year-old monarch bounced right back up and kept going, inspiring his men to carry on the fight. Christian's stubborn determination during this battle is commemorated in Denmark's national anthem. Shrapnel put out Christian's eye. No problem: The warrior king with a knack for heroic publicity stunts had the shrapnel bits removed from his eye and forehead and made into earrings as a gift for his mistress. The earrings hang in the case with his blood-stained clothes (easy to miss, right side). Christian lived to be 70 and fathered 25 children (with two wives and three mistresses). Before moving on, you can peek into Christian's private bathroom—elegantly tiled with Delft porcelain.

Proceed into the **Dark Room.** Here you'll see wax casts of royal figures. This was the way famous and important people were portrayed back then. (If the wax casts aren't here, they're likely out in the corridor.) The chair (possibly gone for restoration) is a forerunner of the whoopee cushion. When you sat on it, metal cuffs pinned your arms down, allowing the prankster to pour water down the back of the chair (see hole)—making you "wet your pants." When you stood up, the chair made embarrassing tooting sounds.

The **Marble Room** (which may be closed for restoration) has a particularly impressive inlaid marble floor. Imagine the king meeting emissaries here in the center, with the emblems of Norway (right), Denmark (center), and Sweden (left) behind him.

The end room, called the **King's Chamber,** was used by Christian's first mistress. You might want to shield children from the sexually explicit art in the case next to the door you just passed. Notice the tamer ceiling painting, with an orchestra looking down on you as they play.

The long **stone passage** leading to the staircase exhibits an intriguing painting (by the door to the King's Chamber) showing the crowds at the coronation of Christian's son, Frederick III. After Christian's death, a weakened Denmark was invaded, occupied, and humiliated by Sweden (Treaty of Roskilde, 1658). Copenhagen alone held out through the long winter of 1658-1659 (the Siege of Copenhagen), and Sweden eventually had to withdraw from the country. During

the siege, Frederick III distinguished himself with his bravery. He seized upon the resulting surge of popularity as his chance to be anointed an absolute, divinely ordained monarch (1660). This painting marks that event—study it closely for slice-of-life details. Next, near the ticket-taker, a sprawling family tree makes it perfectly clear that Christian IV comes from good stock. Notice the tree is labeled in German—the second language of the realm.

The queen had a hand-pulled elevator, but you'll need to hike up two flights of stairs to the throne room.

Throne Room (Third Floor): The **Long Hall**—considered one of the best-preserved Baroque rooms in Europe—was great

for banquets. The decor trumpets the accomplishments of Denmark's great kings. The four corners of the ceiling feature the four continents known at the time. (America—at the far-right end of the hall as you enter—was still considered pretty untamed; notice the decapitated head with the arrow sticking out of it.) In the center, of course, is the proud seal of the Danish Royal Family. The tapestries, designed for this room, are from the late 1600s. Effective propaganda, they show the Danes defeating their Swedish rivals on land and at sea. The king's throne—still more propaganda for two centuries of "absolute" monarchs—was made of "unicorn horn" (actually narwhal tusk from Greenland). Believed to bring protection from evil and poison, the horn was the most precious material in its day. The queen's throne is of hammered silver. The 150-pound lions are 300 years old.

The small room to the left holds a delightful **royal porcelain** display with Chinese, French, German, and Danish examples of the "white gold." For five centuries, Europeans couldn't figure out how the Chinese made this stuff. The difficulty in just getting it back to Europe in one piece made it precious. The Danish pieces, called "Flora Danica" (on the left as you enter), are from a huge royal set showing off the herbs and vegetables of the realm.

On your way back down, the middle floor is worth a look.

Middle Floor: Circling counterclockwise, you'll see more fine clocks, fancy furniture, and royal portraits. The queen enjoyed her royal lathe (with candleholders for lighting and pedals to spin it hidden away below; in the Christian IV Room). The small mirror room (up the stairs from the main hall) was where the king played Hugh Hefner—using mirrors on the floor to see what was under those hoop skirts. In hidden cupboards, he had a fold-out bed and a handy escape staircase.

Back outside, turn right and find the stairs leading down to the...

Royal Danish Treasury (Castle Basement): The palace was a royal residence for a century and has been the royal vault right up until today. As you enter, first head to the right, into the **wine cellar,** with thousand-liter barrels and some fine treasury items. The first room has a vast army of tiny golden soldiers, and a wall lined with fancy rifles. Heading into the next room, you'll see fine items of amber (petrified tree resin, 30-50 million years old) and ivory. Study the large box made of amber (in a freestanding case, just to the right as you enter)—the tiny figures show a healthy interest in sex.

Now head back past the ticket-taker and into the main part of the treasury, where you can browse through exquisite royal knickknacks.

The diamond- and pearl-studded **saddles** were Christian IV's—the first for his coronation, the second for his son's wedding. When his kingdom was nearly bankrupt, Christian had these constructed lavishly—complete with solid-gold spurs—to impress visiting dignitaries and bolster Denmark's credit rating.

The next case displays **tankards.** Danes were always big drinkers, and to drink in the top style, a king had narwhal steins (#4030). Note the fancy Greenland Inuit (Eskimo) on the lid (#4023). The case is filled with exquisitely carved ivory. On the other side of that case, what's with the mooning snuffbox (#4063)? Also, check out the amorous whistle (#4064).

Drop by the case on the wall in the back-left of the room: The 17th century was the age of **brooches.** Many of these are made of freshwater pearls. Find the fancy combination toothpick and ear spoon (#4140). Look for #4146: A queen was caught having an affair after 22 years of royal marriage. Her king gave her a special present: a golden ring—showing the hand of his promiscuous queen shaking hands with a penis.

Step downstairs, away from all this silliness. Passing through the serious vault door, you come face-to-face with a big, jeweled **sword.** The tall, two-handed, 16th-century coronation sword was drawn by the new king, who cut crosses in the air in four directions, symbolically promising to defend the realm from all attacks. The cases surrounding the sword contain everyday items used by the king (all solid gold, of course). What looks like a trophy case of gold records is actually a collection of dinner plates with amber centers (#5032).

Go down the steps. In the center case is Christian IV's **coronation crown** (from 1596, seven pounds of gold and precious stones, #5124), which some consider to be the finest Renaissance crown in Europe. Its six tallest gables radiate symbolism. Find

the symbols of justice (sword and scales), fortitude (a woman on a lion with a sword), and charity (a nursing woman—meaning the king will love God and his people as a mother loves her child). The pelican, which according to medieval legend pecks its own flesh to feed its young, symbolizes God sacrificing his son, just as the king would make great sacrifices for his people. Climb the footstool to look inside—it's as exquisite as the outside. The shields of various Danish provinces remind the king that he's surrounded by his realms.

Circling the cases along the wall (right to left), notice the fine enameled lady's goblet with traits of a good woman spelled out in Latin (#5128) and above that, an exquisite prayer book (with handwritten favorite prayers, #5134). In the fifth window, the big solid-gold baptismal basin (#5262) hangs above tiny oval silver boxes that contained the royal children's umbilical cords (handy for protection later in life, #5272); two cases over are royal writing sets with wax, seals, pens, and ink (#5320).

Go down a few more steps into the lowest level of the treasury and last room. The two **crowns** in the center cases are more modern (from 1670), lighter, and more practical—just gold and diamonds without all the symbolism. The king's crown is only four pounds, the queen's a mere two.

The cases along the walls show off the **crown jewels.** These were made in 1840 of diamonds, emeralds, rubies, and pearls from earlier royal jewelry. The saber (#5540) shows emblems of the realm's 19 provinces. The sumptuous pendant features a 19-carat diamond cut (like its neighbors) in the 58-facet "brilliant" style for maximum reflection (far-left case, #5560). Imagine these on the dance floor. The painting shows the coronation of Christian VIII at Frederiksborg Chapel in 1840. The crown jewels are still worn by the queen on special occasions several times a year.

▲**Rosenborg Gardens**—Rosenborg Castle is surrounded by the royal pleasure gardens and, on sunny days, a minefield of sunbathing Danish beauties and picnickers. While "ethnic Danes" grab the shade, the rest of the Danes worship the sun. When the royal family is in residence, there's a daily changing-of-the-guard mini-parade from the Royal Guard's barracks adjoining Rosenborg Castle (at 11:30) to Amalienborg Castle (at 12:00). The Queen's Rose Garden (across the moat from the palace) is a royal place for a picnic. The fine statue of Hans Christian Andersen in the park—erected while he was still alive (and approved by him)—is meant to symbolize how his stories had a message even for adults.

▲National Gallery of Denmark (Statens Museum for Kunst)—The museum fills a stately building with Danish and European paintings from the 14th century through today. This is particularly worthwhile for the chance to be immersed in great art by the Danes, and to see its good collection of French Modernists.

Cost and Hours: Permanent collection-free, special exhibits-95 kr, Tue-Sun 10:00-17:00, Wed until 20:00, closed Mon, Sølvgade 48, tel. 33 74 84 94, www.smk.dk.

Visiting the Museum: The ground floor holds special exhibits; the second floor has collections of Danish and Nordic artists from 1750 to 1900, and European art from 1300 to 1800; and the Danish and International Art after 1900 is spread between the second and third floors.

Head first to the Danish and Nordic artists section, and pick up the excellent floor plan that suggests a twisting route through

the collection. Take the time to read the descriptions in each room, which put the paintings into historical context. In addition to Romantic works by well-known, non-Danish artists (such as the Norwegian J. C. Dahl and the German Caspar David Friedrich), this is a chance to learn about some very talented Danish painters not well known outside their native land. Make a point to meet the "Skagen Painters," including Anna Ancher, Michael Ancher, Peder Severin Krøyer, and others (find them in the section called "The Modern Breakthrough I-II"). This group, with echoes of the French Impressionists, gathered in the fishing village of Skagen on the northern tip of Denmark, surrounded by the sea and strong light, and painted heroic folk-fishermen themes in the late 1800s. Also worth seeking out are the canvases of Laurits Andersen Ring, who portrayed traditional peasant scenes with modern style; and Jens Ferdinand Willumsen, who pioneered "Vitalism" (celebrating man in nature). Other exhibits are cleverly organized by theme, such as gender or the body.

In the 20th-century section, the collection of early French Modernism is particularly impressive (with works by Matisse, Picasso, Braque, and more). This is complemented with works by

Danish artists, who, inspired by the French avant-garde, introduced new, radical forms and colors to Scandinavian art.

Christianshavn

Across the harbor from the old town, Christianshavn is one of the most delightful districts in town to explore. A little background helps explain what you'll see.

Copenhagen's planned port, Christianshavn, was vital to Danish power in the 17th and 18th centuries. Denmark had always been second to Sweden when it came to possession of natural resources, so the Danes tried to make up for it by acquiring resource-rich overseas colonies. They built Christianshavn (with Amsterdam's engineering help) to run the resulting trade business—giving this neighborhood a "little Amsterdam" vibe today.

Since Denmark's economy was so dependent on trade, the port town was the natural target of enemies. When the Danes didn't support Britain against Napoleon in 1807, the Brits bombarded Christianshavn. In this "blackest year in Danish history," Christianshavn burned down. That's why today there's hardly a building here that dates from before 1807.

Christianshavn remained Copenhagen's commercial center until the 1920s, when a modern harbor was built. Suddenly, Christianshavn's economy collapsed and it became a slum. Cheap prices attracted artsy types, giving it a bohemian flavor.

In 1971, several hundred squatters took over an unused military camp and created the Christiania commune (described later). City officials looked the other way because back then, no one cared about the land. But by the 1980s, the neighborhood had become gentrified, and today it's some of priciest real estate in town. (A small apartment costs around $300,000.) Suddenly developers are pushing to take back the land from squatters, and the very existence of Christiania is threatened.

Christianshavn prices are driven up by wealthy locals (who pay about 60 percent of their income in taxes) paying too much for apartments, renting them cheaply to their kids, and writing off the loss. Demand for property is huge. Prices have skyrocketed. Today the neighborhood is inhabited mostly by rich students and young professionals. Apart from pleasant canalside walks and trendy restaurants to enjoy, there are two things to see in Christianshavn: Our Savior's Church (with its fanciful tower) and Christiania (before it's gone).

▲Our Savior's Church (Vor Frelsers Kirke)

The church recently reopened after a restoration, which has left it gleaming inside and out. Its bright Baroque interior (1696) is shaped like a giant cube. The magnificent pipe organ is supported

COPENHAGEN

by elephants (a royal symbol of the prestigious Order of the Elephant). Looking up to the ceiling, notice elephants also sculpted into the stucco of the dome, and a little one hanging from the main chandelier. Best of all, you can climb the unique spiral spire (with an outdoor staircase winding up to its top—398 stairs in all) for great views of the city and of the Christiania commune below.

Cost and Hours: Church interior-free, open daily 11:00-15:30 but may close for special services; church tower-35 kr; July-mid-Sept Mon-Sat 10:00-19:00, Sun 10:30-19:00; April-June and mid-Sept-Nov daily until 16:00; closed Dec-March and in bad weather; bus #2A, #19, or Metro: Christianshavn, Sankt Annægade 29, tel. 41 66 63 57, www.vorfrelserskirke.dk.

○ **Spin-Tour from the Top of Our Savior's Church:** Climb up until you run out of stairs. As you wind back down, look for these landmarks:

The modern windmills are a reminder that Denmark generates 20 percent of its power from wind. Below the windmills is a great aerial view of the Christiania commune. Beyond the windmills, across Øresund (the strait that separates Denmark and Sweden), stands a shuttered Swedish nuclear power plant. The lone skyscraper in the distance—the first and tallest skyscraper in Scandinavia—is in Malmö, Sweden. The Øresund Bridge made Malmö an easy 35-minute bus or train ride from Copenhagen (it's become a bedroom community, with much cheaper apartments making the commute worthwhile).

Farther to the right, the big red-roof zone is Amager Island. Five hundred years as the city's dumping grounds earned Amager the nickname "Crap Island." Circling on, you come to the towering Radisson Blu hotel. The area beyond it is slated to become a forest of skyscrapers—the center of Europe's biomedical industry.

Downtown Copenhagen is decorated with several striking towers and spires. The tower capped by the golden ball is a ride in Tivoli Gardens. Next is City Hall's pointy brick tower. The biggest building, with the three-crown tower, is Christiansborg Palace. The Børsen (old stock exchange) is just beyond, with its unique dragon-tail tower. Behind that is Nyhavn. Just across from that and the new Playhouse is the dramatic new Opera House (with the flat roof and big, grassy front yard).

Christiania

If you're interested in visiting a freewheeling community of alternative living, Christiania is a ▲▲▲ sight.

In 1971, the original 700 Christianians established squatters' rights in an abandoned military barracks just a 10-minute walk from the Danish parliament building. A generation later, this "free city" still stands—an ultra-human mishmash of idealists, hippies, potheads, non-materialists, and happy children (600 adults, 200 kids, 200 cats, 200 dogs, 2 parrots, and 17 horses). There are even a handful of Willie Nelson-type seniors among the 180 remaining here from the original takeover. And an amazing thing has happened: The place has become the third-most-visited sight among tourists in Copenhagen. Move over, *Little Mermaid.*

"Pusher Street" (named for the sale of soft drugs here) is Christiania's main drag. Get beyond this touristy side of Christiania, and you'll find a fascinating, ramshackle world of moats and earthen ramparts, alternative housing, cozy tea houses, carpenter shops, hippie villas, children's playgrounds, peaceful lanes, and people who believe that "to be normal is to be in a straitjacket." (A local slogan claims, *"Kun døde fisk flyder med strømmen"*—"Only dead fish swim with the current.") Be careful to distinguish between real Christianians and Christiania's motley guests—drunks (mostly from other countries) who hang out here in the summer for the freedom. Part of the original charter guaranteed that the community would stay open to the public.

Hours and Tours: Christiania is open all the time (main entrance is down Prinsessegade behind the Our Savior's Church spiral tower in Christianshavn). You're welcome to snap photos, but ask residents before you photograph them. Guided tours leave from the front entrance of Christiania at 15:00 (just show up, 30 kr, 1.5 hours, daily late June-Aug, only Sat-Sun rest of year, in English and Danish, tel. 32 57 96 70).

The Community: Christiania is broken into 14 administrative neighborhoods on a former military base. The land is still owned by Denmark's Ministry of Defense. Locals build their homes but don't own the land; there's no buying or selling of property. When someone moves out, the community decides who will be invited in to replace that person. A third of the adult population works on the outside, a third works on the inside, and a third doesn't work much at all.

There are nine rules: no cars, no hard drugs, no guns, no

COPENHAGEN

Christiania

To Holmen & Opera House

Peaceful walk to residential areas

BROBERGSGADE

OVERGADEN

MAIN ENTRANCE GATE

To Christianshavns Canal

PRINCESSE-GADE

OTHER ENTRANCE

BADMANDSSTRÆDE

THE GRAY HALL

REFSHALEVEJ

CHRISTIANIA

"PUSHER STREET"

LANGGADEN

⑦

⑥

①

③

②

④

⑤

ULRIKS-BASTION RAMPARTS

PATH

To Our Savior's Church

SANKT ANNÆ GADE

Stadsgraven (former moat)

Rabbit Island

To Airport

100 Meters

100 Yards

① Carl Madsens Plads
② Green Hall
③ Nemoland
④ Månefiskeren Café
⑤ Morgenstedet Vegetarian Café
⑥ Spiseloppen Restaurant
⑦ Tour Departure Point

explosives, and so on. The Christiania flag is red and yellow because when the original hippies took over, they found a lot of red and yellow paint onsite. The three yellow dots in the flag are from the three "i"s in Christiania (or, some claim, the "o"s in "Love, Love, Love").

The community pays the city about $1 million a year for utilities and has about $1 million a year more to run its local affairs. A few "luxury hippies" have oil heat, but most use wood or gas. The ground here was poisoned by its days as a military base, so nothing is grown in Christiania. There's little industry within the commune (Christiania Cykler, which builds fine bikes, is an exception—www.pedersen-bike.dk). The community has one mailing address (for 25 kr/month, you can receive mail here). A phone chain provides a system of communal security (they have had bad experiences calling the police). Each September 26, the day those first squatters took over the barracks in 1971, Christiania has a big birthday bash.

Tourists are entirely welcome here, because they've become a major part of the economy. Visitors react in very different ways to the place. Some see dogs, dirt, and dazed people. Others see a haven of peace, freedom, and no taboos. Locals will remind judgmental Americans (whose country incarcerates more than a quarter of the world's prison inmates) that a society must make the choice: Allow for alternative lifestyles...or build more prisons.

Even since its inception, Christiania has been a political hot potato. No one in the Danish establishment wanted it. And no

one had the nerve to mash it. In the last decade, Christiania has connected better with the rest of society—such as paying for its utilities and taxes. But when Denmark's conservative government took over in 2001, they vowed to "normalize" Christiania (with pressure from the US), and in recent years police have regu-

larly conducted raids on pot sellers. There's talk about opening the commune to market forces and developing posh apartments to replace existing residences, according to one government plan. But Christiania has a legal team, and litigation will likely drag on for many years.

Many predict that Christiania will withstand the government's challenge, as it has in years past. The community, which also calls itself Freetown, fended off a similar attempt in 1976 with the help of fervent supporters from around Europe. *Bevar Christiania*—"Save Christiania"—banners fly everywhere, and locals are confident that their free way of life will survive. As history has shown, the challenge may just make this hippie haven a bit stronger.

Orientation Tour: Passing under the gate, take Pusher Street directly into the community. The first square—a kind of market square (souvenirs and marijuana-related stuff)—is named Carl Madsens Plads, honoring the lawyer who took the squatters' case to the Danish supreme court in 1976 and won. Beyond that is Nemoland (a food circus, on the right). A huge warehouse called the Green Hall (Den Gronne Hal) is a recycling center and hardware store (where people get most of their building materials) that does double duty at night as a concert hall and as a place where children work on crafts. If you go up the stairs between Nemoland and the Green Hall, you'll climb up to the ramparts that overlook the canal.

On the left beyond the Green Hall, a lane leads to the Måne-fiskeren café, and beyond that, to the Morgenstedet vegetarian

COPENHAGEN

restaurant. Beyond these recommended restaurants, you'll find yourself lost in the totally untouristy, truly local residential parts of Christiania, where kids play in the street and the old folks sit out on the front stoop—just like any other neighborhood. Just as St. Mark's Square isn't the "real Venice," the hippie-druggie scene on Pusher Street isn't the "real Christiania"—you can't say you've experienced Christiania until you've strolled these back streets.

A walk or bike ride through Christiania is a great way to see how this community lives. When you leave, look up—the sign above the gate says, "You are entering the EU."

Smoking Marijuana: Pusher Street was once lined with stalls selling marijuana, joints, and hash. Residents intentionally destroyed the stalls in 2004 to reduce the risk of Christiania being disbanded by the government. (One stall was spared and is on display at the National Museum.) Walking along Pusher Street today, you may witness policemen or deals being made—but never at the same time. You may also notice wafts of marijuana smoke and whispered offers of "hash" during your visit. And, in fact, on my last visit there was a small stretch of Pusher Street dubbed the "Green Light District" where pot was being openly sold (signs acknowledged that this activity was still illegal, and announced three rules here: 1. Have fun; 2. No photos; and 3. No running—"because it makes people nervous"). However, purchasing and smoking may buy you more time in Denmark than you'd planned—possession of marijuana is illegal. With the recent police crackdown on marijuana sales, the street price has skyrocketed, crime has crept into the scene, and someone was actually murdered in a drug scuffle near Christiania—problems unthinkable in mellower times.

About hard drugs: For the first few years, junkies were toler-

ated. But that led to violence and polluted the mellow ambience residents envisioned. In 1979, the junkies were expelled—an epic confrontation in the community's folk history now—and since then the symbol of a fist breaking a syringe is as prevalent as the leafy marijuana icon. Hard drugs are emphatically forbidden in Christiania.

Eating in Christiania: The people of Christiania appreciate good food and count on tourism as a big part of their economy. Consequently, there are plenty of decent eateries. Most of the restaurants are closed on Monday (the community's weekly holiday). **Pusher Street** has a few grungy but tasty falafel stands, as well as a popular burger bar. **Nemoland** is the hangout zone—a fun collection of stands peddling Thai food, burgers, *shawarma*, and other fast hippie food with great, tented outdoor seating (30-110-kr meals). Its stay-a-while atmosphere comes with backgammon, foosball, bakery goods, and fine views from the ramparts. **Månefiskeren** ("Moonfisher Bar") looks like a modern-day Brueghel painting, with billiards, chess, snacks, and drinks (Tue-Sun 10:00-23:00, closed Mon). **Morgenstedet** ("Morning Place") is a good, cheap vegetarian café with a mellow, woody interior and a rustic patio outside (75-100-kr meals, Tue-Sun 12:00-21:00, closed Mon, left after Pusher Street). **Spiseloppen** is *the* classy, good-enough-for-Republicans restaurant in the community (closed Mon).

Greater Copenhagen

Carlsberg Brewery—Denmark's beloved source of legal intoxicants, Carlsberg welcomes you to its visitors center for a self-guided tour and a half-liter of beer.

Cost and Hours: 65 kr, Tue-Sun 10:00-17:00, closed Mon, last entry one hour before closing; catch the local train to Enghave, or bus #18, #26, or #6A; enter at Gamle Carlsbergvej 11 around corner from brewery entrance, tel. 33 27 13 14, www.visit carlsberg.dk.

Open-Air Folk Museum (Frilandsmuseet)—This park, part of the National Museum, is filled with traditional Danish architecture and folk culture.

Cost and Hours: Free, late April-late Oct Tue-Sun 10:00-17:00, closed Mon and off-season, outside of town in the suburb of Lyngby, S-tog: Sorgenfri and 10-minute walk to Kongevejen 100, tel. 33 13 44 11.

Bakken—Danes gather at Copenhagen's *other* great amusement park, Bakken.

Cost and Hours: Free; late June-mid-Aug daily 12:00-24:00, shorter hours April-late June and mid-Aug-mid-Sept; closed mid-Sept-March; S-tog: Klampenborg, then walk 10 minutes through the woods; tel. 39 63 73 00, www.bakken.dk.

Dragør—If you don't have time to get to the idyllic island of Ærø, consider a trip a few minutes out of Copenhagen to the fishing village of Dragør (bus #350S from Nørreport). For information, see www.dragoer.dk.

Shopping in Copenhagen

Shops are generally open Monday through Friday from 10:00 to 19:00 and Saturday from 9:00 to 16:00 (closed Sun). While big department stores dominate the scene, many locals favor the characteristic, small artisan shops and boutiques.

Uniquely Danish souvenirs to look for include intricate paper cuttings with idyllic motifs of swans, flowers, or Christmas themes; mobiles with everything from bicycles to Viking ships (look for the quality Flensted brand); and the colorful artwork (posters, postcards, T-shirts, and more) by Danish artist Bo Bendixen.

For a street's worth of shops selling **"Scantiques,"** wander down Ravnsborggade from Nørrebrogade.

Copenhagen's colorful **flea markets** are small but feisty and surprisingly cheap (May-Nov Sat 8:00-14:00 at Israels Plads; May-Sept Fri and Sat 8:00-17:00 along Gammel Strand and on Kongens Nytorv). For other street markets, ask at the TI.

The city's top **department stores** (Illum at Østergade 52, and Magasin du Nord at Kongens Nytorv 13) offer a good, if expensive, look at today's Denmark. Both are on the Strøget and have fine cafeterias on their top floors. The department stores and the Politiken Bookstore on Rådhuspladsen have a good selection of maps and English travel guides.

The section of the Strøget called **Amagertorv** is a highlight for shoppers. The Royal Copenhagen store here sells porcelain on three floors (Mon-Fri 10:00-19:00, Sat 10:00-17:00, Sun 12:00-17:00). The first floor up features figurines and collectibles. The second floor has a free museum with demonstrations and a great video (10 minutes, plays continuously, English only). In the basement, proving that "even the best painter can miss a stroke," you'll find the discounted seconds. Next door, Illums Bolighus shows off three floors of modern Danish design (Mon-Fri 10:00-19:00, Sat 9:00-17:00, Sun 10:00-17:00, shorter hours off-season).

Shoppers who like jewelry look for amber, known as "gold of the North." Globs of this petrified sap wash up on the shores of all the Baltic countries. **House of Amber** has a shop and a tiny two-room museum with about 50 examples of prehistoric insects trapped in the amber (remember *Jurassic Park*?) under magnifying glasses. You'll also see remarkable items made of amber, from necklaces and chests to Viking ships and chess sets (25 kr, daily May-Aug 10:00-19:00, Sept-April 10:00-18:00, museum closes 30 minutes earlier, at the top of Nyhavn at Kongens Nytorv 2; 4 other locations sell amber, but only the Nyhavn location houses a museum as well). If you're visiting Rosenborg Castle, you'll see even better examples of amber craftsmanship in its treasury.

For stylish and practical items of Danish design, check out

the boutique in the **Danish Design Center**.

If you buy anything substantial (300 kr, about $60) from a shop displaying the **Danish Tax-Free Shopping** emblem, you can get a refund of the Value-Added Tax, roughly 20 to 25 percent of the purchase price (VAT is "MOMS" in Danish). If you have your purchase mailed, the tax can be deducted from your bill. For details, call 32 52 55 66, and see "Getting a VAT Refund" in the Introduction.

Nightlife in Copenhagen

Neighborhoods: The **Meatpacking District,** which I've listed for its restaurants, is also one of the city's most up-and-coming destinations for bars and nightlife. On warm evenings, **Nyhavn** canal becomes a virtual nightclub, with packs of young people hanging out along the water, sipping beers. **Christiania** always seems to have something musical going on after dark. **Tivoli** has evening entertainment daily from mid-April through late September.

Venues: Copenhagen Jazz House is a good bet for live jazz (closed Mon, Niels Hemmingsensgade 10, tel. 33 15 26 00, check website for schedule, www.jazzhouse.dk). For blues, try the **Mojo Blues Bar** (70 kr Fri-Sat, otherwise no cover, nightly 20:00-5:00, music starts at 21:30, Løngangsstræde 21c, tel. 33 11 64 53, schedule in Danish on website, www.mojo.dk).

Jazz Cruises: Canal Tours Copenhagen offers 1.5-hour jazz cruises along the canals of Copenhagen. You can bring a picnic dinner and drinks on board and enjoy a lively night on the water surrounded by Danes (140 kr, June-Aug Thu and Sun at 19:00, Sept-Dec and April-May only Sun at 15:00, no tours Jan-March, departs from Canal Tours Copenhagen dock at Nyhavn, tel. 32 96 30 00). Call to reserve on July and August evenings; otherwise try arriving 20 to 30 minutes in advance.

Event and Live Music Listings: For the latest, check at the TI and pick up *The Copenhagen Post* (comes out on Thu, free at TI and some hotels, also sold at newsstands, www.cphpost.dk).

Sleeping in Copenhagen

I've listed a few big business-class hotels, the best budget hotels in the center, cheap rooms in private homes in great neighborhoods an easy bus ride from the station, and a few backpacker dorm options.

Big Copenhagen hotels have an exasperating pricing policy. Their high rack rates are actually charged only about 20 or 30 days a year (unless you book in advance and don't know better). As

COPENHAGEN

Sleep Code

(6 kr = about $1, country code: 45)
S = Single, **D** = Double/Twin, **T** = Triple, **Q** = Quad, **b** = bathroom, **s** = shower. Breakfast is generally included at hotels (unless you get a deeply discounted room rate), but not at private rooms or hostels. You can assume that staff speak English and credit cards are accepted unless otherwise noted.

To help you sort easily through these listings, I've divided the accommodations into three categories, based on the highest rack-rate price for a standard double room with bath during high season:

$$$ Higher Priced—Most rooms 1,000 kr or more.
$$ Moderately Priced—Most rooms between 600-1,000 kr.
$ Lower Priced—Most rooms 600 kr or less.

Prices can change without notice; verify the hotel's current rates online or by email.

---

hotels are swamped at certain times, they like to keep their gouging options open. Therefore, you'll need to check their website for deals or be bold enough to simply show up and use the TI's booking service to find yourself a room on their push list (ask at their desk, 100-kr fee). The TI swears that, except for maybe 10 days a year, you can land yourself a deeply discounted room in a three- or four-star business-class hotel in the center. That means a 1,400-kr double with American-style comfort for about 900 kr, including a big buffet breakfast.

Note that at the big hotels, some rates include breakfast, while the cheapest rates may not (you'll pay extra if you want breakfast).

Hotels in Central Copenhagen

Prices include breakfast unless noted otherwise. All of these hotels are big and modern, with elevators and non-smoking rooms upon request, and all accept credit cards. Beware: Many hotels have rip-off phone rates even for local calls.

Near Nørreport

$$$ Ibsens Hotel is a stylish 118-room hotel in a charming neighborhood away from the main train station commotion and a short walk from the old center (on average Sb-1,000-1,200 kr, Db-1,100-1,400 kr, very slushy rates flex with demand—ask about discounts when booking or check website; higher prices are for larger rooms, third bed-300 kr, great bikes-150 kr/24 hours, entirely non-smoking, free Internet access and Wi-Fi, parking-185 kr/day,

Vendersgade 23, S-tog: Nørreport, tel. 33 13 19 13, fax 33 13 19 16, www.ibsenshotel.dk, hotel@ibsenshotel.dk).

$$ Hotel Jørgensen is a friendly little 30-room hotel in a great location just off Nørreport with some cheap, grungy rooms and some good-value, nicer rooms. A good budget option, it's a bit worn around the edges. While the lounge is welcoming, the halls are a narrow, tangled maze (basic S-575 kr, Sb-675 kr, very basic D-675 kr, nicer Db-850 kr, cheaper off-season, extra bed-200 kr, free Wi-Fi, Rømersgade 11, tel. 33 13 81 86, fax 33 15 51 05, www .hoteljoergensen.dk, hoteljoergensen@mail.dk). They also rent 175-kr dorm beds to those under 35 (4-12 beds per room, sheets-30 kr).

Near Nyhavn
$$$ 71 Nyhavn has 150 smallish, rustic, but very classy rooms in a pair of beautifully restored, early-19th-century brick warehouses located at the far end of the colorful Nyhavn canal. With a professional, polite staff, lots of old brick and heavy timbers, and plenty of style, it's a worthwhile splurge (Sb-1,000-1,500 kr, Db-1,500-2,000 kr, 200 kr more for canal-view "superior" rooms, 400 kr more for larger "executive" rooms, rates vary depending on demand, some rates include breakfast—otherwise 170 kr, air-con in one of the buildings, free Internet access and Wi-Fi, next to the new Playhouse at Nyhavn 71, tel. 33 43 62 00, fax 33 43 62 01, www.71nyhavnhotel.dk, 71nyhavnhotel@arp-hansen.dk).

$$ Hotel Bethel Sømandshjem ("Seamen's Home"), run by a Lutheran association, is a calm and stately former seamen's hotel facing the boisterous Nyhavn canal and offering 29 tired but cozy rooms at the most reasonable rack rates in town. While the decor is college-dorm-inspired, the hotel boasts a kind, welcoming staff and feels surprisingly comfortable once you settle in. Plus, the colorful Nyhavn neighborhood is a great place to "come home" to after a busy day of sightseeing. Book long in advance (Sb-645 kr, large Sb-845 kr, Db-845 kr, larger "good" Db-945 kr, biggest corner Db-1,045 kr, extra bed-200 kr, free Internet access and Wi-Fi, Metro to Kongens Nytorv, facing bridge over the canal at Nyhavn 22, tel. 33 13 03 70, fax 33 15 85 70, www.hotel-bethel.dk, info @hotel-bethel.dk).

Behind the Train Station
The area behind the train station mingles elegant old buildings, trendy nightspots, and a hint of modern sleaze. The main drag running away from the station, Iseldgade, has long been Copenhagen's red-light district; but increasingly, this area is gentrified and feels safe (in spite of the few remaining, harmless sex shops). These hotels are also extremely handy to the up-and-coming Meatpacking District restaurant zone.

COPENHAGEN

Copenhagen Hotels & Restaurants

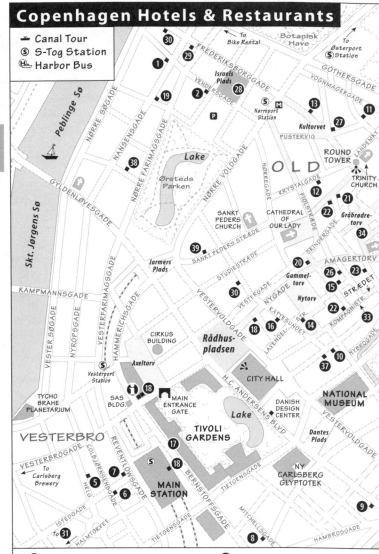

1	Ibsens Hotel	11	Restaurant Schønnemann
2	Hotel Jørgensen	12	Café Halvvejen
3	71 Nyhavn Hotel	13	Slagteren ved Kultorvet
4	Hotel Bethel Sømandshjem	14	Rest. & Café Nytorv
5	Axel Hotel	15	Sorgenfri
6	Star Hotel	16	Domhusets Smørrebrød
7	Hotel Nebo	17	Andersen Bakery
8	Cab-Inn City	18	Lagkagehuset Bakeries (4)
9	Danhostel Copenhagen City	19	Nansens Bakery
10	Danhostel Copenhagen Downtown	20	Konditori La Glace

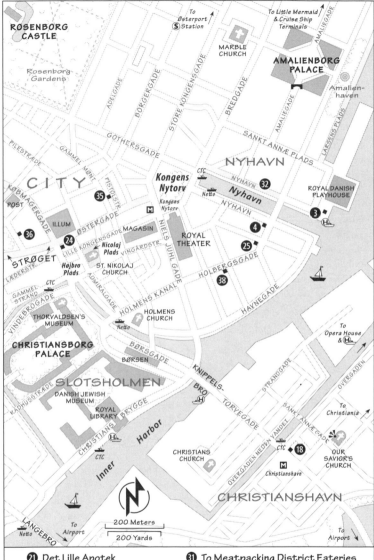

21 Det Lille Apotek

22 Riz-Raz Veg. Buffet (2)

23 Tight Restaurant

24 Café Norden

25 Holberg No. 19

26 Københavner Caféen

27 The Ricemarket

28 Torvehallerne KBH

29 Café Klimt

30 Halifax Burgers (2)

31 To Meatpacking District Eateries

32 Nyhavn Eateries

33 Kompagnistræde Eateries

34 Gråbrødretorv Eateries

35 Netto Supermarket

36 Copenhagen Jazz House

37 Mojo Blues Bar

38 Bike Rentals (2)

39 Bike Copenhagen with Mike

$$$ Axel Hotel and **$$$ Carlton Hotel,** operated by the Guldsmeden ("Dragonfly") company, have more character than most—a restful spa-like ambience decorated with imported Balinese furniture, and an emphasis on sustainability and organic materials. I've listed average prices, but rates can change dramatically, depending on when you book—check their website for the best deals (Axel: Sb-845-975 kr, Db-985-1,145 kr, breakfast-165 kr, 129 rooms, request a quieter back room overlooking the pleasant garden, free Internet access and Wi-Fi, restful spa area with sauna and Jacuzzi-295 kr/person per stay, a block behind the train station at Helgolandsgade 7, tel. 33 31 32 66, fax 33 31 69 70, booking @hotelguldsmeden.com; Carlton: a bit cheaper than Axel, 64 rooms, Vesterbrogade 66, tel. 33 22 15 00, fax 33 22 15 55, carlton@ hotelguldsmeden.com). They share a website: www.hotelgulds-meden.com.

$$ Star Hotel has 134 charmless, cookie-cutter rooms at reasonable prices. Rates vary with the season and online specials (Sb-555-1,100 kr, Db-800-1,555 kr but usually around 950-1,000 kr, breakfast included in some rates—otherwise 65 kr, elevator, free Internet access and Wi-Fi, Colbjørnsensgade 13, tel. 33 22 11 00, star@copenhagenstar.dk).

$$ Hotel Nebo, a secure-feeling refuge with a friendly welcome and 84 comfy rooms, is a half-block from the station (S-420 kr, Sb-650-700 kr, D-650-845 kr, Db-950 kr, most rates include breakfast—otherwise 60 kr, cheaper Oct-April, periodic online deals, extra bed-150 kr, elevator, free Internet access, pay Wi-Fi, Istedgade 6, tel. 33 21 12 17, fax 33 23 47 74, www.nebo.dk, nebo @nebo.dk).

$$ Wake Up Copenhagen offers new, compact, slick, and stylish rooms (similar to but a notch more upscale-feeling than Cab-Inn, described next). The rates can range wildly (Db-600-2,400 kr), and their pricing structure is like the airlines' in that the further ahead and less flexibly you book, the less you pay (average rates are about Sb-500 kr, Db-800 kr). Rooms that are higher up—with better views and quieter—are also more expensive, and you can pay 200 kr extra for a larger room. It's in a desolate no-man's-land behind the station, between the train tracks and the harbor—about a 15-minute walk from the station or Tivoli, but ideal for biking (breakfast-60 kr, elevator, free Wi-Fi, bike rental, Carsten Niebuhrs Gade 11, tel. 44 80 00 00, fax 44 80 00 01, www. wakeupcopenhagen.com—book on this site for best rates, wakeup-copenhagen@arp-hansen.dk).

A Danish Motel 6

$$ Cab-Inn is a radical innovation and a great value, with several locations in Copenhagen (as well as Odense, Aarhus, and

elsewhere): identical, mostly collapsible, tiny but comfy, cruise-ship-type staterooms, all bright, molded, and shiny, with TV, coffee-pot, shower, and toilet. Each room has a single bed that expands into a twin-bedded room with one or two fold-down bunks on the walls. It's tough to argue with this kind of efficiency (general rates: teensy "economy" Sb-485 kr, Db-615 kr; still small "standard" Sb-545 kr, Db-675 kr, flip-down bunk Tb-805 kr; larger "commodore" Sb-645 kr, Db-775 kr; relatively gigantic "captain's" Sb-745 kr, Db-875; larger family rooms also available, breakfast-60 kr, easy parking-60 kr, free Internet access and Wi-Fi, www.cabinn.com). The best of the bunch is **Cab-Inn City,** with 350 rooms and a great central location (no economy rooms here; a short walk south of the main train station and Tivoli at Mitchellsgade 14, tel. 33 46 16 16, fax 33 46 17 17, city@cab inn.com). Two more, nearly identical Cab-Inns are a 15-minute walk northwest of the station: **Cab-Inn Copenhagen Express** (86 rooms, Danasvej 32-34, tel. 33 21 04 00, fax 33 21 74 09, express@ cabinn.com) and **Cab-Inn Scandinavia** (201 rooms, some quads, Vodroffsvej 55, tel. 35 36 11 11, fax 35 36 11 14, scandinavia@cabinn. com). The newest and largest is **Cab-Inn Metro,** near the Ørestad Metro station (710 rooms, some quads, on the airport side of town at Arne Jakobsens Allé 2, tel. 32 46 57 00, fax 32 46 57 01, metro@ cabinn.com).

Rooms in Private Homes

At about 600 kr or so per double, staying in a private home can be a great value. While these accommodations offer a fine peek into Danish domestic life, the experience can be as private or as social as you want it to be. Hosts generally speak English, and you'll get a key and can come and go as you like. Rooms generally have no sink, and the bathroom's down the hall. They usually don't include breakfast, but you'll have access to the kitchen. I've listed an agency with a website that represents scores of fine places and—if you'd rather book direct—a good B&B in Christianshavn.

$ Bed & Breakfast Denmark has served as a clearinghouse for local B&Bs since 1992. Peter Eberth and his staff take a 20-30 percent cut (the "deposit" you pay) but monitor quality. Given the high cost of hostels and hotels and the way local B&B hosts come and go, this is a fine and worthwhile service. Peter's website lets you choose the type and location of place best for you and gives you the necessary details when you pay. He has piles of good local

COPENHAGEN

Christianshavn

1 Esben Juhl Rooms
2 Ravelinen Restaurant
3 Bastionen & Løven Rest.
4 Lagkagehuset Bakery
5 Spicy Kitchen Indian
6 Spiseloppen Restaurant

rooms in central apartments (D-400 kr, Db-500-600 kr). He's located near the station at Sankt Peders Stræde 41, but there's no reason to visit his office (tel. 39 61 04 05, www.bbdk.dk).

$ Esben Juhl rents two spic-and-span, bright rooms in his beautiful Christianshavn apartment, close to the harbor and canal. You'll be sharing Esben's bathroom, and if he books both rooms, he'll actually be sleeping out in the living room; if these sound like too-close quarters, look elsewhere. But Esben is soft-spoken and kind, and enjoys treating his guests like houseguests, making this a good opportunity to connect with a local (S-400 kr, D-500 kr, extra bed-150 kr, includes light breakfast, cash only, free Wi-Fi, David Balfours Gade 5, Metro: Christianshavn, tel. 32 57 39 08, mobile 27 40 12 15, mail@esju.dk).

Hostels

Copenhagen energetically accommodates the young vagabond on a shoestring. Hostels are the best value for those who travel alone, bring their own sheets, and make their own breakfast. Otherwise they can cost 250 kr per night per person.

$ Danhostel Copenhagen City, an official HI hostel, is the hostel of the future. This huge harborside skyscraper (1,004 beds on 16 stories) is clean, modern, non-smoking, and a 10-minute

walk from the train station and Tivoli. Some rooms on higher floors have panoramic views over the city (available on a first-come, first-served basis). This is your best bet for a clean, basic, and inexpensive room in the city center (dorm beds in 6-bed rooms with bathrooms-135-195 kr— some co-ed, some separate; Sb/Db/Qb-495-720 kr, price depends on demand, sheets and towel-60 kr, breakfast-74 kr, nonmembers pay 35 kr/night extra, elevator, lockers, kitchen, self-service laundry, pay Internet access, free Wi-Fi, rental bikes, H. C. Andersen Boulevard 50, tel. 33 11 85 85, www.danhostelcopenhagencity .dk,copenhagencity@danhostel.dk).

$ Danhostel Copenhagen Downtown is beautifully located on a pleasant street right in the city center, a few steps from Slotsholmen Island and two blocks from the Strøget. Its 300 beds are a bit institutional, but it comes with a guest kitchen and a colorful, fun hangout bar, which doubles as the reception (rates vary with demand, bunk in 4- to 10-bed dorm-100-215 kr, D-250-450 kr, 100 kr more for a private bathroom, nonmembers pay 35 kr extra, sheets-30 kr, breakfast-65 kr, free Wi-Fi, Vandkunsten 5, tel. 70 23 21 10, www.copenhagendowntown.com, info@copen hagendowntown.com).

$ City Public Hostel houses travelers late May through August; the rest of the year, it's a latchkey program for local kids. It's well-run, welcomes people of all ages, and has a great location behind the Copenhagen City Museum on Vesterbrogade. With its sprawling grassy front yard, you can even forget you're in the middle of a big city (130 kr/bed in massive 66-bed room, 140 kr/bed in 32- or 22-bed dorm, 160 kr/bed in 12-bed dorm, 170 kr/bed in 10- or 6-bed dorm, sheets-40 kr, no breakfast, relaxing lounge, 10-minute walk behind main train station at Absalonsgade 8, tel. 33 31 20 70, www.citypublichostel.dk, info @citypublichostel.dk).

$ Danhostel Copenhagen Amager, an official HI hostel, is on the edge of town (dorm bed-145 kr, S-360 kr, Sb-460 kr, D-390 kr, Db-490 kr, T-520 kr, Tb-580 kr, Q-630 kr, Qb-680 kr, nonmembers pay 35 kr extra, sheets-45 kr, breakfast-55 kr, family rooms, no curfew, excellent facilities, Internet access, self-serve laundry, Vejlands Allé 200, tel. 32 52 29 08, fax 32 52 27 08, www.danhostelcopenhagen.dk, copenhagen@danhostel.dk). To get from downtown to the hostel, take the Metro (Metro: Bella Center, then 10-minute walk).

Eating in Copenhagen

Cheap Meals

For a quick lunch, try a *smørrebrød*, a *pølse*, or a picnic. Finish it off with a pastry.

Smørrebrød

Denmark's 300-year-old tradition of open-face sandwiches survives. Find a *smørrebrød* take-out shop and choose two or three that look good (about 20 kr each). You'll get them wrapped and ready for a park bench. Add a cold drink, and you have a fine, quick, and very Danish lunch. Tradition calls for three sandwich courses: herring first, then meat, and then cheese. Downtown, you'll find these handy local alternatives to Yankee fast-food chains. They range from splurges to quick stop-offs.

Between Copenhagen University and Rosenborg Castle

My three favorite *smørrebrød* places are particularly handy when connecting your sightseeing between the downtown Strøget core and Rosenborg Castle.

Restaurant Schønnemann is the foodies' choice—it has been written up in international magazines and frequently wins awards for "Best Lunch in Copenhagen." It's a cozy cellar restaurant crammed with small tables—according to the history on the menu, people "gather here in intense togetherness." The sand on the floor evokes a bygone era when passing traders would leave their horses out on the square while they lunched here. You'll need to reserve to get a table, and you'll pay a premium for their *smørrebrød* (50-130 kr). At these prices, the sandwiches had better be a cut above...fortunately, they deliver (two lunch seatings Mon-Sat: 11:30-14:00 and 14:14-17:00, closed Sun, no dinner, Hauser Plads 16, tel. 33 12 07 85).

Café Halvvejen is a small mom-and-pop place serving traditional lunches and open-face sandwiches in a woody and smoke-stained café, lined with portraits of Danish royalty. You can eat inside or at an outside table in good weather (50-70 kr *smørrebrød*, 80-100-kr main dishes, food served Mon-Sat 12:00-15:00, closed Sun, next to public library at Krystalgade 11, tel. 33 11 91 12). In the evening, it becomes a hip and smoky student hangout, though no food is served.

Slagteren ved Kultorvet, a few blocks northwest of the university, is a small butcher shop with bowler-hatted clerks selling good, inexpensive sandwiches to go for about 35 kr. Choose from ham, beef, or pork (sorry—no vegetarian options, Mon-Thu 8:00-17:30, Fri 8:00-19:00, Sat 8:00-14:00, closed Sun, just off Kultorvet square at #4 Frederiksborggade, look for gold bull's head hanging outside).

Near Gammeltorv/Nytorv

Restaurant and Café Nytorv has pleasant outdoor seating on Nytorv (with cozy indoor tables available nearby) and a great deal on a *smørrebrød* sampler for about 179 kr—perfect for two people to share. This "Copenhagen City Plate" gives you a selection of the traditional sandwiches and extra bread on request (daily 9:00-22:00, Nytorv 15, tel. 33 11 77 06). **Sorgenfri** offers a local experience in a dark, woody spot just off the Strøget (80-100 kr, Mon-Sat 11:00-20:45, Sun 12:00-18:00, Brolæggerstræde 8, tel. 33 11 58 80). Or consider **Domhusets Smørrebrød** (Mon-Fri 8:00-15:00, closed Sat-Sun, off the City Hall end of the Strøget at Kattesundet 18, tel. 33 15 98 98).

COPENHAGEN

The *Pølse*

The famous Danish hot dog, sold in *pølsevogne* (sausage wagons) throughout the country, is another typically Danish institution

that has resisted the onslaught of our global, prepackaged, fast-food culture. Study the photo menu for variations. These are fast, cheap, tasty, and, like their American cousins, almost worthless nutritionally. Even so, what the locals call the "dead man's finger" is the dog Danish kids love to bite.

There's more to getting a *pølse* than simply ordering a "hot dog" (which in Copenhagen simply means a sausage with a bun on the side, generally the worst bread possible). The best is a *ristet* (or grilled) hot dog *med det hele* (with the works). Employ these other handy phrases: *rød* (red, the basic boiled weenie), *medister* (spicy, better quality), *knæk* (short, stubby, tastier than *rød*), *brød* (a bun, usually smaller than the sausage), *svøb* ("swaddled" in bacon), *Fransk* (French style, buried in a long skinny hole in the bun with sauce). *Sennep* is mustard and *ristet løg* are crispy, fried onions. Wash everything down with a *sodavand* (soda pop).

By hanging around a *pølsevogn*, you can study this institution. Denmark's "cold feet cafés" are a form of social care: People who have difficulty finding jobs are licensed to run these wiener-mobiles. As they gain seniority, they are promoted to work at more central locations. Danes like to gather here for munchies and *pølsesnak*—the local slang for empty chatter (literally, "sausage talk"). And traditionally, after getting drunk, guys stop here for a hot dog and chocolate milk on the way home—that's why the stands stay open until the wee hours.

For sausages a cut above (and from a storefront—not a cart), stop by the little grill restaurant **Andersen Bakery,** directly across the street from the train station (next to the Tivoli entrance). The menu is limited—either pork or veal/beef—but the ingredients are high-quality and the weenies are tasty (50-kr gourmet dogs, daily 7:00-19:00, Bernstorffsgade 5, tel. 33 75 07 35).

Picnics

Throughout Copenhagen, small delis *(viktualiehandler)* sell fresh bread, tasty pastries, juice, milk, cheese, and yogurt (drinkable, in tall liter boxes). Two of the largest supermarket chains are **Irma** (in arcade on Vesterbrogade next to Tivoli) and **Super Brugsen. Netto** is a cut-rate outfit with the cheapest prices. And, of course, there's the ever-present **7-Eleven** chain, with branches seemingly on every corner; while you'll pay a bit more here, there's a reason they're called "convenience" stores—and they also serve pastries and hot dogs.

Pastry

The golden pretzel sign hanging over the door or windows is the Danes' age-old symbol for a bakery. Danish pastries, called *wienerbrød* ("Vienna bread") in Denmark, are named for the Viennese bakers who brought the art of pastry-making to Denmark, where the Danes say they perfected it. Try these bakeries: **Lagkagehuset** (multiple locations around town; the handiest options include one right in the train station, another nearby inside the TI, one along the Strøget at Frederiksborggade 21, and another on Torvegade just across from the Metro station in Christianshavn) and **Nansens** (on corner of Nansensgade and Ahlefeldtsgade, near Ibsens Hotel). For a genteel bit of high-class 1870s Copenhagen, pay a lot for a coffee and a fresh Danish at **Konditori La Glace,** just off the Strøget at Skoubogade 3.

Dine with the Danes

For a unique experience and a great opportunity to meet locals in their homes, consider having this organization arrange a dinner for you with a Danish family. You get a homey two-course meal with lots of conversation. Some effort is made to match your age and interests, but not occupations. Book online at least a week in advance (400 kr per person, www.dinewiththedanes.dk, tel. 26 85 39 61). Fill out an online questionnaire, and you'll be contacted by email a day or two later.

Restaurants

I've listed restaurants in three areas: the downtown core, the funky Christianshavn neighborhood across the harbor, and the trendy "Meatpacking District" behind the train station. Most of my suggestions in the high-rent downtown are tired but reliable Danish classics. For a broader range of Copenhagen's culinary scene of today, it's worth the short walk to the Meatpacking District.

Due to the high cost of water in Denmark, it's common to be charged for tap water with your meal if you do not order any other beverage. You'll often save money by paying with cash; many Danish restaurants charge a fee for credit-card transactions (about 2-5 percent).

In the Downtown Core

Det Lille Apotek ("The Little Pharmacy") is a reasonable, candlelit place. It's been popular with locals for 200 years, and now it's also quite touristy. Their specialty is "Stone Beef," a big slab of tender, raw steak plopped down and cooked in front of you on a scalding-hot soapstone. Cut it into smaller pieces and it's cooked within minutes (sandwich lunches, traditional dinners for 125-190 kr, nightly from 17:30, just off the Strøget, between Frue Church and Round Tower at Store Kannikestræde 15, tel. 33 12 56 06).

Riz-Raz Vegetarian Buffet has two locations in Copenhagen: around the corner from the canal boat rides at Kompagnistræde 20 (tel. 33 15 05 75) and across from Det Lille Apotek at Store Kannikestræde 19 (tel. 33 32 33 45). At both places, you'll find a healthy all-you-can-eat Middle Eastern/Mediterranean/vegetarian buffet lunch for 79 kr (cheese but no meat, great falafel, daily 11:30-16:00) and an even bigger dinner buffet for 99 kr (16:00-24:00). The wonderfully varied and very filling dinner buffet has to be the best deal in town. Use lots of plates and return to the buffet as many times as you like. They also offer à la carte and meat options for 65-95 kr. Tap water is 8 kr per jug.

Tight resembles a trendy gastropub, serving an eclectic international array of cuisine in a split-level maze of hip rooms that mix old timbers and brick with bright colors. You can only order a fixed-price meal here, unless you want their prizewinning burger (two courses-225 kr, three courses-275 kr, burger-140 kr; Mon-Thu 17:00-22:00, Fri 17:00-23:00, Sat 12:00-23:00, Sun 12:00-22:00, just off the Strøget at Hyskenstræde 10, tel. 33 11 09 00).

Café Norden, very Danish with modern "world cuisine" and fine pastries, is a big, venerable institution overlooking Amagertorv by the heron fountain. They have good light meals and salads, and great people-watching from window seats on the second floor (120-160-kr sandwiches and salads, 150-160-kr main dishes, huge splittable portions, daily 9:00-24:00, order at bar, Østergade 61, tel. 33 11 77 91).

Holberg No. 19, a cozy American-run café with classic ambience, sits just a block off the tourist crush of the Nyhavn canal. With a loose, friendly, low-key vibe, it offers more personality and lower prices than the tourist traps along Nyhavn (60-95-kr salads and sandwiches, order at the bar, Mon-Fri 10:00-22:00, Sat 10:00-20:00, Sun 10:00-18:00, sometimes opens at 8:00, Holberg 19, tel. 33 14 01 90).

Københavner Caféen, cozy and a bit tired, feels like a ship captain's dining room. The staff is enthusiastically traditional, serving local dishes and elegant open-face sandwiches for a good value. Lunch specials (80-100 kr) are served until 17:00, when the more expensive dinner menu kicks in (plates for 120-200 kr, daily, kitchen closes at 22:00, at Badstuestræde 10, tel. 33 32 80 81).

The Ricemarket, an unpretentious Asian fusion bistro, is buried in a modern cellar between the Strøget and Rosenborg Castle. It's the more affordable (and more casual) side-eatery of a popular local restaurant, and offers a break from Danish food (65-95-kr small dishes, 115-185-kr big dishes, 95-kr lunch special includes drink, Mon-Sat 11:00-22:00, Sun 11:00-21:00, Hausergade 38 near Kultorvet, tel. 35 35 75 30).

Illum and **Magasin du Nord** department stores serve cheery, reasonable meals in their cafeterias. At Illum, eat outside at tables along the Strøget, or head to the elegant glass-domed top floor (Østergade 52). Magasin du Nord (Kongens Nytorv 13) also has a great grocery and deli in the basement.

Also try **Restaurant and Café Nytorv** at Nytorv 15 or **Sorgenfri** at Brolæggerstræde 8 (both are described under *"Smørrebrød,"* earlier).

In Christianshavn

This neighborhood is so cool, it's worth combining an evening wander with dinner, even if you're not staying here. It's a 10-minute walk across the bridge from the old center, or a 3-minute ride on the Metro. Choose one of my listings, or simply wander the blocks between Christianshavntorv, the main square, and the Christianshavn Canal—you'll find a number of lively neighborhood pubs and cafés.

Ravelinen Restaurant, on a tiny island on the big road 100 yards south of Christianshavn, serves traditional Danish food at reasonable prices to happy local crowds. Dine indoors or on the lovely lakeside terrace (which is tented and heated, so it's comfortable even on blustery evenings). This is like Tivoli without the kitsch and tourists (70-130-kr lunch dishes, 180-280-kr dinners, mid-April-late Dec daily 11:30-21:00, closed off-season, Torvegade 79, tel. 32 96 20 45).

The Latest Culinary Phe-noma-non

Foodies visiting Denmark probably already know that Copenhagen is home to the planet's top-rated restaurant. In 2010 and 2011, San Pellegrino and *Restaurant* magazine named noma the "Best Restaurant in the World." With the closure of El Bulli near Barcelona in 2011, noma has emerged as *the* reservation to get in the foodie universe. Chef René Redzepi is a pioneer in the burgeoning "New Nordic" school of cooking, which combines modern nouvelle cuisine and molecular gastronomy techniques with locally sourced (and, in some cases, foraged) ingredients from Denmark and other Nordic lands. So, while they use sophisticated cooking methods, they replace the predictable French and Mediterranean ingredients with Nordic ones. The restaurant's name comes from the phrase *nordisk mad* (Nordic food).

But noma, which is located at the northern edge of the trendy Christianshavn district (Strandgade 93, tel. 32 96 32 97), is not cheap. The seven-course *menu* runs 1,500 kr; accompanying wines add 950 kr to the bill. A couple going for the whole shebang is looking at spending close to $800. And even if you're willing to take the plunge, you have to plan ahead—noma is booked up around three months ahead. Check their website (www.noma.dk) for the latest procedure; you'll likely need to call on a specific date, at 10:00 in the morning Copenhagen time, about three months before your desired reservation...and hope you get through. You can also put your name on their waiting list, using their online form.

If you can't commit that far out (or don't want to spend that much), many of the top restaurants in Copenhagen (including Kødbyens Fisekebar, listed on page 85) are run by former chefs from noma—giving you at least a taste of culinary greatness.

Bastionen & Løven, at the little windmill (Lille Mølle), serves gourmet Danish nouveau cuisine with a French inspiration from a small but fresh menu, on a Renoir terrace or in its Rembrandt interior. The classiest, dressiest, and most gourmet of all my listings, this restaurant fills a classic old mansion. Reservations for indoor dining are required; they don't take reservations for outdoor seating, as weather is unpredictable (65-165-kr lunches, 170-185-kr dinners, 325-kr three-course meal, daily 11:30-24:00, walk to end of Torvegade and follow ramparts up to restaurant, at south end of Christianshavn, Christianshavn Voldgade 50, tel. 32 95 09 40).

Lagkagehuset is everybody's favorite bakery in Christianshavn. With a big selection of pastries, sandwiches, excellent fresh-baked bread, and award-winning strawberry tarts, it's a great place for breakfast or picnic fixings (pastries for less than 20 kr, take-out coffee for 30 kr, daily 6:00-19:00, Torvegade 45).

Ethnic Strip on Christianshavn's Main Drag: Torvegade, which is within a few minutes' walk of the Christianshavn Metro station, is lined with appealing and inexpensive ethnic eateries, including Italian, cheap kebabs, Mexican (thriving with a nightly 109-kr buffet), Chinese, and more. **Spicy Kitchen** serves cheap and good Indian food—tight and cozy, it's a hit with locals (55-70-kr plates, Mon-Sat 17:00-23:00, Sun 14:00-23:00, Torvegade 56).

In Christiania: Spiseloppen ("The Flea Eats") is a wonderfully classy place in Christiania. It serves great 135-165-kr vegetarian meals and 175-260-kr meaty ones by candlelight. It's gourmet anarchy—a good fit for Christiania, the free city/squatter town (Tue-Sun 17:00-22:00, closed Mon, occasional live music on weekends, reservations often necessary Fri-Sat; 3 blocks behind spiral spire of Our Savior's Church, on top floor of old brick warehouse, turn right just inside Christiania's main gate, enter the wildly empty warehouse, and climb the graffiti-riddled stairs; tel. 32 57 95 58).

Near Nørreport
The following eateries are near the recommended Ibsens and Jørgensens hotels.

Torvehallerne KBH is in a pair of new, modern, glassy market halls right on Israel Plads. In addition to produce, fish, and meat stalls, it has several inviting food counters where you can sit to eat a meal, or grab something to go. I can't think of a more enjoyable place in Copenhagen to browse for a meal than this upscale food court (prices vary per place, Tue-Thu 10:00-19:00, Fri 10:00-20:00, Sat 9:00-17:00, Sun 10:00-15:00, most places closed Mon, Frederiksborggade 21).

Café Klimt is a tight and thriving place, noisy and lit with candles. A young, hip crowd gathers here under the funky palm tree for modern world cuisine—salads, big pastas, burgers, omelets, and brunch until 16:00 (80-150 kr, daily 9:30-24:00, later Fri-Sat, Frederiksborggade 29, tel. 33 11 76 70).

Halifax, part of a small local chain, serves up "build-your-own" burgers, where you select a patty, a side dish, and a dipping sauce for your fries (100-125 kr, daily 12:00-22:00, Sun until 21:00, Frederiksborggade 35, tel. 33 32 77 11). They have another location just off the Strøget (at Larsbjørnsstræde 9).

In the Meatpacking District (Kødbyen)
Literally "Meat Town," Kødbyen is an old warehouse zone huddled up against the train tracks behind the main station. There are

three color-coded sectors—brown, gray, and white—each one a cluster of old industrial buildings. The brown zone, closest to the station, is a row of former slaughterhouses that has been converted into gallery space. At the far end is the white zone (Den Hvide Kødby), which has been overtaken by some of the city's most trendy and enjoyable eateries, mingling with surviving offices and warehouses for the local meatpacking industry. All of the places I list here are within a few steps of each other (except for the Mother pizzeria, a block away).

The curb appeal of this area is zilch (it looks like, well, a meatpacking district), but inside, these restaurants are bursting with life and flavor. While youthful and trendy, this scene is also very accessible—as much yuppie as it is avant-garde. Most of these eateries are in buildings with old white tile; this, combined with the considerable popularity of this area, can make the dining rooms quite loud. These places can fill up, especially on weekends (when it's virtually impossible to get a table if you just show up)—be sure to reserve ahead.

It's a very close stroll from the station: If you go south on the bridge called Tietgens Bro, which crosses the tracks just south of the station, and carry on for about 10 minutes, you'll run right into the area. Those sleeping in the hotels behind the station just stroll five minutes south. Or you can ride the S-tog to the Dybbølsbro stop, which is also just on the edge of this area.

Kødbyens Fisekebar ("Fish Bar"), one of the first and still the most acclaimed restaurant in the Meatpacking District, is run by a former chef from the famous noma restaurant (see sidebar). Focusing on small, thoughtfully composed plates of modern Nordic seafood, the Fiskebar has a stripped-down white interior with a big fish tank and a long cocktail bar surrounded by smaller tables. It's extremely popular (reservations are essential), and feels a bit too trendy for its own good. While the prices are high, so is the quality; diners are paying for a taste of the "New Nordic" style of cooking that's so in vogue here (100-145-kr small plates, 200-245-kr main dishes; Tue-Thu 17:30-24:00, Fri 15:30-24:00, Sat 12:00-2:00 in the morning, Sun 12:00-15:30, closed Mon; Flæsketorvet 100, tel. 32 15 56 56).

BioMio, in the old Bosch building, is a fresh take on an old cafeteria: First, claim a table (don't be afraid to share—Danes don't bite—and make a note of your table number). Then pick up a plastic card from the front desk to keep track of your purchases. Select your meal from the 100

percent organic, eclectic menu (with "world fusion" food—curries, wok dishes, Moroccan meatballs, and so on). Survey the line of chefs working in the open kitchen, choose which one you want to cook your meal, and place your order directly with him or her. Buy your drinks at the bar, and return to your seat to wait for your food to be delivered. When you're finished, just bring your card to the cashier to settle up. While prices are high for a self-service model, it's a unique experience, with fun ambience and good, healthy food (55-kr small plates, 105-185-kr dinners with big portions, 100-kr two-course lunch available Mon-Fri, open daily 12:00-23:00, Halmtorvet 19, tel. 33 31 20 00).

Paté Paté, next door to BioMio, is a tight, rollicking bistro in a former pâté factory. While a wine bar at heart, it also has a full menu of pricey, carefully prepared modern cuisine and a cozy atmosphere rare in the Meatpacking District (85-115-kr starters, 165-195-kr main dishes, Mon-Sat 9:00-24:00, closed Sun, Slagterboderne 1, tel. 39 69 55 57).

Mother is a pizzeria named for the way the sourdough for their crust must be "fed" and cared for to flourish. You can taste that care in the pizza, which has a delicious tangy crust. Out front are comfortable picnic benches, while the interior curls around the busy pizza oven and chefs pulling globs of dough that will become the basis for your pizza (30-kr bruschetta, 75-140-kr pizzas, a block beyond the other restaurants listed here at Høkerboderne 9, tel. 22 27 58 98).

Nose2Tail Madbodega (*mad* means "food") prides itself on locally sourced, sustainable cooking, using the entire animal for your meal (hence the name). You'll climb down some stairs into an unpretentious white-tiled cellar (50-kr small plates, 70-180-kr large plates, Mon-Sat 18:00-24:00, closed Sun, Flæsketorvet 13A, tel. 33 93 50 45).

Other Central Neighborhoods to Explore

To find a good restaurant, try simply window-shopping in one of these inviting districts.

Nyhavn's harbor canal is lined with a touristy strip of restaurants set alongside its classic sailboats. Here thriving crowds are served mediocre, overpriced food in a great setting. On any sunny day, if you want steak and fries (120 kr) and a 50-kr beer, this can be fun. On Friday and Saturday, the strip becomes the longest bar in the world.

Kompagnistræde is home to a changing cast of great little eateries. Running parallel to the Strøget, this street has fewer tourists and lower rent, and encourages places to compete creatively for the patronage of local diners.

Gråbrødretorv ("Grey Friars' Square") is perhaps the most popular square in the old center for a meal. It's like a food court, especially in good weather. Choose from Italian, French, or Danish. Two respected steakhouses are **Jensen's Bøfhus** (100-kr burgers, 120-220-kr main dishes) and the pricier **Bøf & Ost** (170-250-kr main dishes). **Skildpadden** ("The Turtle") is a student hit, with make-it-yourself sandwiches (69 kr, choose the type of bread, salami, and cheese you want) and a 49-kr salad bar, plus draft beer (30 kr, or 22 kr after 16:00—sort of a reverse happy hour). It's in a cozy cellar with three little tables on the lively square (Mon-Fri 11:30-22:30, Sat-Sun 11:30-20:30, Gråbrødretorv 9, tel. 33 13 05 06).

Istedgade and the surrounding streets behind the train station (just above the Meatpacking District) are home to an assortment of inexpensive ethnic restaurants. You will find numerous kebab, Chinese, Thai, and pizza places. The area can be a bit seedy, especially right behind the station, but walk a few blocks away to take your pick of inexpensive, ethnic eateries frequented by locals.

Copenhagen Connections

By Train or Bus

From Copenhagen by Train to: Hillerød/Frederiksborg (6/hour, 40 minutes on S-tog), **Roskilde** (1-3/hour, 30 minutes), **Humlebæk** (Louisiana modern-art museum; 4/hour, 36 minutes), **Helsingør** (3/hour, 50 minutes), **Odense** (3/hour, 1.75 hours), **Ærøskøbing** (5/day, 2.75 hours to Svendborg with a transfer in Odense, then 1.25-hour ferry crossing to Ærøskøbing), **Billund/Legoland** (hourly, 2.25 hours to Vejle, then take buses #43, #143, #166, or #179 to Billund, allow 3.5 hours total), **Aarhus** (1-2/hour, 3 hours), **Malmö** (3/hour, 35 minutes), **Stockholm** (almost hourly, 5-6 hours on high-speed train, some with a transfer at Malmö or Lund, reservation required; overnight service available but requires a change in Lund), **Växjö** (8/day, 2.5-3 hours), **Kalmar** (12/day, 3.5-4 hours, transfer in Alvesta), **Oslo** (2/day, 8 hours, transfer at Göteborg; for night train—which runs in summer only—take 35-minute train to Malmö, Sweden, www.sj.se, then easy transfer to direct night train), **Berlin** (5/day, 7 hours, reservation required, one direct, others change in Hamburg), **Amsterdam** (9/day, 11-18 hours, most require multiple changes, 1 direct night train), and **Frankfurt/Rhine** (4/day, 9-11 hours, most change in Hamburg). Train info tel. 70 13 14 15 (for English, press 1 for general information and tickets, and 2 for international trains). DSB (or Danske Statsbaner), Denmark's national railway, www.rejseplanen.dk.

By Bus: Taking the bus to **Stockholm** is cheaper but more time-consuming than taking the train (2/day, 9 hours, www.swe bus.se).

By Cruise Ship

More than half a million people visit Copenhagen via cruise ship each year. For a wealth of online information for cruise-ship passengers, see www.cruisecopenhagen.com. For more in-depth cruising information, pick up my *Rick Steves' Northern European Cruise Ports* guidebook.

Cruise Ports

Most cruise ships use one of two main terminals, both north of downtown—**Frihavnen** ("Freeport"), about three miles from the city center, and **Langelinie Pier,** about a mile closer to downtown (but a pleasant 10-minute walk north of *The Little Mermaid* site). A few cruises put in at **Toldbod,** even closer to town (just in front of Amalienborg Palace). The **Copenhagen Ferry Terminal,** located between the Frihavnen and Langelinie piers, serves DFDS ferries to and from Oslo (see "By Overnight Boat to Oslo," later).

Getting Downtown: Handy public **bus #26** connects both Langelinie and Frihavnen to downtown every 20 minutes (24 kr, buy ticket on board, possible to pay in euros or US dollars on this bus line only). Bus #26 does not run on weekends, when you'll have to consider one of the other options described next.

Langelinie and Frihavnen are both within about a 15-minute walk of a **train** station on Copenhagen's S-tog suburban rail line (Frihavnen is near the Nordhavn station, while Langelinie is near Østerport station). From either station, you can hop on a train headed downtown (buy a 24-kr ticket at machine on platform, then take any train headed in direction: Køge, Frederikssund, Ballerup, or Høje Taastrup; ride to the "København H" stop for the main train station).

From either terminal, you can also take a **taxi** (figure around 160 kr into downtown from Langelinie, or 200 kr from Frihavnen), or take a **hop-on, hop-off bus tour**. From Frihavnen, most cruise lines offer a **shuttle bus** straight to Kongens Nytorv and/or Rådhuspladsen (City Hall Square), generally for a fee. From Langelinie, you can **walk** into town (explained later).

Port Details: Neither port area has much in the way of services (such as ATMs); make your way downtown, then find what you need there.

Langelinie Pier, closer to the city, is intuitive and user-friendly: a long, skinny pier with one road and a row of ships. Bus #26 (on weekdays) stops at three points along the road. Otherwise, you can walk: Head to the base of the pier, cross to the mainland, then either bear left to find *The Little Mermaid,* or right to circle around Kastellet Fortress and find Østerport train station for a speedy train downtown. From *The Little Mermaid,* you can walk in about 15 minutes to Amalienborg Palace, then 10 more minutes to the colorful Nyhavn canal.

Frihavnen, a bit farther out, is a sprawling industrial zone with several cruise piers (called Sundkaj, Orientkaj, Fortkaj, and—farther to the north—Levantkaj and a brand-new cruise terminal in the works). The first three piers are all within an easy 5- to 10-minute walk of the port gate (just follow the thick blue line painted on the sidewalk); from the more distant Levantkaj, the cruise line offers a free shuttle bus to the gate. Exiting the port gate, you can bear right to find the stop for bus #26; or bear left out to the main road, then turn left, walk a long block, cross the street, duck under the underpass, and turn left along a residential street to find the Nordhavn train station (for the speedy train downtown).

By Overnight Boat to Oslo

Luxurious DFDS Seaways cruise ships leave nightly from Copenhagen for Oslo, and from Oslo for Copenhagen. The 16-hour sailings leave at 17:00 and arrive at 9:30 the next day. So you can spend seven hours in Norway's capital and then return to Copenhagen, or take this cruise from Oslo and do Copenhagen as a day trip...or just go one-way in either direction.

Cruise Costs: Cabins vary dramatically in price depending on the day and season (most expensive on weekends and late June-mid-Aug; cheapest on weekdays and Oct-April). For example, a bed in a four-berth "Seaways" shoehorn economy cabin starts at 410 kr per person one-way for four people traveling together (500 kr with a window); a luxurious double "Commodore class" cabin higher on the ship starts at 950 kr per person one-way (and includes a TV, minibar, and free breakfast buffet). A "mini-cruise" round-trip with a day in Oslo and no meals starts at 598 kr per person in an economy double cabin. All cabins have private bathrooms inside.

Onboard Services: DFDS Seaways operates two ships on this route—the MS *Pearl of Scandinavia* and the MS *Crown of Scandinavia.* Both offer all the cruise-ship luxuries: big buffets for breakfast (129 kr) and dinner (239 kr), gourmet restaurants (359-kr three-course meals), a kids' playroom, pool (indoor on the *Crown,* indoor and outdoor on the *Pearl*), sauna, nightclubs, pay Wi-Fi, satellite phone, and tax-free shopping. There are no ATMs on board. Cash advances are available at the shipboard exchange desk. All shops and restaurants accept credit cards as well as euros, dollars, and Danish, Swedish, and Norwegian currency.

Reservations: Reservations are smart in summer and on weekends. Advance bookings get the best prices. Book online or call DFDS Seaway's Danish office at 33 42 30 10 (Mon-Fri 8:30-17:00, www.dfdsseaways.us), or, in the US, call 800-533-3755 (www.dfdsseawaysusa.com).

Port Details: The **Copenhagen Ferry Terminal** (a.k.a. DFDS Terminalen) is a short walk north of *The Little Mermaid* site. The terminal is open daily 9:00-17:00 (luggage lockers available).

Getting Downtown: Shuttle bus #20E meets arriving ships from Oslo (daily 9:30-10:15). It goes first to Østerport station (far from downtown but on the S-tog line—easy connection to the main train station, with some recommended hotels and the start of my self-guided walk), then to Kongens Nytorv (on the Metro line and near Nyhavn and other recommended hotels); from either stop, you can connect to Nørreport station (with additional recommended hotels).

To reach the ferry terminal *from* the city center, catch bus #20E at Kongens Nytorv (free for cruise passengers, coordinated with sailing schedule; daily 14:00-16:00, departs every 10-30 minutes, arrives at the terminal 11 minutes later). Or take the S-tog from downtown in the direction of Hellerup or Hillerød to the Nordhavn station. Exit the station, cross under the tracks, and hike toward the water; you'll see the ship on your right.

NEAR COPENHAGEN

*Roskilde • Frederiksborg Castle • Louisiana •
Karen Blixen Museum • Kronborg Castle*

Copenhagen's the star, but there are several worthwhile sights nearby, and the public transportation system makes side-tripping a joy. Visit Roskilde's great Viking ships and royal cathedral. Tour Frederiksborg, Denmark's most spectacular castle, and slide along the cutting edge at Louisiana—a superb art museum with a coastal setting as striking as its art. Blixen fans can get *Out of Africa* at the author's home. At Helsingør, do the dungeons of Kronborg Castle before heading on to Sweden.

Planning Your Time

Roskilde's Viking ships and Frederiksborg Castle are the area's essential sights. Each one takes a half-day, and each one is an easy commute from Copenhagen in different directions (30-40-minute train ride, then a 20-minute walk or short bus ride). You'll find fewer tour-bus crowds in the afternoon. While you're in Roskilde, you can also pay your respects to the tombs of the Danish royalty.

If you're choosing between castles, Frederiksborg is the beautiful showpiece with the opulent interior, and Kronborg—darker and danker—is more typical of the way most castles really were. Both are dramatic from the outside, but Kronborg—overlooking the raging sea channel to Sweden—has a more scenic setting. Castle collectors can hit both in a day (see the two-castle day plan, later).

Louisiana is the obvious choice for art-lovers; the Karen Blixen Museum is for her admirers.

Drivers can visit these sights on the way into or out of Copenhagen. By train, do day trips from Copenhagen, then sleep while

NEAR COPENHAGEN

traveling to and from Copenhagen to Oslo (by boat, or by train via Malmö, Sweden) or Stockholm (by train via Malmö). Consider getting a Copenhagen Card, which covers your transportation to all of the destinations in this chapter, as well as admission to Roskilde Cathedral, Frederiksborg Castle, and the Karen Blixen Museum (but not the Roskilde Viking Museum, Kronborg Castle, or Louisiana).

A Two-Castle Day (plus Louisiana) by Public Transportation: You can see both Frederiksborg and Kronborg castles, plus Louisiana Art Museum, in one busy day. (This works best on Tue-Fri, when Louisiana is open until 22:00.) Ride the 9:05 train from Copenhagen to Hillerød, then hop on the awaiting bus to Frederiksborg Castle; you'll hear the 10:00 bells and be the first tourist inside. Linger in the sumptuous interior for a couple of hours, but get back to the station in time for the 12:30 (weekdays only) or 13:00 (any day) train to Helsingør, a 15-minute walk from Kronborg Castle. Either munch your picnic lunch on the train, or—if it's a nice day—save it for the ramparts of Kronborg Castle. If you're castled out, skip the interior (saving the ticket price, and more time for Louisiana) and simply enjoy the Kronborg grounds and Øresund views before catching a train south toward Copenhagen. Hop off at Humlebæk for Louisiana.

Getting Around

All of these sights except Roskilde are served by Copenhagen's excellent commuter-train (S-tog) system (covered by the Copenhagen Card and by the "24-hour ticket" and "7-day flexicard" that cover greater Copenhagen; not covered by the City Pass, which includes only zones 1-4). All of the train connections (including the line to Roskilde) depart from the main train station; but be aware that most lines also stop at other Copenhagen stations, which may be closer to your hotel (for example, the Nørreport station near Ibsens and Jørgensen hotels). Check the schedules carefully to avoid needlessly going to the main train station.

At the main train station, the S-tog lines do not appear on the overhead schedule screens (which are for longer-distance destinations); simply report to tracks 9-10 to wait for your train (there's a schedule at the head of those tracks).

Roskilde

Denmark's roots, both Viking and royal, are on display in Roskilde (ROSS-killa), a pleasant town 18 miles west of Copenhagen.

Eight hundred years ago, Roskilde was the seat of Denmark's royalty—its center of power. Today the town that introduced Christianity to Denmark in A.D. 980 is most famous for hosting northern Europe's biggest annual rock/jazz/folk festival (early July, www.roskilde-festival .dk). Wednesday and Saturday are flower/flea/produce market days (8:00-14:00).

Getting There: Roskilde is an easy side-trip from Copenhagen by train (1-3/hour, 30 minutes). Trains headed to Ringsted, Nykøbing, or Lindholm all stop in Roskilde (which is an intermediate stop you won't see listed on departure boards).

Orientation to Roskilde

Tourist Information

Roskilde's helpful TI is on the main square, not far from the cathedral (Mon-Fri 10:00-17:00—closes Fri at 16:00 in off-season, Sat 10:00-13:00, closed Sun; Stændertorvet 1, tel. 46 31 65 65, www.visitroskilde.com).

Arrival in Roskilde

There are no lockers at the train station (or nearby), but the TI—about a 5-minute walk away—will take your bags for a few hours if you ask nicely (they'll likely charge 25 kr).

From the train station, consider this circular route: First you'll head to the TI, then the nearby cathedral, and finally down to the harborfront museum. Exit straight out from the station, and walk down to the bottom of the square. Turn left (at the Kvickly supermarket) on the pedestrianized shopping street, Algade. After about four blocks, you emerge into the main square, Stændertorvet. The TI is straight ahead, and the cathedral is to your right. After visiting the cathedral, you'll head about 10 minutes downhill (through a pleasant park) to the Viking Museum: Facing the cathedral facade, turn left and head down the path through the park. When you emerge at the roundabout, continue straight through it to reach the museum.

If you want to go directly from the station to the Viking Museum, you can ride a bus.

Sights in Roskilde

▲▲Roskilde Cathedral

Roskilde's imposing 12th-century, twin-spired cathedral houses the tombs of all of the Danish kings and most of the queens (38 royals in all; pick up the essential map as you enter). If you're a fan of Danish royalty or of evolving architectural styles, it's thrilling; even if you're neither, Denmark's "Westminster Abbey" is still interesting. It's a stately, modern-looking old church with great marblework, paintings, wood carvings, and an engaged congregation that makes the place feel very alive (particularly here in largely unchurched Scandinavia).

Cost and Hours: 60 kr; April-Sept Mon-Sat 9:00-17:00, Sun 12:30-17:00; Oct-March Tue-Sat 10:00-16:00, Sun 12:30-16:00, closed Mon; often closed Sat and

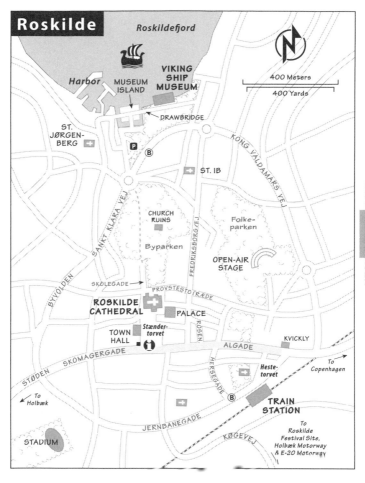

Sun afternoons for baptisms and weddings; free organ concerts offered July-Aug Thu at 20:00; tel. 46 35 16 24, www.roskildedom kirke.dk.

⊃ **Self-Guided Tour:** Begun in the 1170s by Bishop Absalom (and completed in 1280), Roskilde Cathedral was cleared of its side chapels and altars by the Reformation iconoclasts—leaving a blank slate for Danish royals to fill with their tombs. The highlight here is slowly strolling through a half-millennium's worth of royal chapels, representing a veritable textbook's worth of architectural styles.

Before entering, face the towering facade. The main door—called the **King's Door**—was installed only in 2010, and depicts the 12 apostles (each with a symbol that hints at his identity). This door is used by the congregation only to leave special services; the only people who may enter through this door are members of the royal family.

Notice the freestanding brick chapel to the left. This holds the remains of Denmark's last king, **Frederik IX** (1899-1972), and his wife Ingrid. While all of the other monarchs are inside, Frederik—who was an avid sailor in his youth—requested to be buried here, with a view of the harbor.

Now go around the right side, buy a ticket, and go inside. We'll take a clockwise spin through the interior to see the significant royal burial chapels. While this tour is not chronological, neither are the tombs.

NEAR COPENHAGEN

First head to the middle of the nave and look at the **inside of the King's Door**—a glittering-gold, highly stylized relief showing the scene after the Resurrection when Jesus breaks bread in the company of some apostles—who until this point, had not recognized him (their mouths hang agape at their realization).

Walking a few steps to the right, then looking high above, you can see the silly little **glockenspiel** that makes a racket at the top of every hour.

Continue through the left aisle and into the big chapel housing some of the cathedral's most recent additions (from the late 19th through early 20th centuries). The next chapel toward the front will eventually ("Not soon," hope the Danes) have a new tenant: It has recently been restored to house the tomb of the current queen, **Margrethe II,** and her husband Henrik. She teamed up with an artist to design her own tomb (there is likely a model on display). Her body will reside in the stepped area at the bottom, upon which stand three columns representing the far-flung Danish holdings: one made of basalt from the Faroe Islands, another of marble from Greenland, and the third of stone from Denmark proper. Topping the columns are elephants (symbols of Danish royalty) and a semitransparent glass tomb, symbolizing the unpredictability of life.

The next chapel, of St. Andrew, is a modern addition to the church, with a glittering mosaic over the altar. Standing in front of this chapel, look across the nave to see the gorgeous 16th-century Baroque organ.

The next, larger chapel (up the stairs behind the small wooden organ) dates from the era of **Christian IV,** the larger-than-life 17th-century king who created modern Denmark. Christian also left his mark on Roskilde Cathedral, building the altarpiece, pulpit, distinctive twin towers...and this chapel. In here you'll see a fine statue of the king, by Bertel Thorvaldsen; a large 3-D painting with Christian IV wearing his trademark eye patch, after losing his eye in battle; and his rather austere tomb (black with silver trim, surrounded by several others).

Head into the nave and climb up the stairs into the choir area, taking in the gorgeous gilded altarpiece and finely carved stalls.

Behind the altar is the ornately decorated tomb of **Margrethe I,** the Danish queen who added Norway to her holdings by marrying Norwegian King Håkon VI in 1363. Buried in a nearby column are the supposed remains of Harold (read the Latin: *Haraldus*) Bluetooth, who ruled more than a millennium ago (r. 958-985 or 986), made Roskilde the capital of his realm, and converted his subjects to Christianity.

Go down the stairs and through the little door, and circle around the apse (area behind the altar), noticing more fine tombs behind Margrethe's. Hooking back around toward the front, dip into the many more chapels you'll pass, including the grand, textbook-Neoclassical tomb of Frederik V (with white pillars, gold trim, and mourning maidens in ancient Greek gowns); and the room housing elaborate, canopied Baroque tombs. Imagine: Each king or queen commissioned a tomb that suited his or her time—so different, yet all so grand.

▲▲▲Viking Ship Museum (Vikingeskibsmuseet)

Vik literally means "shallow inlet," and "Vikings" were the people who lived along those inlets. Roskilde—and this award-winning museum—are strategically located along one such inlet. (They call it a "fjord," but it's surrounded by much flatter terrain than the Norwegian fjords.) Centuries before Europe's Age of Exploration, Viking sailors navigated their sleek, sturdy ships as far away as the Mediterranean, the Black Sea, the Persian Gulf,

and the Americas. This museum displays five different Viking ships, which were discovered in the Roskilde fjord and painstakingly excavated, preserved, and pieced back together beginning in the 1960s. The ships aren't as intact or as ornate as those in Oslo, but this museum does a better job of explaining shipbuilding. The outdoor area (on "Museum Island") continues the experience, with a chance to see modern-day Vikings creating replica ships, chat with an old-time ropemaker, and learn more about the excavation. The English descriptions are excellent—it's the kind of museum where you want to read everything.

Cost and Hours: 100 kr, price drops to 70 kr Oct-April when many outdoor exhibits are closed, open daily late June-Aug 10:00-17:00, Sept-late June 10:00-16:00, tel. 46 30 02 00, www.vikingeskibsmuseet.dk.

Tours: Free 45-minute tours in English run late June-Aug daily at 12:00 and 15:00; May-late June and Sept Sat-Sun at 12:00; none off-season.

Boat Ride: The museum's workshop has re-created working replicas of all five of the ships on display here, plus others. For an extra 80 kr, you can go for a fun hour-long sail around Roskilde's harbor in one of these replica Viking vessels (frequent departures—up to 7/day—in summer, fewer off-season, ask about schedule when you arrive or call ahead).

Eating: The "summer café" on Museum Island has 25-40-kr cakes and sandwiches; the bigger restaurant, in the large modern building, has 45-kr lunch sandwiches and 175-225-kr dinners.

Getting There: It's on the harbor at Vindeboder 12. From the train station, catch bus #216 or #607 toward Boserup (hourly, 7-minute ride). From the cathedral, it's a 10-minute downhill walk.

Visiting the Museum: The museum has two parts: the Viking Ship Hall, with the remains of the five ships; and, across the drawbridge, Museum Island with workshops, replica ships, and more exhibits.

As you enter the **Viking Ship Hall,** check the board for the day's activities and demonstrations (including shipbuilding, weaving, blacksmithing, and minting). Consider buying the 20-kr guidebook, and request the 14-minute English movie introduction.

The core of the exhibit is the remains of those five ships. These vessels were deliberately sunk a thousand years ago to block an easy channel into this harbor (leaving open only the most challenging approach—virtually impossible for anyone but a local to navigate). The ships, which are named for the place where they were found (Skuldelev), represent an impressively wide range of Viking shipbuilding technology. *Skuldelev 1* is a big, sail-powered ocean-going trade ship, with a crew of six to eight men and lots of cargo; it's like the ship Leif Eriksson took to America 1,000 years ago. *Skuldelev 2* is a 100-foot-long, 60-oar longship; loaded with 65 or 70 bloodthirsty warriors, it struck fear into the hearts of foes. It's similar to the ones depicted in the Bayeux Tapestry in Normandy, France. *Skuldelev 3* is a modest coastal trader that stayed closer to home (wind-powered with oar backup, similar to #1 in design). *Skuldelev 5* is a smaller longship—carrying about 30 men, it's the little sibling of #2. And *Skuldelev 6* is a small fishing vessel—a row/sail hybrid that was used for whaling and hunting seals. (There's no #4 because they originally thought #2 was two different ships...and the original names stuck.)

Exhibits in the surrounding rooms show the 25-year process of excavating and preserving the ships, explain a step-by-step attack and defense of the harbor, and give you a chance to climb aboard a couple of replica ships for a fun photo op. You'll also see displays describing the re-creation of the *Sea Stallion*, a replica of the big longship (#2) constructed by modern shipbuilders using ancient techniques. A crew of 65 rowed this to Dublin, Ireland, in 2007, and then back to Roskilde in the summer of 2008. You can watch a 20-minute film of their odyssey.

Leaving the hall, cross the drawbridge to **Museum Island.** Replicas of all five ships—and others—bob in the harbor; you can

actually climb on board the largest, the *Sea Stallion*. At the boatyard, watch modern craftsmen re-create millennium-old ships using the original methods and materials. Poke into the various workshops, with exhibits on tools and methods. The little square called *Tunet* ("Gathering Place") is ringed by traditional craft shops—basketmaker, ropemaker, blacksmith, woodcarver—which are sometimes staffed by workers doing demonstrations. In the archaeological workshop, exhibits explain how they excavated and preserved the precious timbers of those five ships.

Frederiksborg Castle

Frederiksborg Castle, rated ▲▲, sits on an island in the middle of a lake in the cute town of Hillerød. This grandest castle in Scandinavia is often called the "Danish Versailles." Built from 1602 to 1620, Frederiksborg was the castle of Denmark's King Christian IV. Much of it was reconstructed after an 1859 fire, with the normal Victorian over-the-top flair, by the brewer J. C. Jacobsen and his Carlsberg Foundation.

You'll still enjoy some of the magnificent spaces of the castle's heyday: The breathtaking grounds and courtyards, the sumptuous chapel, and the regalia-laden Great Hall. But most of the place was turned into a fine museum in 1878. Today it's the Museum of National History, taking you on a chronological walk through the story of Denmark from 1500 until today (the third/top floor covers modern times). The countless musty paintings are a fascinating scrapbook of Danish history—it's a veritable national portrait gallery, with images of great Danes from each historical period of the last half-millennium.

A fine path leads around the lake, with ever-changing views of the castle. The traffic-free center of Hillerød is also worth a wander (just outside the gates of the castle, toward train station).

Tourist Information: Hillerød's **TI,** with a good town map and brochures for the entire North Zealand region, is in the free-standing white house next to the castle parking lot (to the left as you face the main castle gate; Mon-Fri 9:30-16:00, closed Sat-Sun except open Sat in July 9:30-13:30, likely closed Oct-April, Frederiksværksgade 2A, tel. 48 24 26 26, www.visitnordsjaelland.com). Because the TI is inside an art gallery, if the TI is "closed" while the gallery is open, you can still slip inside and pick up a town map and brochures.

Getting There: From Copenhagen, take the S-tog to Hillerød (line E, 6/hour, 40 minutes). From the Hillerød station, you can enjoy a pleasant 20-minute walk to the castle (see next page), or catch bus #301 or #302 (free with S-tog ticket or Copenhagen Card, buses are to the right as you exit station, ride three stops to Frederiksborg Slot bus stop). Drivers will find easy parking at the castle.

When you're exiting the station, bear left down the busy road

(Jernbanegade) until the first big intersection, where you'll turn right. After a couple of blocks, where the road curves to the left, keep going straight; from here, bear left and downhill to the pleasant square Torvet, with great views of the castle and a café pavilion. At this square, turn left and walk through the pedestrianized shopping zone directly to the castle gate.

After your visit, if you'd like to continue directly to Helsingør (with Kronborg Castle), hop on the regional train (departs from track 16 at Hillerød station, Mon-Fri 2/hour, Sat-Sun 1/hour, 30 minutes). From Helsingør, it's a quick trip on the S-tog to Humlebæk and Louisiana Art Museum.

Cost and Hours: 75 kr, daily April-Oct 10:00-17:00, Nov-March 11:00-15:00. Take advantage of the free, extensive, informative (if fairly dry) iPod audioguide; ask for it when you buy your ticket. My tour, below, zooms in on the highlights, but the audioguide is more extensive. There are also posted explanations and/or borrowable English descriptions in many rooms, but—like the audioguide—these tend to be quite dry (tel. 48 26 04 39, www .dnm.dk).

Eating: You can picnic in the castle's moat park or enjoy the elegant **Spisestedet Leonora** at the moat's edge (65-90-kr *smørrebrød* and sandwiches, 90-kr salads, 105-125-kr hot dishes, 148-kr brunch buffet Sun until 13:00, open daily 10:00-17:00, slow service, tel. 48 26 75 16).

◑ Self-Guided Tour: From the entrance of the castle complex, it's an appropriately regal approach to the king's residence. You can almost hear the clopping of royal hooves as you walk over the moat and through the first island (which housed the stables and small businesses needed to support a royal residence). Then walk down the winding (and therefore easy-to-defend) lane to the second island, which was home to the domestic and foreign ministries. Finally, cross over the last moat to the main palace, where the king lived.

Main Courtyard: Survey the castle exterior from the Fountain of Neptune in the main courtyard. Christian IV imported Dutch architects to create this "Christian IV style," which you'll see all over Copenhagen. The brickwork and sandstone are products of the local clay and sandy soil. The building, with its horizontal lines, triangles, and squares, is generally in Renaissance style, but notice how this is interrupted by a few token Gothic elements on the church's facade. Some say this homey touch was to let the villagers know the king was "one of them."

Go in the door in the middle of the courtyard to buy your ticket, pick up your free audioguide, and put your bag in a locker (mandatory, 20-kr coin required and will be refunded). Be sure to pick up a free floor plan; room numbers will help orient you on this tour. You'll enter the Knights' Parlor, also called The Rose, a long room decorated as it was during the palace's peak of power. Go up the stairs on the left side of this hall to the...

Royal Chapel: Christian IV wanted to have the grandest royal chapel in Europe. For 200 years the coronation place of

Danish kings, this chapel is still used for royal weddings (and is extremely popular for commoner weddings—book long in advance). The chapel is nearly all original, dating back to 1620. As you walk around the upper level, notice the graffiti scratched on the windowpanes by the diamond rings of royal kids visiting for the summer back in the 1600s. Most of the coats of arms show off noble lineage—with a few exceptions we'll get to soon. At the far end of the chapel, the wooden organ is from 1620, with its original hand-powered bellows. (If you like music, listen for hymns on the old carillon at the top of each hour.)

Scan the hundreds of coats-of-arms lining the walls. These belong to people who have received royal orders from the Danish crown (similar to Britain's knighthoods). While most are obscure princesses and dukes, a few interesting (and more familiar) names show up just past the organ. In the first window bay after the organ, look for the distinctive red, blue, black, and green shield of South Africa—marking Nelson Mandela's coat of arms. (Notice he was awarded the highly prestigious Order of the Elephant, usually reserved for royalty.) Around the side of the same column (facing the chapel interior), find the

coats of arms for Dwight D. Eisenhower (with the blue anvil and the motto "Peace through understanding"), Winston Churchill (who already came from a noble line), and Field Marshal Bernard "Monty" Montgomery. Around the far side of this column is the coat of arms for France's wartime leader, Charles de Gaulle.

Leaving the chapel, you step into the king's oratory, with evocative Romantic paintings (restored after a fire) from the mid-19th century.

You'll emerge from the chapel into the museum collection. But before seeing that, pay a visit to the Audience Room: Go through the door in the left corner marked *Audienssalen*, and proceed through the little room to the long passageway (easy to miss).

Audience Room: Here, where formal meetings took place, a grand painting shows the king as a Roman emperor firmly in command (with his two sons prominent for extra political stability). This family is flanked by Christian IV (on the left) and Frederik III (on the right). Christian's military victories line the walls, and the four great continents—Europe, North America, Asia, and Africa—circle the false cupola (notice it's just an attic). Look for the odd trapdoor in one corner with a plush chair on it. This was where they could majestically lower the king to the exit.

Now go back to the museum section, and proceed through the numbered rooms. Spanning three floors and five centuries, this exhaustive (or, for some, exhausting) collection juxtaposes portraits, paintings of historical events, furniture, and other objects from the same time period, all combining to paint a picture of a moment in Danish history. While fascinating, a little goes a long way, so I've selected only the most interesting items to linger over.

First Floor: Proceed to **Room 26,** which is focused on the Reformation. The case in the middle of the room holds the first Bible translated into Danish (from 1550—access to the word of God was a big part of the Reformation). Over the door to the next room is the image of a monk, Hans Tausen, invited by the king to preach the new thinking of the Reformation...sort of the "Danish Martin Luther." Also note the effort noble families put into legitimizing themselves with family trees and family seals.

Pass through Rooms 27, 28, and 29, and into **Room 30**—with paintings telling the story of Christian IV. Directly across from the door you entered is a painting of the chancellor on his death-

bed, handing over the keys to the kingdom to a still-wet-behind-the-ears young Christian IV—the beginning of a long and fruitful career. On the right wall is a painting of Christian's coronation (the bearded gentleman looking out the window in the upper-left corner is Carlsberg brewer and castle benefactor J. C. Jacobsen—who, some 300 years before his birth, was probably not actually in attendance). Room 31 covers the royal family of Charles IV, while the smaller, darkened corner Room 32 displays the various Danish orders; find the most prestigious, the Order of the Elephant.

Hook back through Room 30, go outside on the little passage, and climb up the stairs.

Second Floor: Go to the corner **Room 39,** which has a fascinating golden globe designed to illustrate Polish astronomer Nicolaus Copernicus' bold new heliocentric theory (that the sun, not the earth, was the center of our world). Look past the

constellations to see the tiny model of the solar system at the very center, with a brass ball for the sun and little figures holding up symbols for each of the planets. The mechanical gears could actually make this model move to make the illustration more vivid.

Continue into one of the castle's most jaw-dropping rooms, the **Great Hall** (Room 38). The walls are lined with tapestries and royal portraits (including some modern ones, near the door). The remarkable wood-carved ceilings include panels illustrating various industries. The elevated platform on the left

was a gallery where musicians could play without getting in the way of the revelry.

Head back out and walk back along the left side of the hall. You can go quickly through the rooms numbered in the 40s and 50s (though pause partway down the long hallway; on the left, find the optical-illusion portrait that shows King Frederik V when viewed from one angle, and his wife when viewed from another). At the far end of this section, Room 57 has a portrait of Hans Christian Andersen. Notice that fashion styles have gotten much more modern...suits and ties instead of tights and powdered wigs. It's time to head into the modern world.

Find the modern spiral staircase nearby. Downstairs are late-19th-century exhibits—which are skippable. Instead, head up to the top floor.

Third Floor: This staircase puts you (confusingly) right in the middle of the modern collection. To keep our chronological focus, find your way to Room 70. From here, the museum's focus shifts, focusing more on the art and less on the history. For example, in Room 70, *The Art Critics* shows four past-their-prime, once-rambunctious artists themselves, now leaning back to critique a younger artist's work...happily entrenched in the art institution. Proceed through the collection. Room 73 focuses on Denmark's far-flung Greenland, with a porcelain polar bear and portraits of explorers. Room 74 has a distinctive Impressionist/Post-Impressionist flavor, with a Danish spin. In Room 77, *Ninth of April, 1940* shows the (ultimately unsuccessful) Danish defense against Nazi invaders on that fateful date. Room 82 focuses on the royal family, with a life-size, photorealistic portrait of the beloved Queen Margrethe II. Facing her is her daughter-in-law, Mary Donaldson—who, in this portrait at least, bears a striking resemblance to another young European royal.

Rounding out the collection is one of its most recent works, Peter Carlsen's *Denmark 2009*—a brilliant parody of Eugène Delacroix's famous painting

Liberty Leading the People (a copy of the inspiration is on the facing wall). Carlsen has replaced the stirring imagery of the original with some dubious markers of contemporary Danish life: football flags, beer gut, shopping bags, tabloids, bikini babes, even a Christiania flag. It's a delightfully offbeat (and oh-so-Danish) note to end our visit to this seriously impressive palace.

Louisiana

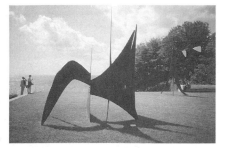

This is Scandinavia's most-raved-about modern-art museum. Located in the town of Humlebæk, beautifully situated on the coast 18 miles north of Copenhagen, Louisiana is a holistic place that masterfully mixes its art, architecture, and landscape.

Cost and Hours: 95 kr, included in a special 176-kr round-trip tour ticket from

Copenhagen—ask at any train station, open Tue-Fri 11:00-22:00, Sat-Sun 11:00-18:00, closed Mon, Gammel Strandvej 13, tel. 49 19 07 19, www.louisiana.dk.

Getting There: Take the train from **Copenhagen** toward Helsingør, and get off at Humlebæk (4/hour, 36 minutes). It's a pleasant 10-minute walk (partly through a forest) to the museum: Exit the station and immediately go left onto Hejreskor Allé, a residential street; when the road curves right, continue straight along the narrow footpath through the trees. After you exit the trail, the museum is just ahead and across the street.

If you're arriving by train from **Helsingør,** take the pedestrian underpass beneath the tracks, then follow the directions above. Louisiana is also connected to Helsingør by bus #388 (runs hourly, stops right at Louisiana as well as at Humlebæk).

If you're coming from **Frederiksborg Castle,** you have two options: You can catch the Lille Nord train from Hillerød to Helsingør, then change there to a regional train heading south to Humlebæk (2/hour, 45 minutes). Alternately, you can take the S-tog toward Copenhagen and Køge, get off at Hellerup, then catch a regional train north toward Helsingør to reach Humlebæk (4/hour, about 1 hour, longer but runs more frequently).

Eating: The cafeteria, with indoor and outdoor seating, is reasonable and welcomes picnickers who buy a drink (80-kr sandwiches at lunch, 120-kr lunch buffet, 150-kr dinner buffet, 30-40-kr cakes).

Visiting the Museum: Wander from famous Chagalls and Picassos to more obscure art (everything is post-1945). Poets spend days here nourishing their creative souls with new angles, ideas, and perspectives. Even those who don't think they're art-lovers can get sucked into a thought-provoking exhibit and lose track of time. There's no permanent exhibit; they constantly organize their substantial collection into ever-changing arrangements, augmented with borrowed and special exhibits (check www .louisiana.dk for the latest)—so that Andy Warhol *Marilyn Monroe* you see on one visit may not be there the next. (One favorite item, French sculptor César's *The Big Thumb*—which is simply a six-foot-tall bronze thumb—isn't going anywhere, since anytime they move it, patrons complain.) There's no audioguide, but everything is labeled in English.

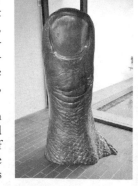

Outside, a delightful sculpture garden sprawls through the grounds, downhill toward the sea. The views over the Øresund, one of the busiest passages in the nautical world, are nearly as inspiring as the art. The museum's floor plan is a big loop, and the seaward side is underground—so as not to block the grand views. It's fun to explore the grounds, peppered with sculptures and made accessible by bridges and steps. The sculptures include items by Alexander Calder, Jean Dubuffet, Joan Miró, and others.

Taken as a whole, the museum is a joy to explore. What you see from the inside draws you out, and what you see from the outside draws you in. The place can't be rushed. Linger and enjoy.

Karen Blixen Museum

Danish writer Karen Blixen, a.k.a. Isak Dinesen of *Out of Africa* fame, lived most of her life in Rungstedlund—her family house in Rungsted, on the Øresund coast. The house, one of the area's finest mansions, is now a museum about her life and writing. For fans of Blixen's works, the house is a ▲▲ sight, though Blixen's dramatic life story and the house's beautiful setting are enough to make a visit enjoyable even for those who've never heard of *Out of Africa*.

Unlike many houses-turned-museums that file you past roped-off doorways, you'll don slippers to pad through the house, mostly unchanged from the time of Blixen's life. Over headphones, listen to Blixen read selections from her own stories as you look out at the same views she enjoyed. She wrote her best-known books (including *Babette's Feast*) in this house, surrounded by mementos of her 17 years in Kenya. Her simple grave is a short walk away through the mansion's backyard gardens.

Cost and Hours: 60 kr; May-Sept Tue-Sun 10:00-17:00, closed Mon; Oct-April Wed-Fri 13:00-16:00, Sat-Sun 11:00-16:00, closed Mon-Tue; tel. 45 57 10 57, www.karen-blixen.dk.

Getting There: From Copenhagen, take the train 30 minutes to Rungsted Kyst (3/hour). From the station, take bus #388, or simply walk 15-20 minutes (follow signs to the house). Rungsted is a short hop away from Humlebæk (7 minutes by train) and Helsingør (20 minutes).

Kronborg Castle

Kronborg Castle is located in Helsingør, a pleasant, salty Danish seaside town that's often confused with its Swedish sister, Helsingborg, just two miles across the channel. Kronborg Castle (also called Elsinore, the Anglicized version of Helsingør) is a ▲▲ sight famous for its tenuous (but profitable) ties to Shakespeare. Most of the "Hamlet" castle you'll see today—a dar-

ling of every big-bus tour and travelogue—was built long after the historical Hamlet died (more than a thousand years ago), and Shakespeare never saw the place. But this Renaissance castle existed when a troupe of English actors performed here in Shakespeare's time (Shakespeare may have known them). These days, various Shakespearean companies from around the world perform *Hamlet* in Kronborg's courtyard each August. Among the actors who've donned the tights here in the title role are Laurence Olivier, Christopher Plummer, Kenneth Branagh, and Jude Law.

To see or not to see? The castle is most impressive from the outside. The free grounds between the walls and sea are great for picnics, with a close-up view of the strait between Denmark and Sweden. If you're heading to Sweden, Kalmar Castle is a better medieval castle. And in Denmark, Frederiksborg (described earlier), which was built as an upgrade to this one, is far more opulent inside. But if Kronborg is handy to your itinerary—or you never met a castle you didn't like—it's worth a visit...even if just for a short romp across the ramparts (no ticket required). Many big-bus tours in the region stop both here and at Frederiksborg (you'll recognize some of the same fellow tourists at both places)—not a bad plan if you're a castle completist.

The town of Helsingør has a **TI** (late June-early Aug Mon-Fri 10:00-17:00, Sat-Sun 10:00-14:00; early Aug-late Sept Mon-Fri 10:00-16:00, Sat 10:00-13:00, closed Sun; rest of year Mon-Fri 10:00-16:00, closed Sat-Sun; tel. 49 21 13 33, www.visithelsingor .dk), a medieval center, the ferry to Sweden, and lots of Swedes who come over for the lower-priced alcohol.

Getting There: Helsingør is a 50-minute train ride from Copenhagen (3/hour). Exit the station out the front door: The TI is on the little square to your left, and the castle is dead ahead along the coast (about a 15-minute walk). Between the station and the castle, you'll pass through a recently renovated harborfront zone with the town's new cultural center and the new home of the maritime museum.

Cost: The wonderful grounds are free, but you'll need a ticket to enter the main building: 75 kr covers the royal apartments and the casements, add the tower/maritime museum for 95 kr; also possible to visit only the casements (30 kr) or only the tower/maritime museum (50 kr). Unless you're a fan of nautical sights, I'd skip the maritime museum and just do the apartments and casements.

Hours: The whole complex is open June-Aug daily 10:00-17:30; April-May and Sept-Oct daily 11:00-16:00; Nov-March Tue-Sun 11:00-16:00, closed Mon; tel. 33 95 42 00, www.kron borgcastle.com.

Tours: Free **tours** in English are offered of the casements (daily at 11:00 and 13:00) and of the royal apartments (daily at 11:30 and 13:30). You can use your mobile device to access a free **audioguide** at the castle, but it takes some tech savvy to make it work; unfortunately, the audioguide isn't available any other way. Dry English descriptions are posted throughout the castle. The equally arid 20-kr printed **guide** (sold at the ticket counter) tries to inject some life into the rooms.

Visiting the Castle: Approaching the castle, pretend you're an old foe of the king, kept away by many layers of earthen ramparts and moats—just when you think you're actually at the castle, you'll find there's another gateway or waterway to pass. On the way in, you'll pass a small model of the complex to help get your bearings. On a sunny day, you could have an enjoyable visit to Kronborg just walking around these grounds and playing "king of the castle," without buying a ticket. Many do.

Finally you'll enter the innermost courtyard of the castle complex. Follow the signs into the ticket desk, buy your ticket, stick your bag in a locker (insert a 20-kr coin, which will be returned), and head upstairs. You'll pop out at the beginning of both the royal apartments and the maritime museum/tower.

Maritime Museum and Tower: I'd give the museum a miss, but if you're a sailor at heart or want to climb the tower, here's the scoop: You'll pass through a seemingly endless series of rooms detailing the salty history of this seafaring nation, with sailor's bric-a-brac, paintings and models of ships and captains, and a few particularly interesting sections (such as the collection of mastheads in the large room, or the small exhibit on

Inuit boats of Greenland). Halfway through, you'll pass through a tight, stone spiral staircase leading up to the top of one of the castle's corner towers, with a fine view of the prickly spires, the town of Helsingør, and the Øresund strait. It's easy to imagine why this was such a strategic point for a fortress—with Sweden so close and the strait so narrow, this passage could be easily monitored from here. Note that the maritime collection will be moved to its brand-new home just around the harbor from the castle, likely by mid-summer of 2013. (When that happens, there's speculation that this space will be filled by an exhibit on Hamlet—a topic that's otherwise in surprisingly short supply in the castle exhibits, given its touristic currency.)

Royal Apartments: Visitors are able to walk through one and a half floors of the complex. The first few rooms are filled with high-tech exhibits, using touchscreens and projected videos to explain the history of the place. You'll learn how, in the 1420s, Danish King Eric of Pomerania built a fortress here to allow for the collection of "Sound Dues," levied on any passing ship hoping to enter the sound of Øresund. This proved hugely lucrative, eventually providing up to two-thirds of Denmark's entire income. By the time of Shakespeare, Kronborg was well-known both for its profitable ability to levy these dues, and for its famously lavish banquets—what better setting for a tale of a royal family unraveling?

Continuing into the apartments themselves, you'll find that the interior is a shadow of its former self; while the structure was rebuilt by Christian IV after a 1629 fire, its rooms were never returned to their former grandeur, making it feel like something of an empty shell. And yet, there are still some fine pieces of furniture and art to see. Frederik II ruled Denmark from the king's chamber in the 1570s; a model shows how it  likely looked back in its heyday. After passing through two smaller rooms, you come to the queen's chamber; from there, stairs lead up to the queen's gallery, custom-built for Queen Sophie to be able to quickly walk directly from her chambers to the ballroom or chapel. Follow her footsteps into the ballroom, a vast hall of epic proportions decorated by a series of paintings commissioned by Christian IV (explained by the board near the entry). At the far end, a model (enlivened by seemingly holographic figures) illustrates how this incredible space must have looked in all its original finery. Beyond the ballroom, the "Little Hall" is decorated with a fine series of

Øresund Region

When the Øresund (UH-ra-soond) Bridge, which connects Denmark and Sweden, opened in July of 2000, it created a dynamic new metropolitan area. Almost overnight, the link forged an economic power with the 12th-largest gross domestic product in Europe. The Øresund region has surpassed Stockholm as the largest metro area in Scandinavia. Now 3.5 million Danes and Swedes—a highly trained and highly technical workforce—are within a quick commute of each other.

The bridge opens up new questions of borders. Historically, southern Sweden (the area across from Copenhagen, called Skåne) had Danish blood. It was Danish for a thousand years before Sweden took it in 1658. Notice how Copenhagen is the capital on the fringe of its realm—at one time it was in the center.

The 10-mile-long link, which has a motorway for cars (the toll is about 300 kr) and a two-track train line, ties together the main islands of Denmark with Europe and Sweden. The $4 billion project consisted of a 2.5-mile-long tunnel, an artificial island called Peberholm, and a 5-mile-long bridge. With speedy connecting trains, Malmö in Sweden is now an easy half-day side-trip from Copenhagen (78 kr each way, 3/hour, 35 minutes). The train drops you at the "Malmö C" (central) station right in the heart of Malmö, and all the important sights are within a short walk. The *Malmö This Week* publication (free from Copenhagen TI) has everything you need for a well-organized visit.

tapestries depicting Danish monarchs. Then wind through several more royal halls, chambers, and bedrooms on your way back down into the courtyard. Once there, go straight across and enter the chapel. The enclosed gallery at the upper-left was the private pew of the royal family.

Casements: You'll enter the underground part of the castle

through a door on the main courtyard (diagonally across from the chapel). While not particularly tight, these passages are very dark and intentionally not very well-lit; a vending machine at the entrance sells 20-kr flashlights (bring yours—or, at least, a bright mobile phone). This extensive network of dank cellars is a double-decker substructure that teemed with activity. The upper level, which you'll see first, was used as servants' quarters, a stable, and a storehouse. The lower level was used to train and barrack soldiers during wartime (an efficient use of so much prime, fortified space). As you explore this creepy, labyrinthine, nearly pitch-black zone (just follow the arrows), imagine the miserably claustrophobic conditions the soldiers lived in, waiting to see some action.

The most famous "resident" of the Kronborg casements was Holger Danske ("Ogier the Dane"), a mythical Viking hero

revered by Danish children. The story goes that if the nation is ever in danger, this Danish superman will awaken and restore peace and security to the land (like King Arthur to the English, Barbarossa to the Germans, and Wenceslas to the Czechs). While this legend has been around for many centuries, Holger's connection to Kronborg was cemented by a Hans Christian Andersen tale, so now everybody just assumes he lives here. In one of the first rooms, you'll see a famous, giant statue of this sleeping Viking...just waiting for things to get *really* bad.

Near Copenhagen Connections

Route Tips for Drivers

Copenhagen to Hillerød (45 minutes) to Helsingør (30 minutes) to Kalmar (4 hours): Just follow the town-name signs. Leave Copenhagen following signs for *E-4* and *Helsingør*. The freeway is great. *Hillerød* signs lead to the Frederiksborg Castle (not to be confused with the nearby Fredensborg Palace) in the pleasant town of Hillerød. Follow signs to *Hillerød C* (for "center"), then *slot* (for "castle"). Though the E-4 freeway is the fastest, the Strandvejen coastal road (152) is pleasant, passing some of Denmark's grandest mansions (including that of Karen Blixen, described earlier).

The 10-mile Øresund Bridge linking Denmark with Sweden (€40 toll, or about 300 kr) lets drivers and train travelers skip nonstop from one country to the next.

If you're nostalgic for the pre-bridge days, the Helsingør-Helsingborg ferry still putters across the Øresund Channel twice hourly (follow the signs to *Helsingborg, Sweden*—freeway leads to dock). Buy your ticket as you roll on board (320 kr one-way for car, driver, and up to nine passengers, increases to 345 kr in summer). Reservations are free but not usually necessary, as ferries depart every 30 minutes (tel. 33 15 15 15, or book online at www.scandlines.dk; also see www.hhferries.se). If you arrive early, you can probably drive onto any ferry. The 20-minute Helsingør-

Helsingborg ferry ride gives you just enough time to enjoy the view of the Kronborg "Hamlet" castle, be impressed by the narrowness of this very strategic channel, and exchange any leftover Danish kroner into Swedish kronor (the ferry exchange desk's rate is decent).

In Helsingborg, follow signs for *E4* and *Stockholm*. The road is good, traffic is light, and towns are all clearly signposted. At Ljungby, road 25 takes you to Växjö and Kalmar. Entering Växjö, skip the first Växjö exit and follow the freeway into *Centrum*, where it ends. It takes about four hours total to drive from Copenhagen to Kalmar.

NEAR COPENHAGEN

CENTRAL DENMARK

Ærø • Odense

The sleepy isle of Ærø is the cuddle after the climax. It's the perfect time-passed world in which to wind down, enjoy the seagulls, and take a day off. Wander the unadulterated cobbled lanes of Denmark's best-preserved 18th-century town. Get Ærø-dynamic and pedal a rented bike into the essence of Denmark. Settle into a world of sailors, who, after the invention of steam-driven boat propellers, decided that building ships in bottles was more their style.

Between Ærø and Copenhagen, drop by bustling Odense, home of Hans Christian Andersen. Its Hans Christian Andersen House is excellent, and with more time, you can also enjoy its other museums (art, town history, trains, folk) and stroll the car-free streets of its downtown.

Planning Your Time

Allow four hours to get from Copenhagen to Ærø (not counting a possible stopover in Odense). All trains stop in Roskilde (with its Viking Ship Museum) and bustling Odense (see the end of this chapter). On a quick trip, you can leave Copenhagen in the morning and do justice to both towns en route to Ærø. (With just one day, Odense and Roskilde together make a long but doable day trip from Copenhagen.)

While out of the way, Ærø is worth the journey. Once there, you'll want two nights and a day to properly enjoy it.

Central Denmark

To Aarhus

Holbæk

Vejle

To Aarhus

Samsø

Kalundborg

To Billund & Jelling

E-45

To Roskilde & Copenhagen

Fredericia

Zealand

Kolding

Odense

Store

Korsør

E-20

To Copenhagen

To Esbjerg & Ribe

Middelfart

E-20

Nyborg

STORE BÆLT BRIDGE

Jutland

Funen

9

8

Bus

Bælt

Lillebælt

43

Kværndrup

Egeskov

Fåborg

8

Svendborg

Als

Langeland

Sønderborg

Ærø

Rudkøbing

Ærøskøbing

Marstal

Lolland

See detail map

GERMANY

E-47

Rødby

50 Kilometers

25 Miles

Puttgarten (GER.)

Ærø

This small (22 by 6 miles) island on the south edge of Denmark is as salty and sleepy as can be. A typical tombstone reads: "Here lies Christian Hansen at anchor with his wife. He'll not weigh until he stands before God." It's the kind of island where baskets of strawberries sit in front of houses—for sale on the honor system.

Ærø statistics: 7,000 residents, 500,000 visitors and 80,000 boaters annually, 350 deer, seven priests, no crosswalks, and three police officers. The three big industries are farming (wheat and dairy), shipping, and tourism—in that order. Twenty percent of the Danish fleet still resides on Ærø, in the town of Marstal. But jobs are scarce, the population is slowly dropping, and family farms are consolidating into larger units.

Ærø, home to several windmills and one of the world's largest solar power plants, is going "green." They hope to become completely wind- and solar-powered. Currently, nearly half the island's heat and electricity is provided by renewable sources, and most of its produce is organically grown. New technology is expected to bring Ærø closer to its goal within the next few years.

Getting Around Ærø

On a short visit, you won't need to leave Ærøskøbing, except for a countryside bike ride—everything is within walking or pedaling distance. But if you have more time or want to explore the rest of the island, you can take advantage of Ærø's **bus** network. Buses leave from a stop just above the ferry dock (leaving the ferry, walk up about a block and look right). Ærø recently made its main bus line, #790, free for visitors (Mon-Fri hourly until about 19:00; Sat 4/day; Sun 3-4/day). There are two different branches—one going to Marstal at the east end of the island, and the other to Søby in the west (look for the town name under the bus number). The main reason to take the bus is to go to Marstal on a rainy day to visit its maritime museum.

You can also take a subsidized **taxi** ride to points around the island—but it requires some planning ahead. To use this "Telebus" system, you have to make the trip between 5:00 and 22:00 (from 7:00 on Sat-Sun). At least two hours in advance, call FynBus at 63 11 22 55 to reserve; a ride to anywhere on Ærø costs just 40 kr per person.

Ærøskøbing

Ærøskøbing is Ærø's village in a bottle. It's small enough to be cute, but just big enough to feel real. The government, recognizing the value of this amazingly preserved little town, prohibits modern building anywhere in the center. It's the only town in Denmark protected in this way. Drop into the 1680s, when Ærøskøbing was the wealthy home port of a hundred windjammers. The many Danes and Germans who come here for the tranquility—washing up the cobbled main drag in waves with the landing of each boat—call it the fairy-tale town. The Danish word for "cozy," *hyggelig*, describes Ærøskøbing perfectly.

Ærøskøbing is simply a pleasant place to wander. Stubby little porthole-type houses, with their birth dates displayed in proud decorative rebar, lean on each other like drunk, sleeping sailors. Wander under flickering old-time lamps. Snoop around town. It's OK. Peek into living rooms (if people want privacy, they shut their drapes). Notice the many "snooping mirrors" on the houses—antique locals are following your every move. The harbor now caters to holiday yachts, and on midnight low tides you can almost hear the crabs playing cards.

The town economy, once rich with the windjammer trade, hit the rocks in modern times. Kids 15 to 18 years old go to a boarding school in Svendborg; many don't return. It's an interesting discussion: Should the island folk pickle their culture in tourism, or forget about the cuteness and get modern?

Planning Your Time

You'll regret not setting aside a minimum of two nights for your Ærøskøbing visit. In a busy day you can "do" everything you like—except relax. If ever a place was right for recreating, this is it. I'd arrive in time for an evening stroll, dinner, and the Night Watchman's tour (21:00 nightly in summer). The next morning, do the island bike tour, returning by midafternoon. You can see the town's three museums in less than two hours (but note that they all close by 17:00 in summer, even earlier off-season), then browse the rest of your daylight away. Your second evening is filled with options: Stroll out to the summer huts for sunset, watch the classic sailing ships come in to moor for the evening (mostly Dutch and German boats crewed by vacationers), watch a movie in the pint-sized town cinema, go bowling with local teens, or check out live music in the pub.

Note that during the off-season (basically Sept-May), the town is quite dead and may not be worth a visit. Several shops and restaurants are closed, the Night Watchman's tour stops running, and bad weather can make a bike ride unpleasant.

Orientation to Ærøskøbing

Ærøskøbing is tiny. Everything's just a few cobbles from the ferry landing.

Tourist Information

The TI, which faces the ferry landing, is a clearinghouse for brochures promoting sights and activities on the island, has info on other Danish destinations, can help book rooms, rents small electric cars (300 kr/half-day, 500 kr/day, reserve a day or two in advance, available June-Aug only), and offers Internet access and Wi-Fi (late-June-mid-Aug Mon-Fri 9:00-18:00, Sat 10:00-18:00, Sun 10:00-15:00; off-season Mon-Fri 10:00-16:00, closed Sat-Sun; tel. 62 52 13 00, www.aeroe.dk).

Helpful Hints

Money: The town's only ATM is on Torvet Square.

Internet Access: Try the TI (steady hours) or the library on Torvet Square (sketchy hours).

Laundry: Ærøskøbing's self-service launderette (on Gyden) is looking for a new owner; in the meantime, most of its machines are out of order. You might be able to do laundry, but don't count on it.

Ferries: See "Ærøskøbing Connections" on page 134.

Bike Rental: Pilebækkens Cykler rents bikes year-round at the gas station at the top of the town. Manager Janne loans read-

ers of this book the 25-kr island *cykel* map so they won't get lost (three-speed bikes-55 kr/24 hours, seven-speed bikes-75 kr/24 hours; Mon-Fri 9:00-16:30, Sat 9:00-12:00, closed Sun except in July—when it's open 10:00-13:00; from Torvet Square, go through green door at Søndergade end of square, past garden to next road, in the gas station at Pilebækken 7; tel. 62 52 11 10). **Hotel Ærøhus** rents seven-speed bikes (75 kr/24 hours, 200-kr deposit, open very long hours). The campground also rent bikes (see "Sleeping in Ærøskøbing," later). Most people on Ærø don't bother locking up their bikes—if your rental doesn't have a lock, don't fret.

Shopping: The town is speckled with cute little shops, including a funky flea market shop next to the bakery. Each July, local artisans show their creations in a warehouse facing the ferry landing.

Self-Guided Walk

▲▲▲Welcome to Ærøskøbing

Ideally, take this stroll with the sun low, the shadows long, and the colors rich. Start at the harbor.

Harbor: Loiter around the harbor a bit first. German and Dutch vacationers on grand old sailboats come into port each evening. Because Ærø is only nine miles across the water from Germany, the island is popular with Germans who regularly return to this peaceful retreat.

• *From the harbor and TI, walk up the main street a block and go left on...*

Smedegade: This is the poorest street in town, with the most architectural and higgledy-piggledy charm. Have a close look at

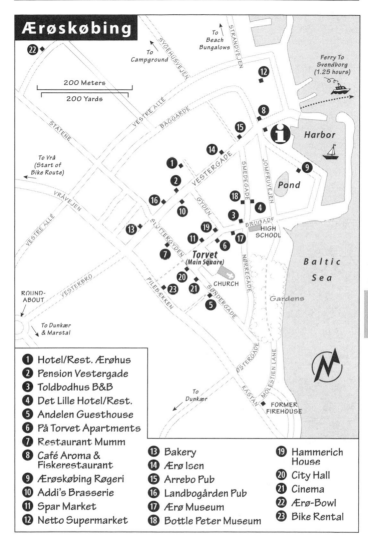

Ærøskøbing

200 Meters
200 Yards

SYGEHUSVEJEN
To Campground
To Beach Bungalows
STRANDVEJEN
Ferry To Svendborg (1.25 hours)

VESTRE ALLÉ
BAGGÅRDE
STATENE

To Vrå (Start of Bike Route)

VRÅVEJEN

YESTRE ALLÉ

VESTERBRO

ROUND-ABOUT
To Dunkær & Marstal

SLOTTEGYDEN
GYDEN
VESTERGADE
SMEDEGADE
JOMFRUVEJEN

Harbor
Pond
Baltic Sea

PILEBÆKKEN
NØRREGADE

Torvet (Main Square)
CHURCH

DRILBADE
HIGH SCHOOL

Gardens

ØSTERGADE
KASTAN
MOLESTIEN LANE

To Dunkær
FORMER FIREHOUSE

CENTRAL DENMARK

1. Hotel/Rest. Ærøhus
2. Pension Vestergade
3. Toldbodhus B&B
4. Det Lille Hotel/Rest.
5. Andelen Guesthouse
6. På Torvet Apartments
7. Restaurant Mumm
8. Café Aroma & Fiskerestaurant
9. Ærøskøbing Røgeri
10. Addi's Brasserie
11. Spar Market
12. Netto Supermarket
13. Bakery
14. Ærø Isen
15. Arrebo Pub
16. Landbogården Pub
17. Ærø Museum
18. Bottle Peter Museum
19. Hammerich House
20. City Hall
21. Cinema
22. Ærø-Bowl
23. Bike Rental

the "street spies" on the houses—clever mirrors letting old women inside keep an eye on what's going on outside. The ship-in-a-bottle Bottle Peter Museum is on the right (described later, under "Sights in Ærøskøbing"). Notice the gutters—some protect only the doorway. Locals find the rounded modern drainpipes less charming than the old-school ones with hard angles. Appreciate the finely carved old doors. Each is proudly unique—try to find two the same. Number 37 (on the left, after Det Lille Hotel), from the 18th century, is Ærøskøbing's cutest house. Its tiny dormer is from some old ship's poop deck. The plants above the door have a traditional purpose—to keep this part of the house damp and slow to burn in case of fire.

Smedegade ends at the Folkehøjskole (folks' high school). Inspired by the Danish philosopher Nikolaj Gruntvig—who wanted people to be able to say "I am good at being me"—it offers people of any age the benefit of government-subsidized cultural education (music, art, theater, and so on).

• *Jog left, then turn right after the school, and stroll along the peaceful, harborside...*

Molestien Lane: This gravel path is lined with gardens, a quiet beach, and a row of small-is-beautiful houses—beginning

with humble and progressing to captain's class. These fine buildings are a reminder that through the centuries, Ærøskøbing has been the last town in Germany, independent, the first town in Denmark...and always into trade—legal and illegal. (The smuggling spirit survives in residents' blood even today. When someone returns from a trip, friends eagerly ask, "And what did you bring back?") Each garden is cleverly and lovingly designed. The harborfront path, nicknamed "Virgin's Lane," was where teens could court within view of their parents.

The dreamy-looking island immediately across the way is a nature preserve and a resting spot for birds making their long journey from the north to the Mediterranean. There's one lucky bull here (farmers raft over their heifers, who return as cows). Rainbows often end on this island—where plague victims were once buried. In the winter, when the water freezes (about once a decade), locals slip and slide over for a visit. The white building you can see at the end of the town's pier was the cooking house, where visiting sailors (who tried to avoid working with open flame on flammable ships) could do their baking.

At the end of the lane stands the former firehouse (with the tall brick tower, now a place for the high school garage band to practice). Twenty yards before the firehouse, a trail cuts left about 100 yards along the shore to a place the town provides for fishermen to launch and store their boats and tidy up their nets. A bench is strategically placed to enjoy the view.

• *Follow the rutted lane inland, back past the firehouse. Turn right and walk a block toward town. At the first intersection, take a right onto...*

Østergade: This was Ærøskøbing's east gate. In the days of German control, all island trade was legal only within the town. All who passed this point would pay various duties and taxes at a tollbooth that once stood here.

As you walk past the traditional houses, peer into living rooms. Catch snatches of Danish life. (After the bend, you can see right through the windows to the sea.) Ponder the beauty of a society with such a keen sense of civic responsibility that fishing permits entrust you "to catch only what you need." You're welcome to pick berries where you like...but "no more than what would fit in your hat."

The wood on these old houses prefers organic coverings to modern paint. Tar painted on beams as a preservative blisters in the sun. An old-fashioned paint of chalk, lime, and clay lets old houses breathe and feel more alive. (It gets darker with the rain and leaves a little color on your fingers.) Modern chemical paint has much less personality.

The first square (actually a triangle, at #55) was the old goose market. Ærøskøbing—born in the 13th century, burned in the 17th, and rebuilt in the 18th—claims (believably) to be the best-preserved town from that era in Denmark. The original plan, with 12 streets laid out by its founder, survives.

• *Leaving the square, stay left on...*

Søndergade: Look for wrought-iron girders on the walls, added to hold together bulging houses. (On the first corner, at

#55, notice the nuts that could be tightened like a corset to keep the house from sagging.) Ærøskøbing's oldest houses (check out the dates)—the only ones that survived a fire during a war with Sweden—are #36 and #32. At #32, the hatch upstairs was where masts and sails were stored for the winter. These houses also have some of the finest doors in town (and in Ærøskøbing, that's really saying something). The red on #32's door is the original paint job—ox blood, which, when combined with the tannin in the wood, really lasts. The courtyard behind #18 was a parking lot in pre-car days. Farmers, in town for their shopping chores, would leave their horses here. Even today, the wide-open fields are just beyond.

• *Wander down to Ærøskøbing's main square...*

Torvet (Main Square): Notice the two pumps. Until 1951, townspeople came here for their water. The linden tree is the town

symbol. The rocks around it celebrate the reunion of a big chunk of southern Denmark (including this island), which was ruled by Germany from 1864 to 1920. See the town seal featuring a linden tree, over the door of the old City Hall (now the library, with Internet stations in former prison cells). Read the Danish on the wall: "With law shall man a country build."

• *Our walk is over. Continue straight (popping into recommended Restaurant Mumm, the best place in town, to make a reservation for dinner). You'll return to the main street (Vestergade) and—just when you need it—the town bakery. If you're ready to launch right into a bike ride, go through the green door right of the City Hall to reach the town's bike-rental place (listed earlier, under "Helpful Hints").*

Sights in Ærøskøbing

Museums

Ærøskøbing's three tiny museums cluster within a few doors of each other just off the main square (if visiting all three, buy the 85-kr combo-ticket; tel. 62 52 29 50, www.arremus.dk). In July, they organize daily chatty tours. While quirky and fun (and with sketchy English handouts), these museums would be much more interesting and worthwhile if they translated their Danish descriptions for the rare person on this planet who doesn't speak *Dansk*. (Your gentle encouragement might help get results.)

Ærø Museum (Ærøskøbing Bymuseum)—This museum fills two floors of an old house with the island's local history, from

seafaring to farming. On the ground floor, you'll see household objects (such as pottery, kitchenware, and tools), paintings, a loom from 1683, and a fun diorama showing an aerial view of Ærøskøbing in 1862—notice the big gardens behind nearly every house. (This museum carries on the tradition with its own garden out back—be sure to go out and explore it before you leave.) Upstairs are 19th-century outfits, lots more paintings, an 18th-century peasant's living room with colorful furniture, and the gear from a 100-year-old pharmacy.

Cost and Hours: 30 kr; late June-Aug Mon-Fri 11:00-16:00, Sat-Sun 11:00-15:00; Sept-late Oct and April-late June daily 11:00-15:00; shorter hours off-season and closed Sat-Sun; Brogade 3-5, www.arremus.dk.

▲**Bottle Peter Museum (Flaske-Peter Samling)**—This fascinating house has 750 different bottled ships. Old Peter Jacobsen,

who made his first bottle at 16 and his last at 85, created some 1,700 total ships-in-bottles in his lifetime. He bragged that he drank the contents of each bottle...except those containing milk. This museum opened in 1943, when the mayor of Ærøskøbing offered Peter and his wife a humble home in exchange for the right to display his works. Bottle Peter died in 1960 (and is most likely buried in a glass bottle), leaving a lifetime of tedious little creations for visitors to squint and marvel at.

Cost and Hours: 40 kr; late June-early Aug daily 10:00-17:00; April-late June and early Aug-late Oct daily 10:00-16:00; shorter hours off-season and closed Sat-Sun; Smedegade 22.

Visiting the Museum: In two buildings facing each other across a cobbled courtyard, you'll see rack after rack of painstaking models in bottles and cigar boxes. Some are "right-handed" and some are "left-handed" (referring to the direction the bottle faced, and therefore which hand the model-maker relied on to execute the fine details)—Bottle Peter could do it all.

In the entrance building, you'll see Peter's "American collection," which he sold to a Danish-American collector so he could have funds to retire. One of Peter's favorites was the "diver-bottle"—an extra-wide bottle with two separate ship models inside: One shipwreck on the "ocean floor" at the bottom of the bottle, and, above that, a second one floating on the "surface." A video shows the artist at work, and nearby you can see some of his tools.

In the second building, you can read some English panels about Peter's life (including his mischievous wit, which caused his friends great anxiety when he had an audience with the king) and see the headstone he designed for his own grave: A cross embedded with seven ships-in-bottles, representing the seven seas he explored in his youth as a seaman.

Hammerich House (Hammerichs Hus)—These 12 funky rooms in three houses are filled with 200- to 300-year-old junk.

Cost and Hours: 30 kr, late May-late Aug daily 12:00-16:00, closed off-season, Gyden 22.

CENTRAL DENMARK

Ærø Island Bike Ride (or Car Tour)

This 15-mile trip shows you the best of this windmill-covered island's charms. The highest point on the island is only 180 feet above sea level, but the wind can be strong and the hills seem long and surprisingly steep. If you'd rather drive the route, you can rent an electric car at the TI (summer only).

As a bike ride, it's good exercise, though it may be more exhausting than fun if you've done only light, recreational cycling at home. You'll pay more for seven gears instead of five, but it's worth it.

Rent your bike in town, and while my map and instructions work, a local cycle map is helpful (free loaner maps if you rent from Pilebækkens Cykler, or buy one at the TI). Bring along plenty of water, as there are few opportunities to fill up (your first good chance is at the WC at the Bregninge church; there are no real shops until downtown Bregninge).

• *Leave Ærøskøbing to the west on the road to Vrå (Vråvejen, signed* Bike Route #90*). From downtown, pedal up the main street (Vestergade) and turn right on Vråvejen; from the bike-rental place on Pilebækken, just turn right and pedal straight ahead—it turns into Vråvejen.*

Leaving Ærøskøbing: You'll see the first of many U-shaped farms, typical of Denmark. The three sides block the wind and store cows, hay, and people. *Gård* (farm) shows up in many local surnames.

At Øsemarksvej, bike along the coast in the protection of the dike built in 1856 to make the once-salty swampland to your left farmable. While the weak soil is good for hay and little else, they get the most out of it. Each winter, certain grazing areas flood with seawater. (Some locals claim this makes their cows produce fatter milk and meat.) As you roll along the dike, the land on your left is about eight feet below sea level. The little white pump house—alone in the field—is busy each spring and summer.

• *At the T-junction, go right (over the dike) toward...*

Borgnæs: The traditional old "straw house" (50 yards down, on left) is a café and shop selling fresh farm products. Just past that, a few roadside tables sell farm goodies on the honor system. Borgnæs is a cluster of modern summer houses. In spite of huge demand, a weak economy, and an aging population, development like this is no longer allowed.

• *Keep to the right (passing lots of wheat fields); at the next T-junction, turn right, following signs for Ø.* Bregningemark *(don't turn off for* Vindeballe*). After a secluded beach, head inland (direction: Ø. Bregninge). Pass the island's only water mill, and climb uphill over the island's 2,700-inch-high summit toward Bregninge. The tallest point on Ærø is called Synneshøj (probably means "Seems High" and it sure*

Ærø Island Bike Ride

To Svendborg

Urehoved

BEACH
BUNGALOWS ■

Drejø

Ommels-
hoved

CHURCH ■   Borgnæs
Bregninge   ▲ Synneshøj

CAMPING

DIKE

•**Ærøskøbing**
(start & end bike ride)

Vrå

Lilleø

VINDEBALLE KRO → ■ ← SHORTCUTS BACK
          TO ÆRØSKØBING
      Vindeballe

Stokkeby

**Vodrup
Klint**
(Cliffs)

Tranderup   Olde

Lille
Rise

Kragnæs

TINGSTEDET
DOLMEN

**Store
Rise** ■

To Marstal
& Maritime
Museum

BREWERY ■

Dunkær

Baltic Sea

3 Kilometers

2 Miles

Vejnæs Nakke

DENMARK

100 KM
50 MI

Odense • • Cope.
          Ærø
GER.

CENTRAL DENMARK

---

does—if you're even a bit out of shape, you'll feel every one of those inches).

Gammelgård: Take a right turn marked only by a *Bike Route #90* sign. The road deteriorates (turns to gravel—and can be slushy

if there's been heavy rain, so be careful). You'll wind scenically and sometimes steeply through "Ærø's Alps," past classic thatched-roofed "old farms" (hence the name of the lane—Gammelgård).

• *At the modern road, turn left (leaving Bike Route #90) and bike to the big village church. Before turning left to roll through Bregninge, visit the church.*

Bregninge Church: The interior of the 12th-century Bregninge church is still painted as a Gothic church would have been. Find the painter's self-portrait (behind the pulpit, right of front pew). Tradition says that if the painter wasn't happy with his pay, he'd paint a fool's head in the church (above third pew on left). Note how the fool's mouth—the hole for a rope tied to the bell—has been worn wider and wider by centuries of ringing. (During services, the ringing bell would call those who were ill and too contagious to be allowed into the church to come for communion—distributed through the square hatches flanking the altar.)

The altarpiece—gold leaf on carved oak—is from 1528, six years before the Reformation came to Denmark. The cranium carved into the bottom indicates it's a genuine masterpiece by Claus Berg (from Lübeck, Germany). This Crucifixion scene is such a commotion, it seems to cause Christ's robe to billow up. The soldiers who traditionally gambled for Christ's robe have traded their dice for knives. Even the three wise men (lower right; each perhaps a Danish king) made it to this Crucifixion. Notice the escaping souls of the two thieves— the one who converted on the cross being carried happily to heaven, and the other, with its grim-winged escort, heading straight to hell. The scene at lower left—a disciple with a bare-breasted, dark-skinned woman feeding her child—symbolizes the Great Commission: "Go ye to all the world." Since this is a Catholic altarpiece, a roll call of saints lines the wings. During the restoration, the identity of the two women on the lower right was unknown, so the lettering—even in Latin—is clearly gibberish. Take a moment to study the 16th-century art on the ceiling (for example, the crucified feet ascending, leaving only footprints on earth). In the narthex, a list of pastors goes back to 1505. The current pastor (Agnes) is the first woman on the list.

• *Now's the time for a bathroom break (public WC in the churchyard). Then roll downhill through...*

Bregninge: As you bike through what is supposedly Denmark's "second-longest village," you'll pass many more U-shaped *gårds*. Notice how the town is in a gully. Imagine pirates trolling along the coast, looking for church spires marking unfortified villages. Ærø's 16 villages are all invisible from the sea—their church spires carefully designed not to be viewable from sea level.

• *About a mile down the main road is Vindeballe. Just before the main part of the village (soon after you pass the official* Vindeballe *sign and the* din fart *sign—which tells you "your speed"), take the* Vodrup Klint *turnoff to the right.*

Vodrup Klint: A road leads downhill (with a well-signed jog to the right) to dead-end at a rugged bluff called Vodrup Klint (WC, picnic benches). If I were a pagan, I'd worship here—the sea, the wind, and the chilling view. Notice how the land steps in sloppy slabs down to the sea. When saturated with water, the slabs of clay that make up the land here get slick, and entire chunks can slide.

Hike down to the foamy beach (where you can pick up some flint, chalk, and wild thyme). While the wind at the top could drag a kite-flyer, the beach below can be ideal for sunbathing. Because Ærø is warmer and drier than the rest of Denmark, this island is home to plants and animals found nowhere else in the country. This southern exposure is the warmest area. Germany is dead ahead.

• *Backtrack 200 yards and follow the signs to* Tranderup. *On the way, you'll pass a lovely pond famous for its bell frogs and happy little duck houses.*

Popping out in Tranderup, you can backtrack (left) about 300 yards to get to the traditional **Vindeballe Kro**—*a handy inn for a stop if you're hungry or thirsty (30-45-kr lunches served daily July-mid-Aug 12:00-14:00, 150-200-kr dinners served daily year-round 18:00-21:00, tel. 62 52 16 13).*

If you're tired or if the weather is turning bad, you can shortcut from here back to **Ærøskøbing:** *Go down the lane across the street from the Vindeballe Kro, and you'll zip quickly downhill across the island to the dike just east of Borgnæs; turn right and retrace your steps back into town.*

But there's much more to see. To continue our pedal, head on into...

Tranderup: Still following signs for *Tranderup*, stay on Tranderupgade parallel to the big road through town. You'll pass a lovely farm and a potato stand. At the main road, turn right. At the Ærøskøbing turnoff (another chance to bail out and head home), side-trip 100 yards left to the big stone (commemorating the return of the island to Denmark from Germany in 1750) and a grand island panorama. Seattleites might find Claus Clausen's rock interesting (in the picnic area, next to WC). It's a memorial to an extremely obscure pioneer from the state of Washington.

• *Return to the big road (continuing in direction: Marstal), pass through Olde, pedal past FAF (the local wheat farmers' co-op facility), and head toward Store Rise (STOH-reh REE-zuh), the next church spire in the distance. Think of medieval travelers using spires as navigational aids.*

Store Rise Prehistoric Tomb, Church, and Brewery: Thirty yards after the Stokkeby turnoff, follow the rough, tree-lined path on the right to the Langdysse (Long Dolmen) Tingstedet, just behind the church spire. This is a 6,000-year-old **dolmen,** an early

Neolithic burial place. Though Ærø once had more than 200 of these prehistoric tombs, only 13 survive. The site is a raised mound the shape and length (about 100 feet) of a Viking ship, and archaeologists have found evidence that indicates a Viking ship may indeed have been burned and buried here.

Ting means assembly spot. Imagine a thousand years ago: Viking chiefs representing the island's various communities gathering here around their ancestors' tombs. For 6,000 years, this has been a holy spot. The stones were considered fertility stones. For centuries, locals in need of virility chipped off bits and took them home (the nicks in the rock nearest the information post are mine).

Tuck away your chip and carry on down the lane to the Store Rise **church.** Inside you'll find little ships hanging in the nave, a fine 12th-century altarpiece, a stick with offering bag and a ting-a-ling bell to wake those nodding off (right of altar), double seats (so worshippers can flip to face the pulpit during sermons), and Martin Luther in the stern keeping his Protestant hand on the rudder. The list in the church allows today's pastors to trace their pastoral lineage back to Doctor Luther himself. (The current pastor, Janet, is the first woman on the list.) The churchyard is circular—a reminder of how churchyards provided a last refuge for humble communities under attack. Can you find anyone buried in the graveyard whose name doesn't end in "-sen"?

The buzz lately in Ærø is its **brewery,** located in a historic brewery 400 yards beyond the Store Rise church. Follow the smell of the hops (or the *Rise Bryggeri* signs). It welcomes visitors with free samples of its various beers. The Ærø traditional brews are available in pilsner (including the popular walnut pilsner), light ale, dark ale, and a typical dark Irish-style stout. The Rise organic brews come in light ale, dark ale, and walnut (mid-June-mid-Sept daily 10:00-14:00; mid-Sept-mid-June Wed-Fri 10:00-14:00, closed Sat-Tue; tel. 62 52 11 32, www.risebryggeri.dk).

• *From here, climb back to the main road and continue (direction: Marstal) on your way back home to Ærøskøbing. The three 330-foot-high modern windmills on your right are communally owned and, as they are a nonpolluting source of energy, state-subsidized. At Dunkær (3 miles from Ærøskøbing), take the small road, signed* Lille Rise, *past the topless windmill. Except for the Lille Rise, it's all downhill from here, as you coast past great sea views back home to Ærøskøbing.*

Huts at the Sunset Beach: Still rolling? Bike past the campground along the Urehoved beach (*strand* in Danish) for a look at the coziest little beach houses you'll never see back in the "big is beautiful" US. This is Europe, where small is beautiful, and the concept of sustainability is neither new nor subversive. (For more details, see "Beach Bungalow Sunset Stroll," later.)

Rainy-Day Options

Ærø is disappointing but not unworkable in bad weather. In addition to the museums listed earlier, you could rent a car (such as the TI's electric cars) to cruise the island. Also, many of the evening options under "Nightlife in Ærøskøbing" (next) are good in bad weather.

If you want to find out more about the island's seafaring history, hop on the free bus #790 to the dreary town of Marstal to visit its fine **Marstal Maritime Museum** (Marstal Søfartsmuseum). Ride the bus all the way to the harbor (about a 20-minute trip), where you'll find the museum. You'll see plenty of model ships, nautical paintings (including several scenes by acclaimed painter Carl Rasmussen), an original ship's galley, a re-created wheelhouse (with steering and navigation equipment), a collection of exotic goods brought back from faraway lands, and a children's area with a climbable mast. Designed by and for sailors, the museum presents a warts-and-all view of the hardships of the seafaring life, rather than romanticizing it (55 kr; July-Aug daily 9:00-18:00; June daily 9:00-17:00; May and Sept-Oct daily 10:00-16:00; Nov-April Mon-Fri 10:00-16:00, Sat 11:00-15:00, closed Sun; Prinsensgade 1, tel. 62 53 23 31, www.marmus.dk).

Nightlife in Ærøskøbing

These activities are best done in the evening, after a day of biking around the island.

▲**Town Walk with Night Watchman**—Each evening in summer, Mr. Jan Pedersen becomes the old night watchman and leads

visitors through town. The hour-long walk is likely in Danish and English—and often in German, too—so you'll hang around a lot. But it's a fine time to be out, meet other travelers, and be charmed by gentle Jan (25 kr, daily late June-late Aug, no tours off-season, meet on Torvet near the church at 21:00, Jan also available as private guide, mobile 40 40 60 13, www.aeroe-turguide.dk, jan.leby @mail.dk).

▲▲**Beach Bungalow Sunset Stroll**—At sunset, stroll to Ærøskøbing's sand beach. Facing the ferry dock, go left, following the harbor. Upon leaving the town, you'll pass the Netto supermarket (convenient for picking up snacks, beer, or wine), a mini-golf course, and a children's playground. In the rosy distance, past a wavy wheat field, is Vestre Strandvejen—a row of tiny, Monopoly-like huts facing the sunset. These tiny beach escapes are privately owned on land rented from the town (no overnight use, WCs at each end). Each is different, but all are stained with merry memories of locals enjoying themselves Danish-style. Bring a beverage or picnic. It's perfectly acceptable—and very Danish— to borrow a porch for your sunset sit. From here, it's a fine walk out to the end of Urehoved (as this spit of land is called).

Cinema—The cute little 30-seat Andelen Theater (a former grain warehouse near Torvet Square) plays movies in their original language (Danish subtitles, closed Mon and in July—when it hosts a jazz festival, new titles begin every Tue). It's run in a charming community-service kind of way. The management has installed heat, so tickets no longer come with a blanket.

Bowling—Ærø-Bowl is a six-lane alley in a modern athletic club at the edge of town. In this old-fashioned town, where no modern construction is allowed in the higgledy-piggledy center, this hip facility is a magnet for young people. One local told me, "I've never seen anyone come out of there without a smile" (hot dogs, junk food, arcade games, kids on dates; Tue-Thu 16:00-22:00, later on Fri-Sat, closed Sun-Mon, Søndergade 28, tel. 62 52 23 06, www .arrebowl.dk).

Pubs—Ærøskøbing's two bars are at the top and bottom of Vestergade. **Arrebo Pub,** near the ferry landing, attracts a young crowd and is *the* place for live music (but no food). The low-key **Landbogården** was recently taken over by a Sri Lankan family who have made it non-smoking and have started serving food— both Indian and Danish dishes (daily for 45-75-kr lunches and 100-160-kr dinners, near the top of Vestergade).

Sleeping in Ærøskøbing

The accommodations scene here is boom or bust. Summer weekends and all of July are packed (book long in advance). It's absolutely dead in the winter. These places come with family-run personality, and each is an easy stroll from the ferry landing.

Sleep Code

(6 kr = about $1, country code: 45)
S = Single, **D** = Double/Twin, **T** = Triple, **Q** = Quad, **b** = bathroom, **s** = shower. Credit cards are accepted (with a 4 percent surcharge), staff speak English, and breakfast is included unless otherwise noted.

To help you sort easily through these listings, I've divided the accommodations into three categories, based on the price for a standard double room with bath during high season:

$$$ Higher Priced—Most rooms 1,000 kr or more.
$$ Moderately Priced—Most rooms between 450-1,000 kr.
$ Lower Priced—Most rooms 450 kr or less.

Prices can change without notice; verify the hotel's current rates online or by email.

In Ærøskøbing

$$$ Hotel Ærøhus is big and sprawling, with 33 uninspired rooms. Although it is less personal and cozy than some of the other listings here, it's the closest thing to a grand hotel in this capital of quaint (S-600 kr, Sb-990 kr, D-800 kr, Db-1,250 kr, free Internet access and Wi-Fi, bike rentals-75 kr/day, possible noise from large dinner parties—ask for a quiet room, tel. 62 52 10 03, fax 62 52 31 68, www.aeroehus.dk, mail@aeroehus.dk, Ole Jensen and family). Their modern holiday apartments nearby are used as overflow accommodations and can be a fine value for groups and families (details on their website).

$$ Pension Vestergade is your best home away from home in Ærøskøbing. It's lovingly run by Susanna Greve and her daughters,

Henrietta and Celia. Susanna, who's fun to talk with and is always ready with a cup of tea, has a wealth of knowledge about the town's history and takes good care of her guests. Built in 1784 for a sea captain's daughter, this creaky, sagging, and venerable eight-room place—with each room named for its particular color scheme—is on the main street in the town center. Picnic in the back garden and get to know Tillie, the live-in dog. Reserve well in advance (singles-600 kr year-round; doubles fluctuate, July: D-990 kr; spring and fall: D-890 kr; winter: D-790 kr; cash only, cuddly hot-water bottles, shared bathrooms, free Internet access and Wi-Fi, Vestergade 44, tel. 62 52 22 98, www.vestergade44 .com, pensionvestergade44@post.tele.dk).

$$ Toldbodhus B&B, a tollhouse from 1770 to 1906, now rents four delightful rooms. Three rooms share two bathrooms in the main house, and a small garden house has a double room with a detached bathroom. Owners Karin and John Steenberg have named and decorated each room after cities they've lived in: Amsterdam, København, London, and Hong Kong. They may be closing after the summer 2013 season (April-Sept: S-750 kr, Db-890 kr; Oct-March: S-650 kr, Db-790 kr; cash only, free Wi-Fi, near harbor on corner of Smedegade at Brogade 8, tel. 62 52 18 11, www.toldbodhus.com, toldbodhus@mail.dk).

$$ Det Lille Hotel is a former 19th-century captain's home with six tidy but well-worn rooms (June-Sept: S/D-950 kr; Oct-May: S/D-850 kr; extra bed-265 kr, free Wi-Fi, Smedegade 33, tel. & fax 62 52 23 00, www.det-lille-hotel.dk, mail@det-lille -hotel.dk).

$$ Andelen Guesthouse, brimming with nautical charm, is in an old warehouse that's been converted into a hotel. The five guest rooms share two bathrooms (S-500 kr, D-600 kr, breakfast-75 kr, free Wi-Fi, Søndergade 28A, tel. 61 60 75 11, www .andelenguesthouse.com, andelenguesthouse@hotmail.com).

$$ På Torvet rents eight newly renovated apartments—each with private kitchen and bathroom—on the main square (Db-750 kr, 200-kr linen and cleaning fee, free Wi-Fi, Torvet 7, tel. 62 52 40 50, www.paatorvet.dk, info@paatorvet.dk).

Outside of Ærøskøbing

$$ Vindeballe Kro, about three miles from Ærøskøbing, is a traditional inn in Vindeballe at the island's central crossroads. Maria and Steen rent 10 straightforward, well-kept rooms (S-450 kr, D-650 kr, tel. 62 52 16 13, www.vindeballekro.dk, mail@vinde ballekro.dk).

$ Ærø Campground is set on a fine beach a few minutes' walk out of town. This three-star campground offers a lodge with a fireplace, campsites, cabins, and bike rental (camping-75 kr/person, 4- to 6-bed cabins-150-300 kr plus per-person fee, bedding-75 kr/ person, open May-Sept; facing the water, follow waterfront to the left; tel. 62 52 18 54, www.aeroecamp.dk, info@aeroecamp.dk).

Eating in Ærøskøbing

Ærøskøbing has a handful of charming and hardworking little eateries. Business is so light that chefs and owners come and go constantly, making it tough to predict the best value for the coming year. As each place has a distinct flavor, I'd spend 20 minutes enjoying the warm evening light and do a strolling survey before making your choice. While there are several simple burger-type joints, I've listed only the serious kitchens. Note that everything closes by 21:00—don't wait too late to eat (if you'll be taking a later ferry from Svendborg to Ærø, either eat before your boat trip or call ahead to reserve a place...otherwise you're out of luck). The only places in town serving food daily during the winter are Addi's Brasserie, Det Lille Hotel, Hotel Ærøhus, and the Landbogården bar (see "Nightlife in Ærøskøbing," earlier).

Restaurant Mumm is where visiting yachters go for a good and classy meal. Portions are huge, and on balmy days their garden terrace out back is a hit. Call ahead to reserve (180-kr daily specials, 80-kr starters, 140-220-kr main courses, daily 16:30-21:00, closed Sun-Mon off-season, near Torvet Square, tel. 62 52 12 12, Peter Sorensen).

Café Aroma, an inexpensive Danish café that feels like a rustic old diner, has a big front porch filled with tables and good, reasonably priced entrées, sandwiches, and burgers for 60-175 kr. Ask about the daily special, which will save you money and is not listed on the confusing menu. Order at the bar (May-Aug daily 11:00-21:00, closed Sept-April, on Vestergade). They also run a high-quality, pricey fish restaurant (aptly named **Fiskerestaurant**) next door.

Ærøskøbing Røgeri serves wonderful smoked fish meals on paper plates and picnic tables. Facing the harbor, it's great for a light meal (50-75 kr for fish with potato salad and bread). Eat there or find a pleasant picnic site at the beach or at the park behind the fish house. A smoked fish dinner and a couple of cold Carlsbergs are a well-earned reward after a long bike ride (May-Sept daily 11:00-18:00, in summer until 20:00, Havnen 15, tel. 62 52 40 07).

Addi's Brasserie is a rare place that's open all year, serving fresh seafood and meat dishes. Eat in the main dining room among portraits of Danish royalty, or in the larger side room (daily lunch and dinner specials, lunch main courses-48-85 kr, dinner main courses-180 kr, daily 12:00-15:00 & 18:00-21:00, across street from Pension Vestergade, Vestergade 39, tel. 62 52 21 43).

Hotel Restaurants: Two hotels in town have dining rooms with good but expensive food; I'd eat at the restaurants I've listed above, unless they're closed. But in a pinch, try these: **Det Lille Hotel** serves meals in an inviting dining room or garden (200-kr daily specials, 70-100-kr starters, 190-240-kr main dishes, daily 12:00-21:00, dinner only off-season—but at least they're open year-round, Smedegade 33, tel. 62 52 23 00, Klaus cooks with attitude). **Hotel Ærøhus** is a last resort, serving creative but pricey French-inspired modern fare in a sprawling complex of dining rooms, big and small (115-kr starters, 225-300-kr main dishes, open daily, on

Vestergade, tel. 62 52 10 03).

Grocery: Buy picnic fixings plus wine and beer at the **Spar Market** (Mon-Fri 9:00-18:00, Sat 9:00-14:00, Sun 10:00-15:00, on Torvet Square) or the bigger **Netto** supermarket (chilled beer and wine—handy for walks to the little huts on the beach at sunset, Mon-Fri 9:00-19:00, Sat 8:00-17:00, closed Sun, kitty-corner from ferry dock).

Bakery: Ærøskøbing's old-school little bakery sells homemade bread, cheese, yogurt, and tasty pastries (Tue-Fri 7:00-17:00, Sat-Sun 7:00-14:00, closed Mon, top of Vestergade).

Ice Cream: Halfway up the main drag (Vestergade), you'll smell fresh-baked waffles and see benches filled with happy ice-cream lickers. **Ærø Isen** serves good ice cream in fresh waffle cones, with whipped cream and jam topping. Their "Ærø-Isen Special" (walnut-maple syrup ice cream topped with whipped cream and maple syrup) is 9 kr more than the other flavors (daily  11:00-21:00). Be sure to check out the gallery behind the shop to see paintings and sculptures featuring local artists.

Ærøskøbing Connections

Ærø-Svendborg Ferry

The ferry ride between **Svendborg,** with connections to Copenhagen, and **Ærøskøbing,** on the island of Ærø, is a relaxing 75-minute crossing. Just get on, and the crew will come to you for your payment. While they accept Danish credit cards, American ones don't work—so be sure to bring enough cash (189 kr round-trip per person, 418 kr round-trip per car—not including driver/passengers, you'll save a little money with round-trip tickets, you can leave the island via any of the three different Ærø ferry routes, ferry not covered by or discounted with railpass).

The ferry always has room for walk-ons, but drivers should reserve a spot in advance, especially on weekends and in summer. During these busy times, reserve as far ahead as you can—ideally at least a week in advance. Car reservations by phone or email are free and easy—simply give your name and license-plate number. If you don't know your license number (i.e., you're reserving from home and haven't yet picked up your rental car), try asking nicely if they're willing to just take your name. They may want you to call them with the number when you pick up your car, but if that's not practical, you can usually just tell the attendant your name before you drive onto the boat (office open Mon-Fri 8:00-16:00, Sat-Sun 9:00-15:30, tel. 62 52 40 00, www.aeroe-ferry.dk, info@aeroe-ferry.dk).

Ferries depart Svendborg daily at 10:15, 13:15, 16:15, 19:15, and 22:30 (plus a 7:15 departure Mon-Fri). Ferries depart Ærøskøbing daily at 8:45, 11:45, 14:45, 17:45, and 20:45 (plus a 5:45 departure Mon-Fri). Drivers with reservations just drive on (be sure to get into the *med* reservations line). If you won't use your car in Ærø, park it in Svendborg (big, safe lot two blocks in from ferry landing, or at the far end of the harbor near the Bendix fish shop). On Ærø, parking is free.

Trains Connecting with Ærø-Svendborg Ferry

The train from **Odense** dead-ends at the Svendborg harbor (2/hour Mon-Sat, 1/hour Sun, 45 minutes; don't get off at the "Svendborg Vest" station—wait until you get to the end of the line, called simply "Svendborg"). Train departures and arrivals are coordinated with the ferry schedule.

Arriving in Svendborg: The ferry leaves Svendborg about five minutes after your train arrives. If you know where you're going, it takes about that long to walk briskly from the station to the dock. Don't dawdle—the boat leaves stubbornly on time, even if the train is a minute or two late. Since trains run every half-hour during summer (except on Sundays), I recommend leaving Odense on an earlier train, so you have a little more time to absorb delays and find your way (in other words, take the train that arrives in Svendborg 35 minutes before your boat). If you're cutting it close, be ready to hop off the train and follow these directions:

To get from the Svendborg train station to the dock, turn left after exiting the train, following the sidewalk between the tracks and the station, then take a left (across the tracks) at the first street, Brogade. Head a block downhill to the harbor, make a right, and the ferry dock is ahead, across from Hotel Ærø. If you arrive early, you can head to the waiting room in the little blue building across the street from the hotel. There are several carry-out restaurants along Brogade, and a few hotels overlooking the ferry line have restaurants.

Departing from Svendborg: All Svendborg trains go to Odense (where you can connect to Copenhagen or Aarhus). Trains leave shortly after the ferry arrives (tight connections for hurried commuters). To reach the train from the Svendborg ferry dock, pass Hotel Ærø and continue a block along the waiting lane for the ferry, turn left and go up Brogade one block, then take a right and follow the sidewalk between the tracks and the train station. A train signed *Odense* should be waiting on the single track (departs at :20 or :50 past each hour).

Odense

Founded in A.D. 988 and named after Odin (the Nordic Zeus),

Odense is the main city of the big island of Funen (Fyn in Danish) and the birthplace of storyteller Hans Christian Andersen (whom the Danes call simply H. C., pronounced "hoe see"). Although the author was born here in poverty and left at the tender age of 14 to pursue a career in the theater scene of Copenhagen, H. C. is Odense's favorite son—you'll find his name and image all over town. He once said, "Perhaps Odense will one day become famous because of me." Today, Odense (OH-then-za) is one of Denmark's most popular tourist destinations.

Orientation to Odense

As Denmark's third-largest city, with 166,000 people, Odense is big and industrial. But its old center, tidy and neatly urbanized,

retains some pockets of the fairy-tale charm it had in the days of H. C. Everything is within easy walking distance, except for the open-air folk museum.

The train station sits at the north end of the town center. A few blocks south runs the main pedestrian shopping boulevard, Vestergade. Near the eastern end of this drag, and a couple of blocks up, is a tight tangle of atmospheric old lanes, where you'll find the Hans Christian Andersen House and town history museum.

Tourist Information

The TI is in the Town Hall (Rådhuset), the big brick palace overlooking the square at the east end of the Vestergade pedestrian street (July-Aug Mon-Fri 9:30-18:00, Sat 10:00-15:00, Sun 11:00-14:00; Sept-June Mon-Fri 9:30-16:30, Sat 10:00-13:00, closed Sun; tel. 63 75 75 20, www.visitodense.com). For all the information

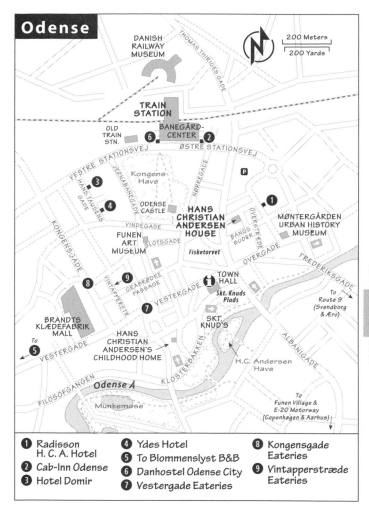

Odense

DANISH RAILWAY MUSEUM

THOMAS THRIGES GADE

200 Meters
200 Yards

TRAIN STATION

OLD TRAIN STN.

6 BANEGÅRD-CENTER **2**

VESTRE STATIONSVEJ

ØSTRE STATIONSVEJ

JERNBANEGADE

HANS TAUSENS GADE

Kongens Have

3

4

ODENSE CASTLE

KONGENSGADE

VINDEGADE

SLOTSGADE

FUNEN ART MUSEUM

HANS CHRISTIAN ANDERSEN HOUSE

NØRREGADE

P

OVERSTRÆDE

OVERGADE

BANGS BODER

1

MØNTERGÅRDEN URBAN HISTORY MUSEUM

FREDERIKSGADE

Fisketorvet

VINTAPPERSTR.

GRÅBRØDRE PASSAGE

9

8

7

VESTERGADE

i TOWN HALL

Skt. Knuds Plads

SKT. KNUD'S

To Route 9 (Svendborg & Ærø)

ALBANIGADE

BRANDTS KLÆDEFABRIK MALL

VESTERGADE

To **5**

HANS CHRISTIAN ANDERSEN'S CHILDHOOD HOME

KLOSTERBAKKEN

H.C. Andersen Have

FILOSOFGANGEN

Odense Å

Munkemose

To Funen Village & E-20 Motorway (Copenhagen & Aarhus)

CENTRAL DENMARK

1 Radisson H. C. A. Hotel
2 Cab-Inn Odense
3 Hotel Domir
4 Ydes Hotel
5 To Blommenslyst B&B
6 Danhostel Odense City
7 Vestergade Eateries
8 Kongensgade Eateries
9 Vintapperstræde Eateries

needed for a longer stop, pick up their excellent and free *Go Odense* guide. If you plan to visit multiple sights, consider the **Odense Pass,** which fully covers the museum at H. C.'s birthplace, city history museum, art museum, railway museum, and open-

air folk museum. It saves you money if you visit at least three sights (159 kr, buy at TI).

Arrival in Odense

The train station is located in the Bånegard Center, a large shopping complex, which also holds the bus station, library (with free Internet access), Galaxy Internet café, shops, eateries, and a movie theater. For a quick visit, check your luggage at the train station (20/40-kr lockers in corridor next to DSB Resjebureau office), pick up a free town map inside the ticket office, jot down the time your train departs, and hit the town (follow signs to *Odense Centrum*).

To make a beeline to the **Hans Christian Andersen House,** turn left out of the station and walk to the corner (at the Cab-Inn). Turn right across the busy street and head one block down Nørregade, then turn left (at the Super Spar market) down Skulkenborg. After one short block, turn right and walk along the highway to the crosswalk by the yellow Oluf Bagers Gård; crossing here will put you at the start of a cute cobbled zone with the Hans Christian Andersen House on your right.

To get to the **TI,** turn right out of the station, cross the busy road, then cut through the Kongens Have (King's Garden) park and head down Jernabanegade. When you come to Vestergade, take a left and follow this fine pedestrian street 100 yards to the TI.

Sights in Odense

Note that some of Odense's museums charge higher admission (about 15-20 kr extra) during school holidays.

▲▲▲**Hans Christian Andersen House**—To celebrate Hans Christian Andersen's 100th birthday in 1904, the city founded this museum in the house where he was born. Today the humble (and rebuilt) house is the corner of an expansive, high-tech museum packed with mementos from the writer's life—and hordes of children and tourists. You could spend several delightful hours here getting into his life story and work. It's fun if you like the man and his tales.

Cost and Hours: 70 kr (30 percent discount if you have a ticket for Fyrtøjet or **Møntergården**—see next two listings), free for kids under 18, daily 10:00-16:00, July-late-Aug until 17:00, Bangs Boder 29, tel. 65 51 46 01, www.museum.odense.dk.

Information: Everything is well described in English. The 50-kr guidebook is unnecessary, but makes a nice souvenir.

Performances: The garden fairy-tale theater—with pleasing vignettes—thrills kids daily in July and early August in the museum garden at 11:00, 13:00, and 15:00, weather permitting (30-minute show in Danish, but fun regardless of language).

Eating: The café next door offers seating indoors and out with sandwiches, burgers, and pancakes (80-120 kr).

Visiting the Museum: At the ticket desk, pick up the floor plan and follow the one-way route through the collection. Touchscreens invite you to delve deeper into specific topics, and

headsets and benches throughout let you to listen to a selection of fairy tales.

You'll kick things off with "**The Age**" exhibit, which considers the era in which Andersen lived (1805-1875), putting the author in his historical context—the time of Abraham Lincoln, Charles Darwin, and Karl Marx. "The Man" paints a portrait of this quirky individual, who was extremely tall and gangly, with a big nose...an ugly duckling, indeed. He spent hours in the mirror perfecting an expression of wry cleverness for photographic portraits (several of which are displayed). You'll learn how bad teeth caused H. C. a lifetime of pain, and how this deeply sensitive, introspective fellow worried about his family history of mental illness even as he astounded the world with his exuberant creativity. "The Art" demonstrates that H. C. was as talented with visual arts as the written word; this darkened room shows off intricate paper cutouts he created (some of which illustrated his tales) and sketches from his travels.

"**The Life**" is a circular exhibit (turn left and proceed counterclockwise, following the footprints) with a step-by-step biography of the writer, accompanied by artifacts from his life. This is arranged around a central Memorial Hall slathered with eight frescoes depicting scenes from H. C.'s past, under a dome filled with natural light. Notice that as the story of his life—starting with a tearful hug to his mother on his departure from Odense at age 14—progresses, the scenes change from daylight to sunset to evening. Under the dome are items relating to H. C.'s fervent crush on the opera singer Jenny Lind: a love letter that he wrote to her, and the champagne glass she used to toast him as her "brother" (a painful rebuff that broke H. C.'s heart—he kept the glass his entire life as a reminder).

Continuing around the biographical section, you'll pass a movie theater with a 13-minute introductory **film** about H. C. (plays every 15 minutes, alternates between Danish and

English).

Don't miss the stairs down into the basement, where you'll find the **"Cabinet of Curiosities"**—several items that belonged to H. C. While some are ordinary (his top hat, pocket watch, pen, shaving kit, lock of hair, vest, and so on), other items have fascinating stories to tell. The 30-foot length of rope was an essential bit of travel gear for H. C., who went around the world; the phobic author kept it in his hotel room so that he could escape in case of fire. Displayed next to his actual bed is an eight-panel screen decorated with impressively detailed sketches by H. C. himself of his travels and his friends (executed while he was stuck in his apartment recovering from illness).

Near the top of the steps, you can enter H. C.'s **birth house,** with descriptions of the people his family lived with and replicas of the type of furniture that likely filled these humble rooms. Later on, the author was highly ashamed of having been born in such a modest house in a very poor neighborhood—the theme of poverty turns up frequently in his works.

Near the end of the exhibit is a recreation of H. C.'s **study** from his apartment in Nyhavn, Copenhagen. You'll exit through "The Works," a library of Andersen's books from around the world (his tales have been translated into nearly 150 languages). The museum gift shop is full of mobiles, cut-paper models, and English versions of Andersen's fairy tales.

Another H. C. House: The writer's childhood home (with a small exhibit of its own) is a few blocks southwest of here, but it's skippable because the main museum here is so excellent and comprehensive.

Fyrtøjet ("Tinderbox")—Next door to the H. C. Andersen House is this privately run, modern, and fun hands-on center for children based on works by H. C. The centerpiece is Fairytale Land, with giant props and sets inspired by the author's tales. Kids can dress up in costumes and get their faces painted at the "magical wardrobe," act out a fairy tale, and do arts and crafts in the "atelier." Ask about performances (generally daily at 12:00 and 14:00; some are in Danish only, but others are done without dialogue).

Cost and Hours: 80 kr for ages 3-69 (free to other ages), 30 percent discount if you have a ticket for the H. C. Andersen House or **Møntergården;** July-mid-Aug daily 10:00-17:00; off-season Fri-Sun 10:00-16:00, closed Mon-Thu; Hans Jensens Stræde 21, tel. 66 14 44 11, www.fyrtoejet.com. On school holidays, there are more activities, the museum is open later (until 17:00), and you'll pay 15 kr extra.

▲**Møntergården (Urban History Museum)**—This well-presented museum, three short blocks from the H. C. Andersen House, fills several medieval buildings with exhibits on the history of Odense. You'll time-travel from prehistoric times (lots of arrow, spear, and ax heads) through to 1660, when the king stripped the town of its independent status. The main exhibit, "Life of the City," fills a stately 17th-century, red house (Falk Gøyes Gård) with a high-tech, well-presented exhibit about Odense in medieval and Renaissance times, covering historical events as well as glimpses of everyday life. Wedged along the side of this building is a surviving medieval lane; at the far end are four miniscule houses which the city used to house widows and orphaned students who couldn't afford to provide for themselves. It's fascinating to squeeze into these humble interiors and imagine that people lived in these almshouses through 1955 (open only in summer, but at other times you can ask at the ticket desk to have them unlocked). A new museum building with expanded exhibits may be open by the time you visit.

Cost and Hours: 50 kr, 30 percent discount if you have a ticket for the H. C. Andersen House or **Fyrtøjet;** Tue-Sun 10:00-16:00, closed Mon; Overgade 48, tel. 65 51 46 01, www.museum .odense.dk.

▲**Danish Railway Museum (Danmarks Jernbanemuseum)**—Conveniently (and appropriately) located directly behind the train

station, this is an ideal place to kill time while waiting for a train—and is worth a look for anyone who enjoys seeing old locomotives and train cars. Here at Denmark's biggest (and only official) rail museum, the huge roundhouse is filled with classic trains, while upstairs you'll walk past long display cases of model trains and enjoy good views down onto the trains. The information is in English, and there are lots of children's activities.

Cost and Hours: 60 kr, daily 10:00-16:00; Dannebrogsgade 24—just exit behind the station, near track 7/8, and cross the street; tel. 66 13 66 30, www.railmuseum.dk.

Funen Art Museum (Fyns Kunstmuseum)—This small, pleasant museum displays Danish art from 1750 to the present. The chronological exhibit starts on the first floor, where you'll see everything from Danish Romanticism (portraits, landscapes, and slice-of-life scenes) to the earliest inklings of Modernism. Down on the ground floor, the collection gets very abstract. Abstraction seems to suit the Danes, skilled as they are with clean, eye-pleasing design. The large central courtyard is filled with temporary exhibits.

Cost and Hours: 50 kr, Tue-Sun 10:00-16:00, closed Mon, Jernbanegade 13, tel. 65 51 46 01, www.museum.odense.dk.

▲Funen Village/Den Fynske Landsby Open-Air Museum—The sleepy gathering of 26 old buildings located about two miles out of town preserves the 18th-century culture of this region. There are no explanations in the buildings, because many school groups who visit play guessing games. Buy the guidebook to make your visit meaningful.

Cost and Hours: 80 kr in summer, 60 kr off-season; July-mid-Aug daily 10:00-18:00; April-June and mid-Aug-late Oct Tue-Sun 10:00-17:00, closed Mon; closed late Oct-March except grounds—but not buildings—open Sun only; bus #110 or #111 from Odense station, or take train to Fruens Bøge station and walk 15 minutes, tel. 65 51 46 01, www.museum.odense.dk.

Sleeping in Odense

(6 kr = about $1, country code: 45)

The demand (and prices) are higher in Odense on weekdays and in winter; in summer and on weekends, you can often get a better deal.

$$$ Radisson H. C. A. Hotel is big, comfortable, and impersonal, with 145 rooms a block from the Hans Christian Andersen House. It's older but nicely updated, and offers great rates every day through the summer (Sb-1,445 kr, Db-1,595 kr, elevator, free Internet access and Wi-Fi, Claus Bergs Gade 7, tel. 66 14 78 00, fax 66 14 78 90, www.radissonblu.com/hotel-odense, hcandersen @radissonblu.com).

$$ Cab-Inn Odense brings its no-frills minimalist economy to town, with 201 simple, comfy, and modern rooms (economy Sb-495 kr, Db-625 kr; standard Sb-545 kr, Db-675 kr; larger "Commodore" Sb-575 kr, Db-705 kr; biggest "Captains Class" Sb-675 kr, Db-805 kr; breakfast-70 kr, elevator, free Internet and Wi-Fi, parking for small cars only-80 kr/day, next to the station at Østre Stationsvej 7-9, tel. 63 14 57 00, www.cabinn.com, odense @cabinn.com).

$$ Hotel Domir, recently remodeled with new bathrooms, has 35 tidy, basic, stylish little rooms along its tiny halls. It's located on a quiet side-street just a few minutes from the train station and features extra soundproofing (Sb-575-695 kr, twin Db-650-745 kr, double bed for 100 kr more, Tb-800-845 kr, price depends on demand, elevator, free Internet access and Wi-Fi, limited parking-50-100 kr/day, free loaner bikes, Hans Tausensgade 19, tel. 66 12 14 27, fax 66 12 14 13, www.domir.dk, booking@domir.dk). They also run **Ydes Hotel,** just down the street, with industrial and metallic simplicity (about 50-70 kr cheaper).

$$ Blommenslyst B&B rents four rooms in two private guesthouses just outside Odense (S-330 kr, D-460 kr, breakfast-70 kr, 10-minute drive from town center, Ravnebjerggyden 31, tel. 65 96 81 88, www.blommenslyst.dk, ingvartsen-speth@post.tele.dk, Marethe and Poul Erik Speth).

Hostel: **$ Danhostel Odense City** is a huge, efficient hostel towering above the train station, with 140 beds in 4- and 6-bed rooms with baths, plus private rooms. "Better" rooms have "better beds and a TV"; the room prices listed here reflect standard/better rooms (dorm bed-250 kr, Sb-450/500 kr, Db-620/670 kr, sheets-60 kr, breakfast-65 kr—it can add up, elevator, pay Internet access, free Wi-Fi, laundry, reception open 8:00-12:00 & 16:00-20:00 but self-service check-in kiosk at other times, Østre Stationsvej 31, tel. 63 11 04 25, odensedanhostel.dk, info@cityhostel.dk).

Eating in Odense

If you are in town for just a short stopover to visit the Hans Christian Andersen House, consider the café at the museum for lunch. Otherwise, Odense's main pedestrian shopping streets, **Vestergade** and **Kongensgade,** offer the best atmosphere and most options for lunch and dinner.

Vintapperstræde is an alleyway full of restaurants just off Vestergade (look for the ornamental entryway). Choose from Danish, Mexican, Italian, and more. Study the menus posted outside each restaurant to decide, then grab a table inside or join the locals at an outdoor table.

Odense Connections

From Odense by Train to: Copenhagen (3/hour, 1.75 hours, some go direct to the airport), **Aarhus** (2/hour, 1.5 hours), **Billund/ Legoland** (2/hour, 50-minute train to Vejle; transfer to bus #43, #143, #166, or #179; allow 2 hours total), **Svendborg/Ærø ferry** (2/hour on Mon-Sat, hourly on Sun, 45 minutes, to Svendborg dock—Ærø ferry runs 5-6/day, 75-minute crossing), **Roskilde** (2/ hour, 70 minutes).

CENTRAL DENMARK

Route Tips for Drivers

Aarhus or Billund to Ærø: Figure about two hours to drive from Billund (or 2.5 hours from Aarhus) to Svendborg. The freeway takes you over a bridge to the island of Funen (or *Fyn* in Danish); from Odense, take the highway south to Svendborg.

Leave your car in Svendborg (at the convenient long-term parking lot two blocks from the ferry dock or at the far end of the harbor near the Bendix fish shop) and sail for Ærø. It's an easy 75-minute crossing; note there are only five or six boats a day. Cars need reservations but walk-on passengers don't.

Ærø to Copenhagen via Odense: From Svendborg, drive north following signs to *Fëborg*, past Egeskov Castle, and on to Odense. For the open-air folk museum (Den Fynske Landsby), leave Route 9 just south of town at Højby, turning left toward Dalum and the Odense campground (on Odensevej). Look for *Den Fynske Landsby* signs (near the train tracks, south edge of town). If you're going directly to the Hans Christian Andersen House, follow the signs.

Continuing toward Copenhagen, you'll take the world's third-longest suspension bridge (Storebælt Bridge, 220-kr toll, 12.5 miles long). Follow signs marked *København* (Copenhagen). If you're following my three-week itinerary by car: When you get to Ringsted, signs point you to Roskilde—aim toward the twin church spires and follow signs for *Vikingskibene* (Viking ships). Otherwise, if you're heading to Copenhagen or the airport, stay on the freeway, following signs to *København C* or to *Dragør/Kastrup Airport*.

JUTLAND

Aarhus • Legoland • Jelling

Jutland (Jylland—pronounced "YEW-lan"—in Danish) is the part of Denmark that juts up from Germany. It's a land of windswept sandy beaches, inviting lakes, Lego toys, moated manor houses, and fortified old towns. In Aarhus, the lively and student-filled capital of Jutland, you can ogle the artwork in one of Denmark's best art museums, experience centuries-old Danish town life in its open-air folk museum, and meet a boggy prehistoric man. After you wander the pedestrian street, settle in to nurse a drink along the canalside people zone. This region is particularly family-friendly. Make a pilgrimage to the most famous land in all of Jutland: the pint-sized kids' paradise, Legoland. The nearby village of Jelling is worth a quick stop to see the ancient rune stones known as "Denmark's birth certificate."

Planning Your Time

Aarhus makes a natural stop for drivers connecting Kristiansand, Norway and Hirtshals, Denmark by ferry. Trains also link Aarhus to Hirtshals, as well as to points south, such as Odense and Copenhagen. Allow one day and an overnight to enjoy this busy port town.

Families will likely want a whole day at Legoland (near the town of Billund), while historians might consider a brief detour to Jelling, just 10 minutes off the main Billund-Vejle road. Both are best by car but are doable by public transportation.

Aarhus

Aarhus (OAR-hoos, sometimes spelled Århus), Denmark's second-largest city, has a population of 243,000 and calls itself the "World's Smallest Big City." I'd argue it's more like the world's biggest little town: easy to handle and easy to like. Aarhus is Jutland's capital and cultural hub. Its Viking founders settled here—where a river hit the sea—in the eighth century, calling their town Aros. Today, modern Aarhus bustles with an impor-

tant university, an inviting café-lined canal, a bursting-with-life pedestrian boulevard (Strøget), a collection of top-notch museums (modern art, open-air folk, and prehistory), and an adorable "Latin Quarter" filled with people living very, very well. Aarhus, a pleasant three-hour train ride from Copenhagen, is worth a stop.

Orientation to Aarhus

Aarhus lines up along its tranquil canal—formerly a busy highway—called Åboulevarden, which runs through the middle of town. The cathedral and lively Latin Quarter are directly north of the canal, while the train station is about five blocks to the south (along the main pedestrianized shopping street—the Strøget). The main museums are scattered far and wide: The ARoS Art Museum is at the western edge of downtown, the Den Gamle By open-air folk museum is a bit farther to the northwest, and the Moesgård Museum (prehistory—and closed for renovation until 2014) is in the countryside far to the south.

Tourist Information

The Aarhus TI has become entirely virtual (www.visitaarhus.com). There's no office and no telephone number; to fill the gap, the local tourist board has installed computer kiosks that access the TI website in various hotel lobbies around town. But if you have a question, try asking your hotelier or other helpful locals. Hotels sell the **Aarhus Card,** which provides small discounts on major sights and free entry to some minor sights, and includes public transportation. This can be a money-saver for busy sightseers (129 kr/1 day, 179 kr/2 days).

Arrival in Aarhus

At Aarhus' user-friendly train station, all tracks feed into a concourse, with ticket offices *(billetsalg)* and a waiting room between tracks 2-3 and 4-5. One direction (marked *Bruun's Galleri*), takes you directly into a shopping mall; the other direction (under the clock), leads into the blocky main terminal hall, with lockers (20-40 kr), fast food, and automated ticket machines. Near the main doors, notice electronic screens showing departure times for upcoming city and regional buses.

To get into town, it's a pleasant 10-minute walk: Exit straight ahead, cross the street, and proceed up the wide, traffic-free shopping street known as the Strøget, which takes you directly to the canal, cathedral, and start of my self-guided walk.

Aarhus Center

Self-Guided Walk

1 Aarhus Cathedral
2 Cathedral Square
3 Hotel Royal
4 Viking Museum
5 Aarhus Theater
6 Church of Our Lady
7 Møllestien
8 Canal (Åboulevarden)

Hotels, Restaurants & Services

9 Villa Provence
10 Hotel Guldsmeden
11 Best Western Hotel Ritz
12 Scandic Plaza Aarhus Hotel
13 Cab-Inn
14 To Danhostel Aarhus
15 City Sleep In
16 Lecoq Restaurant
17 Den Rustikke Brasserie
18 Pilhkjær Restaurant
19 Jacob's Pita Bar
20 Sota Sushi
21 Carlton Brasserie
22 Åboulevarden Canal Eateries
23 Bryggeriet Sct. Clemens
24 Teater Bodega
25 To Launderette

JUTLAND

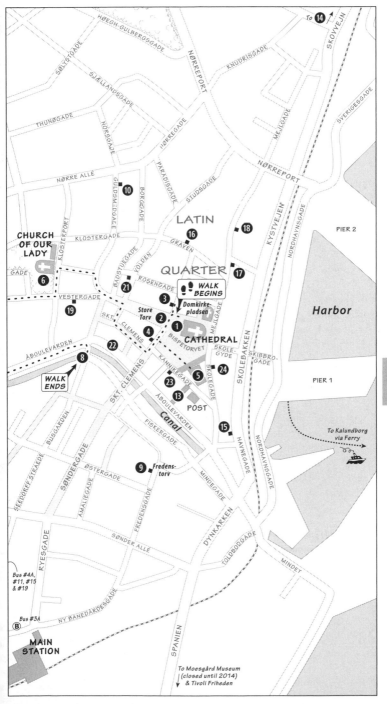

Getting Around Aarhus

The sights mentioned in my self-guided walk and the ARoS Art Museum are all within a 15-minute walk; the Den Gamle By open-air folk museum is a few minutes farther, but still walkable. The Moesgård Museum (prehistory; closed until 2014) and Tivoli Friheden (amusement park) are best reached by bus.

You can buy bus tickets from the coin-op machines on board the bus (a 20-kr, 2-zone ticket covers any of my recommended sights, and is good for 2 hours). Bus drivers are friendly and speak English.

A few local buses leave from in front of the train station, but most depart around the corner, along Park Allé in front of the Town Hall. Bus #3A to the Den Gamle By open-air folk museum leaves from a stop across the street from the station. Other buses leave from in front of the Town Hall, about two blocks away: Cross the street in front of the station, turn left and walk to the first major corner, then turn right up Park Allé; the stops are in front of the blocky Town Hall (with the boxy tower, on the left). From here, buses #4A, #11, #15, and #19 go to Den Gamle By; bus #16 goes to the Tivoli Friheden amusement park; and bus #18 goes to the Moesgård Museum. To help you find your bus stop, look for the handy bus-stop diagram at the start of the Strøget.

Taxis are easy to flag down but pricey (30-kr drop fee).

Helpful Hints

Internet Access: Many hotels, cafés, and restaurants offer free Wi-Fi.

Laundry: An unstaffed, coin-op launderette *(mønt-vask)* is four short blocks south of the train station, on the square in front of St. Paul's Church (daily 7:30-21:00, bring lots of coins—30 kr to wash, about 25 kr to dry, 5 kr for soap, M.P. Bruunsgade 64).

Self-Guided Walk

Welcome to Aarhus

This quick little walk acquaints you with the historic center, covering everything of sightseeing importance except the three big museums (modern art, prehistory, and open-air folk). You'll begin at the cathedral, check out the modest sights in its vicinity, wander the cute Latin Quarter, take a stroll down the "most beautiful street" in Aarhus, and end at the canal. After touring the impressive cathedral, the rest of the walk should take about an hour.

• *Start by touring Aarhus Cathedral.*

▲▲Aarhus Cathedral (Domkirke)

While Scandinavia's biggest church (330 feet long and tall) is typically stark-white inside, it also comes with some vivid decorations dating from before the Reformation.

Cost and Hours: Free entry; May-Sept Mon and Wed-Sat 9:30-16:00, Tue 10:30-16:00; Oct-April Mon and Wed-Sat 10:00-15:00, Tue 10:30-15:00; closed Sun except for services at 12:00 and 17:00; www.aarhus-domkirke.dk.

Visiting the Cathedral: The cathedral was finished in 1520 in all its Catholic glory. Imagine it with 55 side chapels, each dedicated to a different saint and wallpapered with colorful frescos. Bad timing. Just 16 years later, in 1536, the Reformation hit and Protestants cleaned out the church—side altars gone, paintings whitewashed over—and added a pulpit mid-nave so parishioners could hear the sermon. The front pews were even turned away from the altar to face the pulpit (a problem for weddings today).

Ironically, that Lutheran whitewash protected the fine 16th-century Catholic art. When it was peeled back in the 1920s, the fres-

coes were found perfectly preserved. In 1998, the surrounding whitewash was redone, making the old original paintings, which have never been restored, pop. Noble tombs that once lined the floor (worn smooth by years of traffic) now decorate the walls. The fancy text-filled wall medallions are epitaphs, originally paired with tombs. Ships hang from the ceilings of many Danish churches (you'll find a fine example in the left transept)—in this nation of seafarers, there were invariably women praying for the safe return of their sailors.

Step into the enclosed choir area at the front of the church. The main altarpiece, dating from 1479, features the 12 apostles flanking St. Clement (the patron saint of Aarhus and sailors—his symbol is the anchor), St. Anne, and John the Baptist. On top, Jesus is crowning Mary in heaven.

JUTLAND

Head down the stairs to the apse area behind the altar. Find the model of the altarpiece, which demonstrates how the polyptych (many-paneled altarpiece) you just saw can be flipped to different scenes throughout the church year.

Also in this area, look for the fresco in the aisle (right of altar, facing windows) that shows a three-part universe: heaven, earth (at Mass), and—under the thick black line—purgatory...an ugly land with angels and devils fighting over souls. The kid on the gallows illustrates how the medieval Church threatened even little children with ugly damnation. Notice the angels trying desperately to save the damned. Just a little more money to the Church and...I...think...we...can...pull...Grandpa...OUT.

An earlier Romanesque church—just as huge—once stood on this spot. As you exit, notice the tiny, pointy-topped window in the back-right. It survives with its circa-1320 fresco from that earlier church. Even back then—when the city had a population of 1,000—the church seated 1,200. Imagine the entire community (and their dogs) assembled here to pray and worship their way through the darkness and uncertainty of medieval life.

• *Then, standing at the cathedral door, survey the...*

Cathedral Square

The long, triangular square is roughly the shape of the original Viking town from A.D. 770. Aarhus is the Viking word for "mouth of river." The river flows to your left to the beach, which—before modern land reclamation—was just behind the church. The green spire peeking over the buildings dead ahead is the Church of Our Lady (which we'll visit later on this walk). Fifty yards to the right, the nubile caryatids by local  artist Hans Krull decorate the entry to the **Hotel Royal** and town casino. (Krull's wildly decorated bar is just beyond, down the stairs at the corner.)

• *Fifty yards to the left of the church (as you face the square), in the basement of the Nordea Bank, is the tiny...*

Viking Museum

When excavating the site for the bank building in 1960, remains of Viking Aarhus were uncovered. Today you can ride an escalator down to the little bank-sponsored museum showing a surviving bit of the town's original boardwalk *in situ* (where it was found), Viking artifacts, and a murder victim (missing his head)—all well-described in English.

Cost and Hours: Free, open bank hours: Mon-Fri 10:00-16:00, Thu until 17:30, closed Sat-Sun.

• *Leaving the bank, walk straight ahead along the substantial length of the cathedral (brides have plenty of time to reconsider things during their procession) to the fancy building opposite.*

Aarhus Theater

This ornate facade, with its flowery stained glass, is Danish Art Nouveau from around 1900. Under the tiny balcony is the town  seal, featuring towers, the river, St. Clement with his anchor, and St. Paul with his sword. High above, on the roofline, crouches the devil. The local bishop made a stink when this "house of sin" was allowed to be built facing the cathedral. The theater builders had the last say, finishing their structure with this smart-aleck devil triumphing (this was a hit with the secular, modern locals).

• *Return to the square in front of the cathedral.*

Latin Quarter

The higgledy-piggledy old town encompasses the six or eight square blocks in front of the cathedral and to the right. Latin was  never spoken here—the area was named in the 1960s after the cute, boutique-ish, and similarly touristy zone in Paris. Though Aarhus' canal strip is the new trendy spot, the Latin Quarter is still great for shopping, cafés, and strolling. Explore these streets: Volden (named for the rampart), Graven (moat), and Badstuegade ("Bath Street"). In the days when fires routinely decimated towns, bathhouses—with their open fires necessary to heat the water—were located outside the walls. Back in the 15th century, finer people bathed monthly, while everyday riff-raff took their "Christmas bath" once a year.

• *Back at the far end of the cathedral square, side-trip away from the cathedral to the green spire of the...*

Church of Our Lady (Vor Frue Kirke)

The smart brick building you see today is in the Dutch Renaissance style from the 15th century, but this local "Notre-Dame" is the

oldest church in town. After Christianity came to Viking Denmark in 965, a tiny wooden church was built here. The crypt of its 11th-century stone rebuild was discovered in 1955. Four rune stones were also discovered on this site. Enter the church around the back, and climb below the main altar into an evocative arcaded space (c. 1060). Like the Aarhus Cathedral, the church's whitewashed walls are covered with fine epitaph medallions with family portraits. Step through the low door behind the rear pew (on the right with your back to the altar) into the peaceful cloister. With the Reformation, this became a hospital. Today, it's a retirement home for lucky seniors.

Cost and Hours: Free; May-Aug Mon-Fri 10:00-16:00, Sat 10:00-14:00; Sept-April Mon-Fri 10:00-14:00, Sat 10:00-12:00; closed Sun year-round, www.aarhusvorfrue.dk.

• *Walk west on Vestergade to the next street, Grønnegade. Turn left, then take the next right onto...*

Møllestien

Locals call this quiet little cobbled lane the "most beautiful street in Aarhus." The small, pastel cottages—draped in climbing roses and hollyhock in summer—date from the 18th century. Notice the small mirrors on some of the windows. Known as "street spies," they allow people inside to inconspicuously watch what's going on outside.

• *At the end of the lane, head left toward the canal. The park on your right, **Mølleparken**, is a good spot for a picnic. The big, boxy building with the rainbow ring on top is the **ARoS Art Museum** (described later, under "Sights in Aarhus")—consider visiting it now, or backtrack here when the walk is over.*

When you reach the canal, turn left and walk until you get to the concrete bridge. Stand with the Mølleparken toward your right.

Canal (Åboulevarden)

You're standing on the site of the original Viking bridge. The open sea was to the left. A protective harbor was to the right. When attacked, the bridge on this spot was raised, ships were tucked safely away, and townsmen stood here to defend their fleet. Given the choice, they'd let the town burn and save their ships.

In the 1930s, the Aarhus River was covered over to make a new road—an event marked by much celebration. In the 1980s, locals reconsidered the change, deciding that the road cut a boring, people-mean swath through the center of their town. They removed the road, artfully canalized the river, and created a trendy new people zone—the town's place to see and be seen. This strip of modern restaurants ensures the street stays as lively as possible even after the short summer.

• *Your walk is over. Following the canal to the right takes you to* **ARoS Art Museum**, *then to the* **Den Gamle By** *open-air folk museum. Following it to the left takes you past the best of the Aarhus canal zone. Crossing the canal and going straight (with a one-block jog left) gets you to the Strøget pedestrian boulevard, which leads all the way to the train station (where you can catch a bus—either at the station or the Town Hall nearby—to Tivoli Friheden amusement park, the Den Gamle By open-air folk museum, or the Moesgård Museum). All of these sights are described in the next section.*

Sights in Aarhus

▲▲**ARoS**—The Aarhus Art Museum is a must-see sight, both for the building's architecture and for its knack for making cutting-edge art accessible and fun. Everything is described in English. Square and unassuming from the outside, the bright white interior—with its spiral staircase winding up the museum's eight floors—is surprising. The building has two sections, one for the exhibits and one for administration. The halves are divided by a vast atrium, which is free to enter if you just want to peek at the building itself (or to visit the gift shop or café). But to see any of the items described below, you'll have to buy a ticket. In

addition to the permanent collections that I've described, the museum displays an impressive range of temporary exhibits—be sure to find out what's on during your visit.

Cost and Hours: 100 kr; Tue-Sun 10:00-17:00, Wed-Thu until 22:00; closed Mon, ARoS Allé 2, tel. 87 30 66 00, www.aros .dk.

Eating: The lunch café on the museum's ground floor serves 60-125-kr light meals, while the fancier restaurant on the top floor serves 190-kr lunch specials.

Visiting the Museum: After entering at the fourth-floor

lobby, buy your ticket, pick up a museum floor plan, and walk two floors down the spiral staircase (to Floor 2) to find one of the museum's prized pieces: the squatting sculpture called *Boy* (by Australian artist Ron Mueck)—15 feet high, yet astonishingly realistic, from the wrinkly skin on his elbows to the stitching on his shorts.

Next, head down to the lowest level. Here, amid black walls, artists from around the world (including Bill Viola and James Turrell) exhibit their immersive works of light and sound in each of nine spaces *(De 9 Rum)*. In this unique space, you're plunged into the imagination of the artist.

Now ride the elevator all the way to the top floor (Floor 8), then climb up the stairs (or ride a different elevator) to the rooftop.

Here you can enjoy the museum's newest icon: Olafur Eliasson's *Your Rainbow Panorama,* a 150-yard-long, 52-yard-diameter circular walkway enclosed in glass that gradually incorporates all the different colors of the spectrum. The piece provides 360-degree views over the city, while you're immersed in mind-bending, highly saturated hues. (It's "your" panorama because you are experiencing the colors.) This recent addition is a striking contrast to the mostly dark and claustrophobic works you've just seen in the nine spaces down below—yet, like those, it's all about playing with light. It's also practical—from a distance, it can be used by locals throughout the city as a giant compass (provided they know which color corresponds with which direction).

Back on Floor 8, stroll through the manageable permanent collection of works from 1770 to 1930. Paintings dating from the **Danish Golden Age** (1800-1850) are evocative of the dewy-eyed Romanticism that swept Europe during that era: pastoral scenes of flat Danish countryside and seascapes, slices of peasant life, aristocratic portraits, "postcards" from travels to the Mediterranean world, and poignant scenes of departures and arrivals at Danish seaports. The **Danish Modernist** section, next, mostly feels derivative of big-name artists (you'll see the Danish answers to Picasso, Matisse, Modigliani, and others).

Continue down the spiral staircase, past various temporary exhibits. On Floor 5, take a spin through the **contemporary art**

gallery, featuring art (including many multimedia installations) since 1980. Like the rest of this museum, these high-concept, navel-gazing works are well-presented and very accessible.

▲▲**Den Gamle By**—"The Old Town" open-air folk museum has 75 half-timbered houses and craft shops. Unlike other

Scandinavian open-air museums that focus on rural folk life, Den Gamle By is designed to give you the best possible look at Danish urban life in centuries past. A fine botanical garden is next door.

Cost: Because peak-season days offer more activities, the cost depends on the time of year. July-mid-Sept: 125 kr, April-June and mid-Sept-mid-Nov: 100 kr; Jan-March: 50 kr; mid-Nov-Dec: special Christmas themed events and prices.

Hours: Daily July-mid-Sept 10:00-18:00; shorter hours off-season. After hours, the buildings of the open-air museum are locked, but the peaceful park is open (tel. 86 12 31 88, www.den gamleby.dk).

Getting There: Stroll 20 minutes up the canal from downtown, or catch a bus from near the train station: Bus #3A departs directly across the street from the station, while others (#4A, #11, #15, and #19) depart across the street from the Town Hall, on Park Allé.

Eating: This is a perfect place to enjoy a picnic lunch (bring your own, or order a lunch packet at the reception desk by the ticket booth)—outdoor and indoor tables are scattered around the grounds. The only eatery in the park open year-round is the cheery indoor/outdoor Simonsens Have, an inviting cafeteria serving affordable light meals (30-kr sandwiches, three *smørrebrød* for 60 kr). In peak season, you'll have many other options, including *pølse* and other snack stands, a café next to the ticket kiosk, and Wineke's Cellar, an 18th-century public house serving beer, wine, and sandwiches (in the basement of the Mintmaster's Mansion).

Visiting the Museum: At the ticket desk, pick up the free map of the grounds; also pick up the flier listing what's on (and plan your time around taking advantage of those options). Though each building is described with a plaque, and there are maps throughout the park, the 50-kr guidebooklet is a worthwhile investment and a nice souvenir.

The grounds reward an adventurous spirit. They're designed to be explored, so don't be too shy to open doors or poke into seemingly abandoned courtyards—you may find a chatty docent inside, telling their story, answering questions, or demonstrating an

JUTLAND

old-timey handicraft. Follow sounds and smells to discover a whole world beyond the main streets.

The main part of the exhibit focuses on the 18th and 19th centuries. You'll start by heading up Navnløs, then hanging a right at Vestergade (passing a row house and a flower garden with samples for sale) to the canal. Head straight over the bridge and hike up the cute street lined with market stalls, shops, and a bakery until you pop out on the main square, Torvet. The building on the left side of Torvet, the Mayor's House (from 1597), contains a museum upstairs featuring home interiors from 1600 to 1850, including many with gorgeously painted walls. At the top of Torvet is the Mintmaster's Mansion, the residence of a Copenhagen noble (from 1683). Enter around back to tour the boldly colorful, 18th-century Baroque rooms. Under the heavy timbers of the attic is an exhibit about the history of this recently restored building.

Continuing out the far end of Torvet on Søndergade, you enter the 20th century. The streets and shops here evoke the year 1927, including a hardware store and (down Havbogade) a brewery where you can often buy samples (in the courtyard behind). At the end of Søndergade (on the left) is the Legetoj toy museum, with two floors of long hallways crammed with nostalgic playthings.

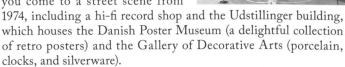

Walking into the next zone, you come to a street scene from 1974, including a hi-fi record shop and the Udstillinger building, which houses the Danish Poster Museum (a delightful collection of retro posters) and the Gallery of Decorative Arts (porcelain, clocks, and silverware).

The area under construction on the right is where they are re-creating a harborfront area from the 1970s (due to open in 2014). Continue down along the construction zone, cross the canal, and turn right (back toward the entrance). You'll pass idyllic pond scenery and the Simonsens Have cafeteria, before winding up at the bridge you crossed earlier.

Moesgård Museum—The museum is closed until 2014, when its brand-new, state-of-the art building is due to open south of town. Billed as "cultural history in a new setting," the sloping build-

ing will emerge from the fields, with grass growing on the roof; in addition to the existing prehistory collection, plans call for new exhibits on ethnography and the Arabian Gulf, plus space for temporary exhibits (tel. 89 42 11 00, www.moesmus.dk).

Tivoli Friheden Amusement Park—The local Tivoli, about a mile south of the train station, offers great fun for the family.

Cost and Hours: 80 kr for entry only, 215 kr includes rides; daily early July-early Aug 11:00-22:00, May-early July and early Aug-Sept weekends only and shorter hours, closed Oct-April except special events; bus #16 from Park Allé near Town Hall, tel. 86 14 73 00, www.friheden.dk.

Sleeping in Aarhus

My recommendations include the following: two tired business hotels facing the train station with rates that flex with demand (a good value if booked in advance and arriving on a weekend or in the summer); two charming hotels with personality; a stripped-down, functional, Motel 6-type place; and two backpacker/student-friendly hostels.

$$$ Villa Provence, named for owners Steen and Annette's favorite vacation destination, is a *petit* taste of France in the center of Aarhus, and makes a very cozy and convenient home base. Its 40 fun-yet-tasteful rooms, decorated with antique furniture and old French movie posters, surround a quiet courtyard. Prices vary depending on the size and elegance of the room (Sb-1,095-2,300 kr, Db-1,295-2,900 kr, free Wi-Fi, parking-125 kr/day, 10-minute walk from station, near Åboulevarden at the end of Fredensgade, Fredens Torv 12, tel. 86 18 24 00, fax 86 18 24 03, www.villaprovence.dk, hotel@villaprovence.dk).

$$$ Hotel Guldsmeden ("Dragonfly") is a small, welcoming, and clean hotel with 27 rooms, fluffy comforters, a delightful stay-awhile garden, and a young, disarmingly friendly staff. A steep staircase takes you to the best rooms (Sb-1,195 kr, Db-1,325 kr), while the cheaper rooms (five rooms sharing two bathrooms) are in a ground-floor annex behind the garden (S-745 kr, D-945 kr; extra bed-250 kr, 10 percent off rooms with private bath with this book based on availability, free Wi-Fi, 15-minute walk or 70-kr taxi from the station, in Aarhus' quiet Latin Quarter at Guldsmedgade 40, tel. 86 13 45 50, fax 86 13 76 76, www.hotelguldsmeden.com, aarhus@hotelguldsmeden.com).

Sleep Code

(6 kr = about $1, country code: 45)
S = Single, **D** = Double/Twin, **T** = Triple, **Q** = Quad, **b** = bathroom, **s** = shower. You can assume credit cards are accepted and breakfast is included unless otherwise noted.

To help you sort easily through these listings, I've divided the accommodations into three categories based on the price for a standard double room with bath during high season:

  $$$ Higher Priced—Most rooms 1,000 kr or more.
  $$ Moderately Priced—Most rooms between 500-1,000 kr.
  $ Lower Priced—Most rooms 500 kr or less.

Prices can change without notice; verify the hotel's current rates online or by email.

$$$ Best Western Hotel Ritz, also across the street from the station, has 67 older but clean rooms. It's a bit less welcoming than my other listings (tiny budget Sb-765 kr, Sb-850-1,200 kr, Db-1,000-1,400 kr, bigger "superior" Db-1,300-1,600 kr, higher rates are for weekdays while lower rates are for weekends and summer, elevator, free Internet access and Wi-Fi, Banegårdspladsen 12, tel. 86 13 44 44, fax 86 13 45 87, www.hotelritz.dk, mail@hotelritz.dk).

$$ Scandic Plaza Aarhus Hotel rents 162 sleek, well-furnished, business-class rooms 100 yards from the station (weekends and summer: Db-800-1,140 kr; weekdays: Db-1,240-1,915 kr; check website for best deals, kids under age 13 free, elevator, free Internet access and Wi-Fi, gym, Banegårdspladsen 14, tel. 87 32 01 00, fax 87 32 01 99, www.scandichotels.com, plaza.aarhus @scandichotels.com). They offer a 12-20 percent discount for pre-paid, nonrefundable "early rate" online bookings.

$$ Cab-Inn, overlooking the atmospheric Åboulevarden canal, is extremely practical. Its 197 simple, minimalist-yet-comfy little rooms each come with a single bed that expands into a twin and one or two fold-down bunks on the walls. The service, like the rooms, is no-nonsense (Sb-495 kr, Db-625-805 kr, Tb-805 kr, Qb-935 kr, breakfast-70 kr, free Wi-Fi, easy parking-80 kr—reserve ahead, rooms overlook boisterous canal or quieter courtyard, Kannikegade 14, tel. 86 75 70 00, fax 86 75 71 00, www.cabinn.dk, aarhus@cabinn.dk).

$ Danhostel Aarhus, an official HI hostel with six-bed dorms and plenty of two- and four-bed rooms, is near the water two miles out of town (dorm bed-200 kr, S/D-380-506 kr, Sb/Db-570-670 kr, price depends on season, nonmembers-35 kr/night extra, sheets-45 kr, towels-10 kr, adult breakfast-59 kr, kids break-fast-29 kr, pay Wi-Fi, laundry, served by several buses from the train station—see website for details, Marienlundsvej 10, tel. 86 21 21 20, www.aarhus-danhostel.dk, info@aarhus-danhostel.dk).

$ City Sleep In, a creative independent hostel, has a shared kitchen, fun living and games room, laundry service, and lockers. It's on a busy road facing the harbor (with thin windows—expect some street noise), a 15-minute hike from the station. It's pretty grungy, but is the only centrally located budget option in town (170 kr/bunk in 4- to 6-bed dorms, D-440 kr, Db-500 kr, extra bed-120 kr, sheets-50 kr, towel-20 kr, breakfast-65 kr, elevator, free Internet access and Wi-Fi; no curfew; reception open daily 8:00-11:00 & 16:00-19:00 & 19:30-21:00, Fri-Sat until 23:00; Havnegade 20, tel. 86 19 20 55, fax 86 19 18 11, www.citysleep-in .dk, sleep-in@citysleep-in.dk).

Eating in Aarhus

Affluent Aarhus has plenty of great little restaurants. All of these are in the old town, within a few minutes' stroll from the cathedral.

In the Latin Quarter

The streets of the Latin Quarter are teeming with hardworking and popular eateries. The street called Mejlgade, along the western edge of downtown, has a smattering of youthful, trendy restaurants that are just far enough off the tourist trail to feel local.

Lecoq is a pricey favorite. Chef/owner Troels Thomsen and his youthful gang (proud alums from a prestigious Danish cooking school) serve up a fresh twist on traditional French cuisine in a single Paris-pleasant yet unassuming 10-table room. They pride themselves on their finely crafted presentation. Reservations are smart (300-kr three-course meals, 200-kr main dishes, 100-kr starters, Thu 16:00-24:00, Fri 15:00-24:00, Sat-Wed 17:00-24:00, Graven 16, tel. 86 19 50 74). The attached bar, with outdoor seating, serves drinks only.

Den Rustikke is a French-style brasserie offering affordable, mostly French dishes, either in the rollicking interior or outside, under a cozy colonnade (45-85-kr lunches, 165-kr three-course dinners, daily 11:30-15:00 & 17:00-late, Mejlgade 20, tel. 86 12 00 95).

Pilhkjær is a bit more sedate, filling a cellar with elegantly casual atmosphere. The menu changes daily and is available only as a 300-kr, three-course meal—no à la carte (Tue-Thu 17:30-22:30, Fri-Sat 17:30-23:30, closed Sun-Mon, at the end of a long courtyard at Mejlgade 28, tel. 86 18 23 30).

Cheap Eats: *Jacob's* **Pita Bar** is a popular spot for pita sandwiches that are a cut above the average *shawarma*. Choose from

JUTLAND

grilled beef, chicken, lamb, ground beef, or turkey and melted cheese, plus your choice of a wide selection of sauces. These sandwiches are great for an inexpensive, quick meal: Sit at the counter, or get your order to go and find a spot to sit on the nearby square, along the canal, or Møllerparken (46-kr pita sandwiches, "menu" with fries and a drink-78 kr, Mon-Thu 11:00-21:00, Fri-Sat 11:00 until late, Sun 17:00-21:00, Vestergade 3, tel. 87 32 24 20). The pita bar is part of the adjacent, decent but overpriced steak house, Jacob's BarBQ (nightly until the wee hours).

Sushi: A few short blocks farther from the action (past the Church of Our Lady), **Sota** is a local favorite for sushi. This split-level sushi bar, in a half-timbered old house, is a sleek Tokyo-Scandinavian hybrid (50-90-kr rolls, 120-190-kr combo meals, pricier splurges available, Mon-Thu 16:00-22:00, Fri-Sat 16:00-23:00, closed Sun, Vestergade 47, tel. 86 47 47 88).

Carlton Brasserie, facing a pretty square, is a solid bet for good Danish and international food in classy (verging on stuffy) surroundings. The restaurant has tables on the square, with more formal seating in back (inviting menu, 135-235-kr plates, 380-kr formal three-course dinner, closed Sun, Rosensgade 23, tel. 86 20 21 22).

Along Åboulevarden Canal

The canal running through town is lined with trendy eateries—all overpriced unless you value making the scene with the locals (and all open daily until late). They have indoor and canalside seating with heaters and blankets, so diners can eat outdoors even when it's cold. Before settling in, cruise the entire strip, giving special consideration to **Cross Café** (with red awnings, right at main bridge) and **Ziggy,** both of which are popular for salads, sandwiches, burgers, and drinks; and **Grappa,** a classy Italian place with 95-135-kr pastas and pizzas, as well as pricier plates. Several places along here serve basic 25-45-kr breakfast buffets, which are popular with students for brunch.

Near the Cathedral

These places, while a bit past their prime and touristy, are convenient and central.

Bryggeriet Sct. Clemens (St. Clement's Brewery), facing the cathedral, is a bright, convivial, fun-loving, and woody land of happy eaters and drinkers. Choose from a hearty menu and eat amid shiny copper vats. If you're dropping by for just a beer, they have enticing 40-80-kr beer snacks—including little *Nürnberger* bratwurst (80-105-kr lunch and light meals; 175-270-kr hearty dinners such as steak, ribs, and fish; Mon-Sat 11:30-24:00, closed Sun, Kannikegade 10-12, tel. 86 13 80 00).

JUTLAND

Teater Bodega is the venerable best bet for traditional Danish—where local men go for "food their wives won't cook." While a bit tired and old-fashioned for Aarhus' trendy young student population, it's a sentimental favorite for old-timers. Facing the theater and cathedral, it's dressy and draped in theater memorabilia (130-230-kr main dishes, 60-110-kr open-face sandwiches at lunch only, Mon-Sat 11:30-22:30, closed Sun, Skolegade 7, tel. 86 12 19 17).

Aarhus Connections

From Aarhus by Train to: Odense (2/hour, 1.5 hours), **Copenhagen** (1-2/hour, 3 hours), **Ærøskøbing** (5-6/day, transfer to ferry in Svendborg, total trip-4.25 hours, sample schedules: 10:27-14:45 or 13:27-17:45), **Hamburg, Germany** (2 direct/day, more with transfers, 5 hours), **Hirtshals/Ferry to Kristiansand, Norway** (hourly, 2.5-3 hours; to meet the Color Line ferry, transfer at Hjørring and continue to Hirtshals Havn; note that railpasses don't cover the Hjørring-Hirtshals train—www.rejseplanen.com—but do give a 50 percent discount; buy your ticket in Hjørring or on board; for the latest ferry schedule, see www.colorline.com).

Route Tips for Drivers
From the Ferry Dock at Hirtshals to Jutland Destinations: From the dock in Hirtshals, drive south (signs to *Hjørring, Ålborg*). It's about 2.5 hours to Aarhus. (To skip Aarhus, skirt the center and follow E45 south.) To get to downtown **Aarhus,** follow signs to the center, then *Domkirke*. Park in the pay lot across from the cathedral. Signs all over town direct you to Den Gamle By open-air folk museum. From Aarhus, it's 60 miles to Billund/Legoland (go south on Skanderborg Road and get on E45; follow signs to *Vejle, Kolding*). For **Jelling,** take the *Vejle N* exit and follow signs to *Vejle,* then veer right on the ring road (following signs to *Skovgade*), then follow Route 442 north. For **Legoland,** take the *Vejle S* exit for Billund (after *Vejle N*—it's the first exit after the dramatic Vejlefjord bridge).

JUTLAND

Legoland

Legoland is Scandinavia's top kids' sight. If you have a child (or are a child at heart), it's a fun stop. This huge park is a happy com-
bination of rides, restaurants, trees, smiles, and 33 million Lego bricks creatively arranged into such wonders as Mount Rushmore, the Parthenon, "Mad" King Ludwig's castle, and the Statue of Liberty. It's a Lego world here, as everything is cleverly related to this popu-
lar toy. If your time in Denmark is short, or if your family has already visited a similar Legoland park in California, England, or Germany, consider skipping the trip. But if you're in the neighbor-
hood, a visit to the mothership of all things Lego will be a hit with kids ages two through the pre-teens.

Cost: 299 kr entry includes all rides (279 kr for kids ages 3-12 and over 65). Legoland generally doesn't charge in the evening (free after 19:30 in July and late Aug, otherwise after 17:30). Tel. 75 33 13 33, www.legoland.dk.

Hours: Generally April-Oct daily 10:00-18:00, until 20:00 Sat-Sun and most of Aug, until 21:00 daily early July-early Aug, closed Nov-March and Wed-Thu in Sept-mid-Oct. Activities close an hour before the park, but it's basically the same place after dinner as during the day, with fewer tour groups.

Crowd-Beating Tips: Legoland is crowded during the Danish summer school vacation, from early July through mid-August. To bypass the ticket line, purchase tickets in advance (simply scan them at the entry turnstile). Advance tickets are sold online at www.legoland.dk (reduced-price family tickets also available), and at many Danish locations (at stores, hotels, and TIs), including the Dagli' Brugsen store in Vandel, just west of Billund. Advance tickets include a 30-kr food-and-drink coupon and a 40-kr coupon for certain special activities.

Money-Saving Deals: If a one-day visit is not enough, you can pay an extra 99 kr (once at the park) to cover the following day's admission. If you hate waiting in lines, consider shelling out for the Express Pass add-on, which allows holders to skip to the front of the (often long) lines for up to eight rides. The cost is based on the user's height—59 kr for kids 100-119 cm tall (3'3"-3'11"), and 99 kr for those 120 cm (3'11") and taller.

Getting There: Legoland, located in the town of Billund, is easiest to visit by car, but doable by public transportation. The nearest train station to Billund is Vejle. Trains arrive at Vejle from **Copenhagen** (hourly, 2.25 hours), **Odense** (2/hour, 50 minutes), and **Aarhus** (3/hour, 45 minutes). At Vejle, catch the bus (generally #43, #143, #166, or #179) to travel the remaining 25 miles to Billund (30-45 minutes). For train and bus details, see www.rejseplanen.dk.

Eating: Surprisingly, the park's restaurants don't serve Legolamb, but there are plenty of other food choices. Prices are high, so consider bringing a picnic to enjoy at one of the several spots set aside for bring-it-yourselfers.

Background: Lego began in 1932 in the workshop of a local carpenter who named his wooden toys after the Danish phrase *leg godt* ("play well"). In 1949, the company started making the plastic interlocking building bricks for which they are world famous. Since then, Lego has continued to expand its lineup and now produces everything from Ninjago ninja warriors to motorized models, Clikits jewelry, board games, and video games—many based on popular movies (*Lego Star Wars, Lego Harry Potter*, etc.)—making kids drool in languages all around the world. According to the company, each person on this planet has, on average, 62 Lego blocks.

Self-Guided Tour

Legoland is divided into eight different "worlds" with fun themes such as Adventure Land, Pirate Land, and Knight's Kingdom.

Pick up a brochure at the entrance and make a plan using the colorful 3-D map. You can see it all in a day, but you'll be exhausted. The Legoredo section (filled with Wild West clichés Europeans will enjoy more than Americans) merits just a quick look, though your five-year-old might enjoy roasting a biscuit-on-a-stick around the fire with a tall, blond park employee wearing a Native American headdress.

A highlight for young and old alike is Miniland (near the entrance), where landscaped gardens are filled with carefully constructed Lego landscapes and cityscapes. Anyone who has ever picked up a Lego block will marvel at seeing representations of the world's famous sights, including Danish monuments, Dutch windmills, German castles, and an amazing representation of the Norwegian harbor of Bergen. Children joyfully watch as tiny Lego boats ply the waters and Lego trains chug merrily along the tracks.

Nearby, kids can go on mellow rides in child-size cars, trains, and boats. A highlight of Miniland is the Traffic School, where young drivers (ages 7-13) learn the rules of the road and get a souvenir license. (If interested in this popular attraction, make a reservation upon arrival.)

More rides are scattered throughout the park. While the rides aren't thrilling by Disneyland standards, most kids will find something to enjoy (parents should check the brochure for strictly enforced height restrictions). The Falck Fire Brigade ride in Lego City invites family participation as you team up to put out a (fake) fire. The Temple is an Indiana Jones-esque Egyptian-themed treasure hunt/shoot-'em-up, and the Dragon roller coaster takes you in and around a medieval castle. Note that on a few rides (including the Pirate Splash Battle), you'll definitely get wet. Special walk-in, human-sized dryers help you warm up and dry off.

The indoor museum features company history, high-tech Lego creations, a great doll collection, and a toy exhibit full of mechanical wonders from the early 1900s, many ready to jump into action with the push of a button. A Lego playroom encourages hands-on fun, and a campground is across the street if your kids refuse to move on.

Nearby: Those looking for water fun with a tropical theme can check out the Aquadome (one of Europe's largest water parks), located outside Legoland in Billund at the family resort of Lalandia (www.lalandia.dk).

Sleeping near Legoland

(6 kr = about $1, country code: 45)
$$$ Legoland Hotel adjoins Legoland (Sb-1,600 kr, Db-1,900 kr, special family deals: 3,000 kr for room big enough for 2 adults and 2 kids, some room prices include 2-day admission to park, prices slightly lower Sept-May or for 2 or more nights, free Wi-Fi, tel. 75 33 12 44, fax 75 35 38 10, www.hotellegoland.dk, hotel@lego land.dk).

$$$ Hotel Svanen is close by, in Billund (standard Sb-1,095 kr, standard Db-1,195 kr, fancier rooms cost more, extra child's bed-100 kr, free Wi-Fi, Nordmarksvej 8, tel. 75 33 28 33, fax 75 35 35 15, www.hotelsvanen.dk, info@hotelsvanen.dk).

$$ Legoland Village is a family hostel-type place offering inexpensive rooms that sleep one to five people (Db-585-985 kr, Tb-895-1,045 kr, Qb-975-1,135 kr, Quint/b-860-1,265 kr, higher prices are for mid-May-late Sept, sheets and towels-70 kr/person, Ellehammers Allé 2, tel. 75 33 27 77, fax 75 33 28 77, www.lego land-village.dk, info@legoland-village.dk).

Private Rooms: Private rooms are key to a budget visit here. In a forest just outside of Billund, Erik and Mary Sort run **$ Gregersminde,** with a great setup: six double rooms, plus a cottage that sleeps up to six people. Their guests enjoy a huge living room, a kitchen, lots of Lego toys, and a kid-friendly yard (S-200-300 kr, Sb 260-390 kr, D-320-350 kr, Db-380-450 kr, cottage-660-750 kr—towels and sheets extra, higher prices are for June-Sept, breakfast-50-60 kr, cash only, 10 percent cheaper for 2 nights or more, free Internet access, rental bikes-15 kr, cash only, leave Billund on Grindsted Road, turn right on Stilbjergvej, go a half-mile to Stilbjergvej 4B, tel. 61 27 33 23, www.gregersminde .dk, info@gregersminde.dk).

Jelling

On your way to or from Legoland, consider a short side-trip to the tiny village of Jelling (pronounced "YELL-ing"), a place of

immense importance in Danish history. Here you'll find two rune stones, set next to a 900-year-old church that's flanked by two enormous, man-made burial mounds. The two stones are often called "Denmark's birth certificate"—the first written record of Denmark's status as a nation-state. An excellent (and free) museum lies just across the street.

Two hours is ample for a visit. If pressed for time, an hour is enough to see the stones and take a quick look at the museum. Note that the museum is closed on Monday.

Jelling is too small for a TI, but the museum staff can answer most questions. If you're here around lunchtime, Jelling is a great spot for a picnic. There are several central eateries and a café and WC inside the museum, and another WC in the parking lot near the North Mound.

Getting There: Drivers can easily find Jelling, just 10 minutes off the main Vejle-Billund road. Train travelers coming from Copenhagen or Aarhus must change in Vejle, which is connected to Jelling by hourly trains (direction: Herning) and bus #211.

Self-Guided Walk

Denmark is proud of being Europe's oldest monarchy and of the fact that Queen Margrethe II, the country's current ruler, can trace her lineage back 1,300 years to this sacred place.

• *Begin your visit at the...*

Kongernes Jelling Museum: Inside this modern, light-filled building you'll find informative exhibits, historical models of the area, and replicas of the rune stones. Kids will love the room in the back on the ground level where they can write their name in the runic alphabet—and the gift shop bristling with wooden swords and Viking garb (free, June-Aug Tue-Sun 10:00-17:00, Sept-May Tue-Sun 12:00-16:00, closed between Christmas and New Year's and on Mon year-round, café, tel. 75 87 23 50, www.kongernes jelling.dk).

• *Cross the street and walk through the graveyard to examine the actual...*

Rune Stones: The stones stand just south of the church. The modern bronze-and-glass structure is designed to protect the stones from the elements while allowing easy viewing.

The smaller stone was erected by King Gorm the Old (a.k.a. Gorm the Sleepy), who ruled Denmark for 40 years in the ninth century. You probably don't read runic so I'll translate: *"King Gorm made this monument in memory of Thyra, his wife, Denmark's salvation."* These are the oldest recorded words of a Danish king, and the first time that the name Denmark is used to describe a country and not just the region.

The **larger stone** was erected by Gorm's son, Harald Bluetooth, to honor his parents, commemorate the conquering of Denmark and Norway, and mark the conversion of the Danes to Christianity. (Bluetooth technology—which transmits electronic data wirelessly—takes its name from Harald, who created the decidedly non-wireless connection between the Danish and Norwegian peoples.)

Harald was a shrewd politician who had practical reasons for being baptized. He knew that if he declared Denmark to be a Christian land, he could save it from possible attack by the predatory German bishops to the south. The inscription reads: *"King Harald ordered this monument made in memory of Gorm, his father, and in memory of Thyra, his mother; that Harald who won for himself all of Denmark and Norway and made the Danes Christian."*

This large stone has three sides. One side reveals an image of Jesus and a cross, while the other has a serpent wrapped around a lion. This is important imagery that speaks to the transition from Nordic paganism to Christianity. These designs carved into the rock were once brightly painted.

• *Go around the back of the church and climb the steps to the 35-foot-high, grass-covered...*

North Mound: According to tradition, Gorm was buried in a chamber inside this mound, with his queen Thyra interred in the smaller mound to the south. But excavations in the 1940s turned up no royal remains in either mound. (In the 1970s, what is believed to be Gorm's body was discovered below the church.) Scan the horizon and mentally remove the trees. Imagine the commanding view this site had in the past. Look north to stones that trace the outline of a ship. Below you lies a graveyard with typically Danish well-manicured plots.

• *Now descend the stairs to the...*

Church: Within the sparse interior, note the ship model hanging from the ceiling, a holdover from a pre-Christian tradition seeking a safe journey for ship and crew. The church, which dates from around 1100, is decorated with restored frescoes. A zig-zag motif is repeated in the modern windows and the inlaid floor. The metal "Z" in the floor marks the spot where Gorm's body lies.

More Jutland Sights

Himmelbjerget and Silkeborg—If you're connecting the Billund and Jelling area with Aarhus, consider this slower but more scenic route north through the idyllic Danish Lake District. (With less time, return to Vejle and take the E45 motorway.)

Himmelbjerget, best seen by car, lies in the middle of Jutland near the town of Silkeborg. Both are about an hour north of Billund (22 miles west of Aarhus). Silkeborg is accessible by train from Aarhus with a change in Skanderborg.

Denmark's landscape is vertically challenged when compared to its mountainous neighbors Norway and Sweden. If you have a hankering to ascend to one of the country's highest points, consider a visit to the 482-foot-tall **Himmelbjerget,** which translates loftily as "The Heaven Mountain." That may be overstating it, but by Danish standards the view's not bad. One can literally drive to the top, where a short trail leads to an 80-foot-tall brick tower. Climb the **tower** (small admission fee, April-Oct daily 10:00-17:00, longer hours July-mid-Sept) for a commanding view. Clouds roll by above a patchwork of green and gold fields while boats ply the blue waters of the lake below. You may see the vintage paddle steamers make the hour-long trip between Himmelbjerget and Silkeborg in season (the dock is accessed by a short hike from the tower down to the lake).

Silkeborg, in the center of the Danish Lake District, has an excellent freshwater aquarium/exhibit/nature park called **AQUA** that's worth a visit, especially if you're traveling with kids (adults-140 kr, kids 3-11-75 kr, free for kids 3 and under; Mon-Fri 10:00-16:00, Sat-Sun 10:00-17:00, longer hours in summer, closed most of Dec; tel. 89 21 21 89, www.ferskvandscentret.dk). Also in Silkeborg, modern-art lovers will enjoy the **Museum Jorn Silkeborg,** featuring colorful abstract works by Asger Jorn—a prominent member of the 1960s' COBRA movement—plus other Danish and foreign art (70 kr, free for kids 18 and under, April-Oct Tue-Sun 10:00-17:00, closed Mon, shorter hours off-season, tel. 86 82 53 88, www.museumjorn.dk).

▲**Ribe**—A Viking port 1,000 years ago, Ribe, located about 30 miles southwest of Billund, is the oldest, and possibly loveliest, town in Denmark. It's an entertaining mix of cobbled lanes and leaning medieval houses, with a fine **cathedral** with modern paintings under Romanesque arches (free entry, tower-10 kr). The **TI** can find accommodations for a booking fee (Torvet 3, tel. 75 42 15 00, www.visitribe.dk), or try **$$ Weis Stue,** a smoky, low-ceilinged, atmospheric inn, which rents primitive rooms and serves good meals (S-395 kr, D-495 kr, no breakfast, across from church, tel. 75 42 07 00, www.weis-stue.dk). Take the free **Night Watchman** tour (daily May-mid-Oct at 22:00, additional tour at 20:00 June-Aug).

PRACTICALITIES

This section covers just the basics on traveling in this region (for much more information, see *Rick Steves' Scandinavia*). You'll find free advice on specific topics at www.ricksteves.com/tips.

Money

Denmark uses the Danish kroner: 1 krone equals about $0.17. To convert prices in kroner to dollars, multiply by two, then drop a zero (e.g., 15 kr = about $3, 100 kr = about $20). Check www.oanda.com for the latest exchange rates.

The standard way for travelers to get kroner is to withdraw money from ATMs using a debit or credit card, ideally with a Visa or MasterCard logo. Before departing, call your bank or credit-card company: Confirm that your card will work overseas, ask about international transaction fees, and alert them that you'll be making withdrawals in Europe. Also ask for the PIN number for your credit card in case it'll help you use Europe's "chip-and-PIN" payment machines (see below); allow time for your bank to mail your PIN to you. To keep your valuables safe while traveling, wear a money belt.

In Denmark, many places will charge you a fee for using a credit card, so it's a good idea to ask before using your card.

Dealing with "Chip and PIN": Much of Europe (including Denmark) is adopting a "chip-and-PIN" system for credit cards, and some merchants rely on it exclusively. European chip-and-PIN cards are embedded with an electronic chip, in addition to the magnetic stripe used on our American-style cards. This means that your credit (and debit) card might not work at automated payment machines, such as those at train and subway stations, toll roads, parking garages, luggage lockers, and self-serve gas pumps. Memorizing your credit card's PIN lets you use it at some chip-and-PIN machines—just enter your PIN when prompted. If a payment machine won't take your card, look for a machine that takes cash or see if there's a cashier nearby who can process your transaction. The easiest solution is to pay for your purchases with cash you've withdrawn from an ATM using your debit card (Europe's ATMs still accept magnetic-stripe cards).

Phoning

Smart travelers use the telephone to reserve or reconfirm rooms, reserve restaurants, get directions, research transportation connections, confirm tour times, phone home, and lots more.

To call Denmark from the US or Canada: Dial 011-45 and then the local number. (The 011 is our international access code, and 45 is Denmark's country code.)

To call Denmark from a European country: Dial 00-45 followed by the local number. (The 00 is Europe's international access code.)

To call within Denmark: Dial the local number.

Tips on Phoning: A mobile phone—whether an American one that works in Denmark, or a European one you buy when you arrive—is handy, but can be pricey. If traveling with a smartphone, switch off data-roaming until you have free Wi-Fi.

To make cheap international calls, you can buy an international phone card in Denmark; these work with a scratch-to-reveal PIN code at any phone, allow you to call home to the US for pennies a minute, and also work for domestic calls.

Another option is buying an insertable phone card in Denmark. These are usable only at pay phones, are reasonable for making calls within the country, and work for international calls as well (though not as cheaply as the international phone cards). However, pay phones are becoming hard to find in Scandinavian countries. You're likely to see them only in railway stations, airports, and medical facilities. Note that insertable phone cards—and most international phone cards—work only in the country where you buy them.

Calling from your hotel-room phone is usually expensive, unless you use an international phone card. For more on phoning, see www.ricksteves.com/phoning.

Making Hotel Reservations

To ensure the best value, I recommend reserving rooms in advance, particularly during peak season. Email the hotelier with the following key pieces of information: number and type of rooms; number of nights; date of arrival; date of departure; and any special requests. (For a sample form, see www.ricksteves.com/reservation.) Use the European style for writing dates: day/month/year. For example, for a two-night stay in July, you could request: "1 double room for 2 nights, arrive 16/07/13, depart 18/07/13." Hoteliers typically ask for your credit-card number as a deposit.

Given the economic downturn, some hotels are willing to deal to attract guests—try emailing several to ask their best price. Most Scandinavian business hotels use "dynamic pricing," which means they change the room rate depending on demand—just like the airlines change their fares. This makes it extremely difficult to predict what you will pay. For many hotels, I list a range of prices. If the rate you're offered is at or near the bottom of my printed range, it's likely a good deal.

In general, hotel prices can soften if you do any of the following: offer to pay cash, stay at least three nights, or mention this book. You can also try asking for a cheaper room or a discount, or offer to skip breakfast. Business-class hotels drop prices to attract tourists with summer rates (late June–early Aug) and weekend rates (Fri, Sat, and sometimes Sun). You need to ask about these discounts.

Eating

Restaurants are often expensive. Alternate between picnics (outside or in your hotel or hostel); cheap, forgettable, but filling cafeteria or fast-food fare ($20 per person); and atmospheric, carefully chosen restaurants popular with locals ($40 per person and up). In Denmark, there is a charge for tap water if you don't order another beverage, and many restaurants charge a fee if you use a credit card.

The *smörgåsbord* (known in Denmark as the *store koldt bord*) is a revered Scandinavian culinary tradition. Seek it out at least once during your visit. Begin with the fish dishes, along with boiled potatoes and *knäckebröd* (crisp bread). Then move on to salads, egg dishes, and various cold cuts. Next it's meatball time! Pour on some gravy as well as a spoonful of lingonberry sauce. Still hungry? Make a point to sample the Nordic cheeses and the racks of traditional desserts, cakes, and custards.

For lunch, you'll find *smørrebrød* shops turning open-face sandwiches into an art form. Shops will wrap these Danish sandwiches up for a perfect picnic in a nearby park. For a quick, cheap meal, try a Danish hot dog *(pølse)*, sold in *pølsevogne* (sausage wagons). Ethnic eateries—Turkish, Greek, Italian, and Asian—offer a good value and a break from Danish fare.

To avoid high restaurant prices for alcohol, many Danes—and tourists—buy their wine, beer, or spirits at any supermarket or corner store, and then drink at a public square; this is legal and openly practiced. A local specialty is *akvavit*, a strong, vodka-like spirit distilled from potatoes and flavored with anise, caraway, or other herbs and spices—then drunk ice-cold. *Salmiakka* is a nearly black licorice-flavored liqueur, and *Gammel Dansk* can be described as Danish bitters for the adventurous.

Service: Good service is relaxed (slow to an American). When you're ready for the bill, ask for the *regningen*. Throughout Denmark, a service charge is included in your bill, so there's no need to leave an additional tip. In fancier restaurants or any restaurant where you enjoy great service, round up the bill (about 5-10 percent of the total check).

Transportation

By Train: In Denmark, the train system is excellent and nearly always a better option than buses. Faster trains are more expensive than slower "regional" trains. To see if a railpass could save you money, check www.ricksteves.com/rail. If you're buying tickets as you go, note that prices can fluctuate. To research train schedules and fares, visit the Danish train websites: www.dsb.dk or www.rejseplanen.dk. Or check out Deutsche Bahn's excellent all-Europe timetable: www.bahn.com.

By Car: It's cheaper to arrange most car rentals from the US. For tips on your insurance options, see www.ricksteves.com/cdw, and for route planning, consult www.viamichelin.com. Bring your driver's license. Local road etiquette is similar to that in the US. Ask your car-rental company about the rules of the road, or check the US State Department website (www.travel.state.gov, click on "International Travel," then specify your country of choice and click "Traffic Safety and Road Conditions"). Use your headlights day and night; it's required in most of Scandinavia. A car is a worthless headache in any big city—park it safely (get tips from your hotelier).

By Boat: Ferries are essential for hopping between the mainland and Denmark's islands, such as Ærø (drivers should reserve in advance for weekends and summer, www.aeroe-ferry.dk). Note that short-distance ferries may take only cash, not credit cards. Advance reservations are also recommended when using overnight boats in summer or on weekends to link Copenhagen to Oslo (www.dfdssea-ways.com). Other worthwhile ferry routes connect northern Denmark to Norway; see www.fjordline.com and www.colorline.com.

Helpful Hints

Emergency Help: To summon the **police** or an **ambulance**, call 112. For passport problems, call the **US Embassy** (in Copenhagen: passport services by appointment only, tel. 33 41 74 00, http://denmark.usembassy.gov). For other concerns, get advice from your hotel.

Theft or Loss: To replace a passport, you'll need to go in person to an embassy (see above). Cancel and replace your credit and debit cards by calling these 24-hour US numbers collect: Visa—tel. 303/967-1096, MasterCard—tel. 636/722-7111, American Express—tel. 336/393-1111. File a police report either on the spot or within a day or two; you'll need it to submit an insurance claim for lost or stolen railpasses or travel gear, and it can help with replacing your passport or credit and debit cards. Precautionary measures can minimize the effects of loss—back up your photos and other files frequently. For more information, see www.ricksteves.com/help.

Time: Europe uses the 24-hour clock. It's the same through 12:00 noon, then keep going: 13:00, 14:00, and so on. Denmark, like most of continental Europe, is six/nine hours ahead of the East/West Coasts of the US.

Holidays and Festivals: Europe celebrates many holidays, which can close sights and attract crowds (book hotel rooms ahead). For info on holidays and festivals in Denmark, check the Scandinavia Tourist Board website: www.goscandinavia.com. For a simple list showing major—though not all—events, see www.ricksteves.com/festivals.

Numbers and Stumblers: What Americans call the second floor of a building is the first floor in Europe. Europeans write dates as day/month/year, so Christmas is 25/12/13. Commas are decimal points and vice versa—a dollar and a half is 1,50, and there are 5.280 feet in a mile. Europe uses the metric system: A kilogram is 2.2 pounds; a liter is about a quart; and a kilometer is six-tenths of a mile.

Resources from Rick Steves

This Snapshot guide is excerpted from the latest edition of *Rick Steves' Scandinavia,* which is one of more than 30 titles in my series of guidebooks on European travel. I also produce a public television series, *Rick Steves' Europe,* and a public radio show, *Travel with Rick Steves.* My website, www.ricksteves.com, offers free travel information, a Graffiti Wall for travelers' comments, guidebook updates, my travel blog, an online travel store, and information on European railpasses and our tours of Europe. If you're bringing a mobile device on your trip, you can download free information from Rick Steves Audio Europe, featuring podcasts of my radio shows, free audio tours of major sights in Europe, and travel interviews about Denmark (via www.ricksteves.com/audioeurope, iTunes, Google Play, or the Rick Steves Audio Europe free smartphone app). You can follow me on Facebook and Twitter.

Additional Resources

Tourist Information: www.goscandinavia.com
Passports and Red Tape: www.travel.state.gov
Packing List: www.ricksteves.com/packlist
Travel Insurance: www.ricksteves.com/insurance
Cheap Flights: www.kayak.com
Airplane Carry-on Restrictions: www.tsa.gov/travelers
Updates for This Book: www.ricksteves.com/update

How Was Your Trip?

If you'd like to share your tips, concerns, and discoveries after using this book, please fill out the survey at www.ricksteves.com/feedback. Thanks in advance—it helps a lot.

Danish Survival Phrases

The Danes tend to say words quickly and clipped. In fact, many short vowels end in a "glottal stop"—a very brief vocal break immediately following the vowel. While I haven't tried to indicate these in the phonetics, you can listen for them in Denmark...and (try to) imitate. Three unique Danish vowels are æ (sounds like the *e* in "egg"), ø (sounds like the German *ö*—purse your lips and say "oh"), and å (sounds like the *o* in "bowl"). The letter *r* is not rolled—it's pronounced farther back in the throat, almost like a *w*. A *d* at the end of a word sounds almost like our *th*; for example, *mad* (food) sounds like "math." In the phonetics, Ī / ī sounds like the long *i* sound in "light."

Hello. (*formal*)	**Goddag.**	goh-DAY
Hi. / Bye. (*informal*)	**Hej. / Hej-hej.**	hī / hī-hī
Do you speak English?	**Taler du engelsk?**	TAY-lehr doo ENG-elsk
Yes. / No.	**Ja. / Nej.**	yeah / nī
Please. (May I?)*	**Kan jeg?**	kan yī
Please. (Can you?)*	**Kan du?**	kan doo
Please. (Would you?)*	**Vil du?**	veel doo
Thank you (very much).	**(Tusind) tak.**	(TOO-sin) tack
You're welcome.	**Selv tak.**	sehl tack
Can I help (you)?	**Kan jeg hjælpe (dig)?**	kan yī YEHL-peh (dī)
Excuse me. (to pass)	**Undskyld mig.**	OON-skewl mī
Excuse me. (Can you help me?)	**Kan du hjælpe mig?**	kan doo YEHL-peh mī
(Very) good.	**(Meget) godt.**	(MĪ-ehl) goht
Goodbye.	**Farvel.**	fah-VEHL
one / two	**en / to**	een / toh
three / four	**tre / fire**	tray / feer
five / six	**fem / seks**	fehm / sehks
seven / eight	**syv / otte**	syew / OH-deh
nine / ten	**ni / ti**	nee / tee
hundred	**hundrede**	HOON-reh
thousand	**tusind**	TOO-sin
How much?	**Hvor meget?**	vor MĪ-ehl
local currency: (Danish) crown	**(Danske) kroner**	(DAHN-skeh) KROH-nah
Where is...?	**Hvor er..?**	vor ehr
..the toilet	**..toilettet**	toh-ee-LEH-teht
men	**herrer**	HEHR-ah
women	**damer**	DAY-mah
water / coffee	**vand / kaffe**	vehn / KAH-feh
beer / wine	**øl / vin**	uhl / veen
Cheers!	**Skål!**	skohl
Can I have the bill?	**Kan jeg få regningen?**	kan yī foh RĪ-ning-ehn

*Because Danish has no single word for "please," they approximate that sentiment by asking "May I?", "Can you?", or "Would you?", depending on the context.

INDEX

INDEX

Audio Europe™

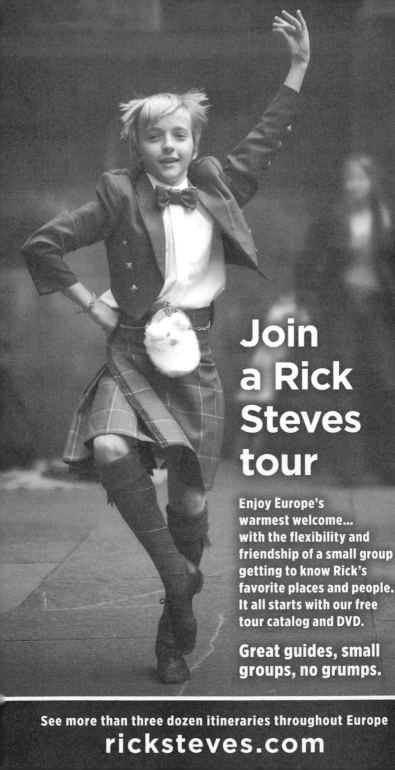

Join a Rick Steves tour

Enjoy Europe's warmest welcome... with the flexibility and friendship of a small group getting to know Rick's favorite places and people. It all starts with our free tour catalog and DVD.

Great guides, small groups, no grumps.

Start your trip at

Free information and great gear to

▶ Explore Europe

Browse thousands of articles, video clips, photos and radio interviews, plus find a wealth of money-saving tips for planning your dream trip. You'll find up-to-date information on Europe's best destinations, packing smart, getting around, finding rooms, staying healthy, avoiding scams and more.

▶ Travel News

Subscribe to our free Travel News e-newsletter, and get monthly updates from Rick on what's happening in Europe!

▶ Travel Forums

Learn, ask, share—our online community of savvy travelers is a great resource for first-time travelers to Europe, as well as seasoned pros.

Rick Steves' Europe Through the Back Door, Inc.

ricksteves.com

turn your travel dreams into affordable reality

▶ Rick's Free Audio Europe™ App

The Rick Steves Audio Europe™ app brings history and art to life. Enjoy Rick's audio tours of Europe's top museums, sights and neighborhood walks—plus hundreds of tracks including travel tips and cultural insights from Rick's radio show—all organized into geographic playlists. Learn more at ricksteves.com.

▶ Great Gear from Rick's Travel Store

Pack light and right—on a budget—with Rick's custom-designed carry-on bags, wheeled bags, day packs, travel accessories, guidebooks, journals, maps and Blu-ray/DVDs of his TV shows.

130 Fourth Avenue North, PO Box 2009 • Edmonds, WA 98020 USA
Phone: (425) 771-8303 • Fax: (425) 771-0833 • ricksteves.com

Rick Steves.

www.ricksteves.com

EUROPE GUIDES

Best of Europe
Eastern Europe
Europe Through the Back Door
Mediterranean Cruise Ports
Northern European Cruise Ports

COUNTRY GUIDES

Croatia & Slovenia
England
France
Germany
Great Britain
Ireland
Italy
Portugal
Scandinavia
Spain
Switzerland

CITY & REGIONAL GUIDES

Amsterdam, Bruges & Brussels
Barcelona
Budapest
Florence & Tuscany
Greece: Athens & the Peloponnese
Istanbul
London
Paris
Prague & the Czech Republic
Provence & the French Riviera
Rome
Venice
Vienna, Salzburg & Tirol

SNAPSHOT GUIDES

Berlin
Bruges & Brussels
Copenhagen & the Best of
   Denmark
Dublin
Dubrovnik
Hill Towns of Central Italy
Italy's Cinque Terre
Krakow, Warsaw & Gdansk
Lisbon
Madrid & Toledo
Milan & the Italian Lakes District
Munich, Bavaria & Salzburg
Naples & the Amalfi Coast
Northern Ireland
Norway
Scotland
Sevilla, Granada & Southern Spain
Stockholm

POCKET GUIDES

Amsterdam
Athens
Barcelona
Florence
London
Paris
Rome
Venice

Rick Steves guidebooks are published by Avalon Travel,
a member of the Perseus Books Group.

NOW AVAILABLE:
eBOOKS, DVD & BLU-RAY

TRAVEL CULTURE

Europe 101
European Christmas
Postcards from Europe
Travel as a Political Act

eBOOKS

*Nearly all Rick Steves guides
are available as eBooks. Check
with your favorite bookseller.*

RICK STEVES' EUROPE DVDs

11 New Shows 2013–2014
Austria & the Alps
Eastern Europe
England & Wales
European Christmas
European Travel Skills & Specials
France
Germany, BeNeLux & More
Greece, Turkey & Portugal
Iran
Ireland & Scotland
Italy's Cities
Italy's Countryside
Scandinavia
Spain
Travel Extras

BLU-RAY

Celtic Charms
Eastern Europe Favorites
European Christmas
Italy Through the Back Door
Mediterranean Mosaic
Surprising Cities of Europe

PHRASE BOOKS & DICTIONARIES

French
French, Italian & German
German
Italian
Portuguese
Spanish

JOURNALS

Rick Steves' Pocket Travel Journal
Rick Steves' Travel Journal

PLANNING MAPS

Britain, Ireland & London
Europe
France & Paris
Germany, Austria & Switzerland
Ireland
Italy
Spain & Portugal

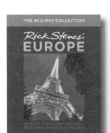

Rick Steves books and DVDs are available at bookstores
and through online booksellers.

Avalon Travel
a member of the Perseus Books Group
1700 Fourth Street
Berkeley, CA 94710

Printed in Canada by Friesens. Updated for second printing July 2013.
Third printing July 2014.

ISBN 978-1-61238-198-5
ISSN 1084-7206

For the latest on Rick's lectures, guidebooks, tours, public radio show, and public television
series, contact Europe Through the Back Door, Box 2009, Edmonds, WA 98020, 425/771-
8303, fax 425/771-0833, www.ricksteves.com, rick@ricksteves.com.

Europe Through the Back Door

Managing Editor: Risa Laib
Editors: Jennifer Madison Davis, Glenn Eriksen, Tom Griffin, Cameron Hewitt, Suzanne
 Kotz, Cathy Lu, John Pierce, Carrie Shepherd, Gretchen Strauch
Editorial Interns: Valerie Gilmore, Rebekka Shattuck, Amanda Zurita
Researchers: Tom Griffin, Cameron Hewitt, Ian Watson
Graphic Content Director: Laura VanDeventer
Maps & Graphics: David C. Hoerlein, Twozdai Hulse, Lauren Mills

Avalon Travel

Senior Editor & Series Manager: Madhu Prasher
Editor: Jamie Andrade
Assistant Editor: Nikki Ioakimedes
Copy Editor: Patrick Collins
Proofreader: Kelly Lydick
Indexer: Stephen Callahan
Production & Typesetting: McGuire Barber Design
Cover Design: Kimberly Glyder Design
Maps & Graphics: Kat Bennett, Mike Morgenfeld, Brice Ticen

Photography: Dominic Bonuccelli, Tom Griffin, Sonja Groset, Cameron Hewitt, David C.
 Hoerlein, Lauren Mills, Rick Steves, Renee Van Drent, Ian Watson, Chris Werner
Cover Photo: Rosenborg Palace Copenhagen, Denmark © Paul Thompson Images / Alamy

ABOUT THE AUTHOR

RICK STEVES

 Since 1973, Rick Steves has spent 100 days every year exploring Europe. Along with writing and researching a bestselling series of guidebooks, Rick produces a public television series *(Rick Steves' Europe)*, a public radio show *(Travel with Rick Steves)*, and an app and podcast *(Rick Steves Audio Europe);* writes a nationally syndicated newspaper column; organizes guided tours that take over 10,000 travelers to Europe annually; and offers an information-packed website (www.ricksteves.com). With the help of his hardworking staff of 80 at Europe Through the Back Door—in Edmonds, Washington, just north of Seattle—Rick's mission is to make European travel fun, affordable, and culturally enlightening for Americans.

Connect with Rick:

facebook.com/RickSteves twitter: @RickSteves

More for your trip!
Maximize the experience with Rick Steves as your guide

Guidebooks
Dozens of European country and city guidebooks

Planning Maps
Use the map that's in sync with your guidebook

Rick's DVDs
Preview where you're going with 6 shows on Scandinavia

Free! Rick's Audio Europe™ App
Hear Scandinavia travel tips from Rick's radio shows

Small-Group Tours
Take a lively Rick Steves tour through Scandinavia

For all the details, visit ricksteves.com